GunDigest PRESENTS

THE ACCURATE HANDGUN

Robert Campbell

Published by

Gun Digest® Books, an imprint of Caribou Media
Gun Digest Media, P.O. Box 12219, Zephyr Cove, NV 89448
www.gundigest.com

To order books or other products call toll-free 1-800-258-0929
or visit us online at **www.gundigeststore.com**

Cover photography by Kris Kandler
All photos by author except where noted

ISBN-13: 978-1-946267-00-9
ISBN-10: 1-946267-00-7

Cover & Design by Dave Hauser
Edited by Corey Graff

Printed in the United States of America

10 9 8 7 6 5 4 3 2 1

TABLE OF CONTENTS

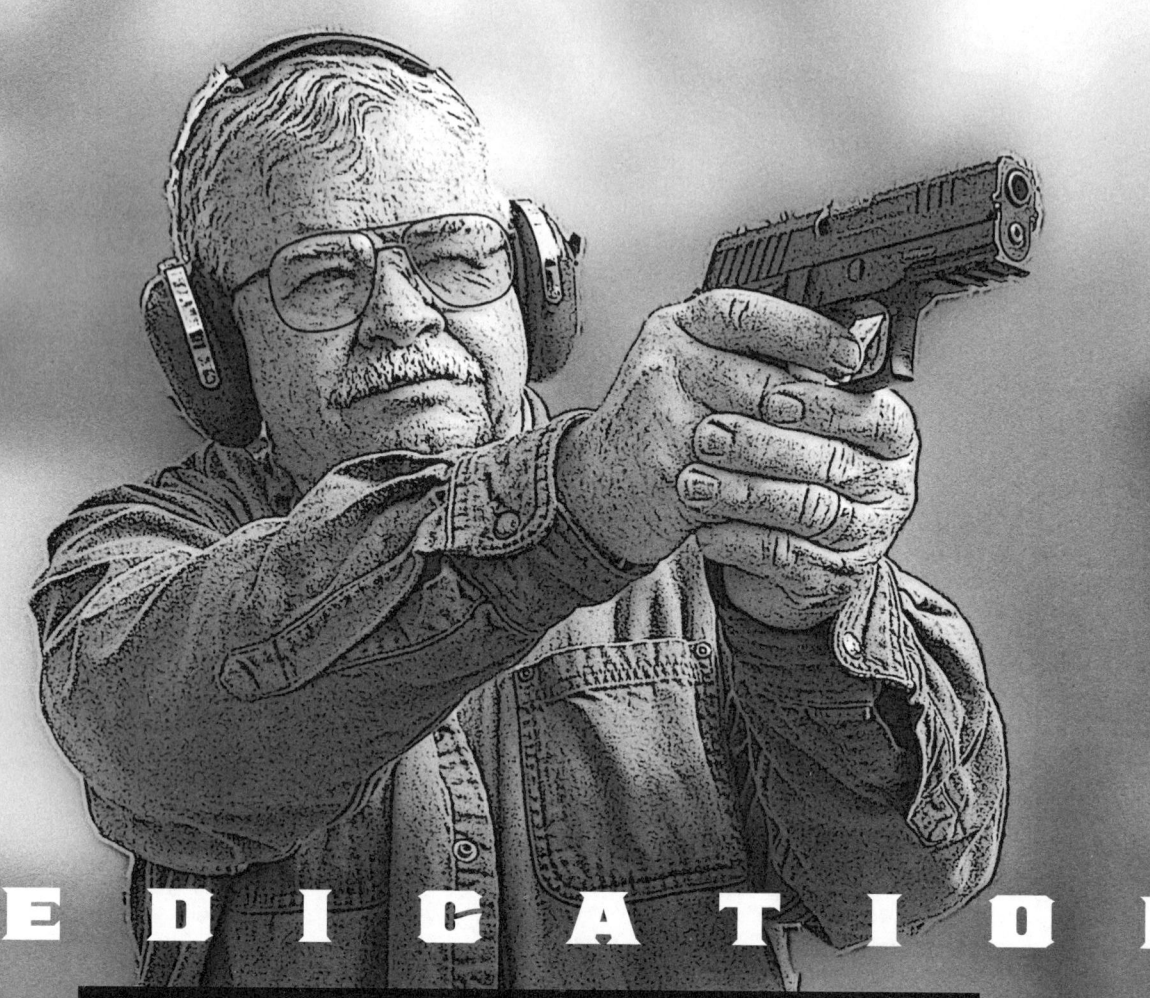

DEDICATION

TO MY SONS.
ALAN IS A BETTER METALWORKER
AND GUNSMITH THAN I EVER WILL BE,
AND MATTHEW A BETTER THINKER
THAN I EVER COULD BE.
TO MY WONDERFUL GRANDCHILDREN.
AND MY DAILY INSPIRATION, JOYCE.
LOVE YOU ALL.

INTRODUCTION

There are many good reasons for owning a handgun. Personal security and a strong sense of self-preservation are among the top ones. Some will practice as little as possible; others will strive to be all they can. This book is for the latter and less crowded group. Some engage in competition, testing the limits of the handgun and ammunition and, most of all, the shooter. These athletes achieve feats of skill and marksmanship that set them apart from most shooters. Some of us appreciate the challenge of hunting game with a handgun and try to master it in turn for small, medium and large game. In every pursuit — from plinking dirt clods and tin cans to long-range silhouette — accuracy is important. I have always been more interested in accuracy than speed and power. A few well-placed big bore bullets in a target mean more to me than a cluster of fifty bullets in a target. A balance of speed, power and accuracy is essential in personal defense, but accuracy is the most important. A miss is a miss; and a slow hit is sometimes as good as a fast hit, but a fast miss is irrelevant.

The handgun is primarily a defensive instrument. All other roles are secondary. Just the same, each individual handgun has a certain appeal based on its attributes and performance. A quality .22-caliber handgun will provide many hours of pleasant recreation. The 1911 .45 is a war winner and the finest personal defense handgun available, and also very accurate in the best examples. Magnum revolvers, such as the Ruger GP100 and Colt Python, have amazing accuracy potential. If you are intrigued by the accuracy potential of such handguns I believe you will profit from studying this book thoroughly. This work is a compilation of much of what I have learned concerning handguns over the past five decades. I hope you enjoy reading it and applying the knowledge found in its pages.

– Bob Campbell

WHAT IS ACCURACY?

This old bullseye gun captures the spirit of handgun accuracy.

Accuracy is a both a measurement and a pursuit. We pursue accuracy and try to find a quality measurement for it that fits our needs. A useful measurement of accuracy is sometimes difficult. Its true value is zero — zero deviation from the center, zero deviation from the target or the desired flight path.

A clock or a pocket watch is deemed to be accurate when it keeps time regularly. We have all had the dying mechanism that ceases to work or the cheap watch that would not keep time. These timepieces have their own measurement of accuracy. Common timepieces sometimes gain or lose a few seconds a year, but atomic clocks do not. Handguns are declared accurate when they have a high level of expectation of hitting the target in trained hands. They are considered good quality when this accuracy is consistent.

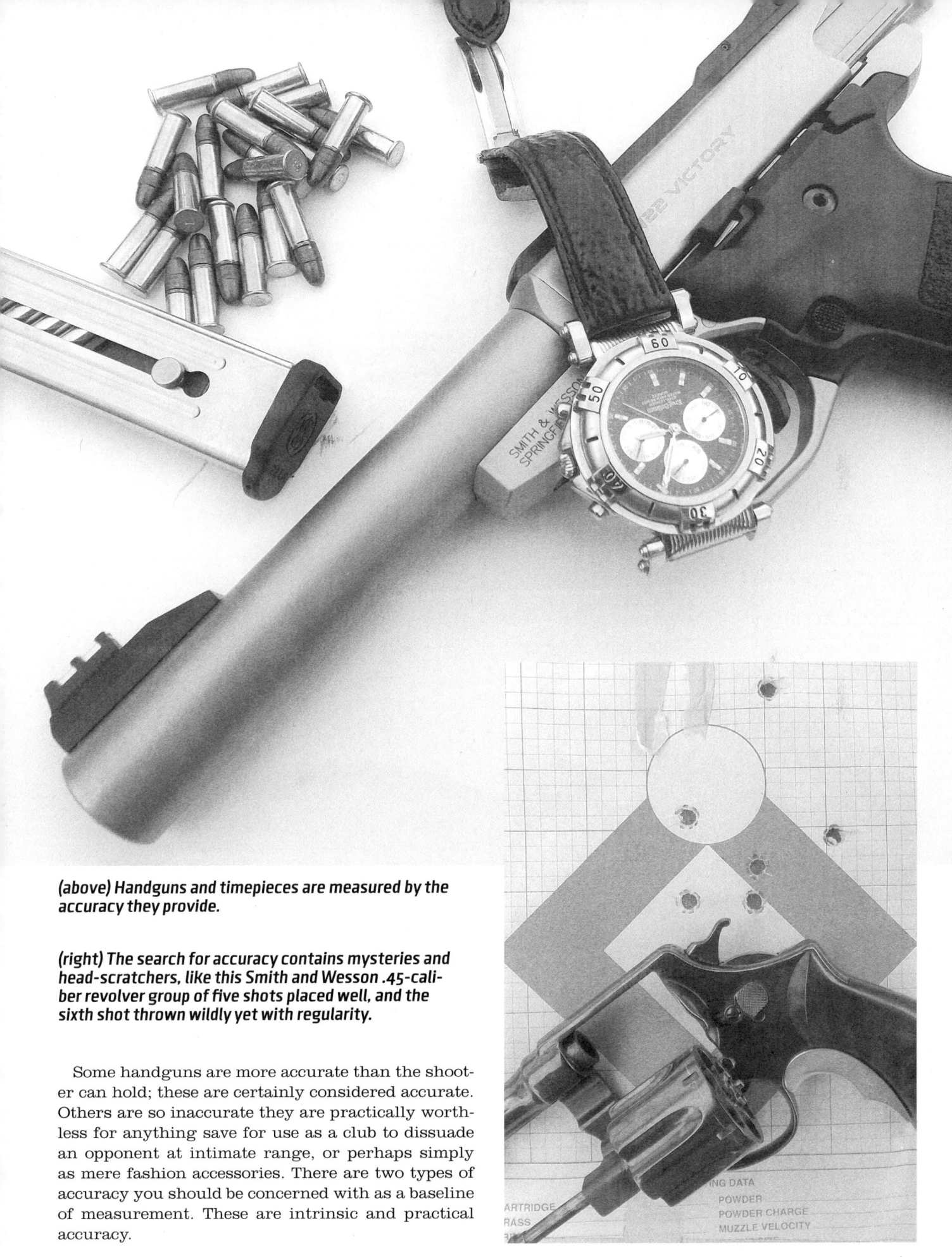

(above) Handguns and timepieces are measured by the accuracy they provide.

(right) The search for accuracy contains mysteries and head-scratchers, like this Smith and Wesson .45-caliber revolver group of five shots placed well, and the sixth shot thrown wildly yet with regularity.

Some handguns are more accurate than the shooter can hold; these are certainly considered accurate. Others are so inaccurate they are practically worthless for anything save for use as a club to dissuade an opponent at intimate range, or perhaps simply as mere fashion accessories. There are two types of accuracy you should be concerned with as a baseline of measurement. These are intrinsic and practical accuracy.

A combination of ergonomics, trigger action, and quality of manufacture make for an accurate handgun. In combat shooting accuracy is relative.

Intrinsic Accuracy

Intrinsic accuracy is the mechanical ability of a handgun to place its shots into a tight group at a given range. A handgun in a factory fixture can be tested for accuracy. The result is better than what you or I could demonstrate on the firing range, although a trained shooter will come very close to these results at times. A handgun without sights or grips would still prove accurate in this firing fixture as the human element is removed from consideration. By the same token, ammunition is often tested in a firing fixture bearing little resemblance to a firearm. These fixtures are heavy and, while they have a chamber and a barrel, there is little else to resemble a firearm. Both the human element and the mechanical element are removed from this type of ammunition testing. The ammunition is evaluated purely on its own merits. This type of testing is important in an institutional setting. During my long shooting life I have yet to use a machine rest. I prefer to stay in touch with reality. I have the greatest respect for the ballistic scientist and his methods. But he has done his work and now I will do mine. I am not capable of setting up a laboratory on the range — at least not with my modest resources — so I am not going to use a machine rest or a firing fixture. But I am appreciative of the work ballistics experts do and am going to make the most of the research they provide us. Such research has led to improvements in handguns and accuracy. Yet, it's up to you to test the practical limits of your own handgun's accuracy.

It is important to follow a consistent procedure from the first shot. This young shooter is receiving instruction from his dad, an NRA instructor and veteran.

Practical Accuracy

The second type is practical accuracy. This is the level of accuracy that a trained shooter will be able to demonstrate with the firearm. A firearm without sights has plenty of intrinsic accuracy but I would not be able to use it to connect with a squirrel in a tree at 10 yards or a deer at 50 yards. Practical accuracy can be defined as the percentage of intrinsic accuracy you are able to demonstrate firing from the solid benchrest position. There are even more angles to this accuracy testing. As an example, when firing off of the benchrest, I am able to control a heavy trigger. A grip frame that is too large for my hands can be addressed with the 'H' grip, which is offset and far from ideal, but I am able to fire the handgun fairly well from the bench with this grip.

Firing offhand is another matter. Some handguns retain a high level of accuracy potential in offhand fire. Others are an aggravation. This qualifying of accuracy has been a lifelong pursuit I find immensely interesting. Some handguns are well-made of good material and very accurate but incapable of placing the bullets in the same hole time after time. There are measurements of accuracy that are useful in comparing one handgun to another. There are also basic requirements of accuracy that have been set in place for over a century. The standard measurement of handgun accuracy is a five-shot

(right) This custom-grade revolver sports aftermarket grips and a hand machined front sight. How accurate is it? Accurate enough.

Shooting from a solid benchrest the author gauges handgun accuracy.

This shooter is using a classic firing position at the 100-yard line with the .45 Colt revolver.

in competition. Others set inaccuracy records! In one instance, Remington revolvers were chambered for the proprietary .44 Remington cartridge. With the introduction of the .44-40 Winchester rifle, Colt chambered their revolvers for the .44-40 WCF cartridge. The writing was on the wall and proprietary cartridges such as the .44 Colt and .44 Remington were doomed in sales. Remington re-chambered unsold .44 Remington revolvers for the new .44-40 cartridge. The bore diameter of the .44 Remington was larger than the .44-40, but the barrels were left unchanged. Despite soft lead bullets that bucked up to engage the rifling, the converted Remington .44-40 revolvers were highly inaccurate, with the average .44 Remington so re-chambered throwing patterns rather than groups at even 10 yards. On the other hand, the U.S. Army demanded that the new service revolver that eventually became the Colt Single Action Army (SAA) be capable of 'dropping an Indian War Pony' at 100 paces. This led to a terrific combination of accuracy and power in the Colt SAA and its .45 Colt cartridge. During many western battles more horses than men were killed, so the accuracy built into the SAA was badly needed. This requirement for accuracy and power was a reason the Colt SAA survived for so long and was such a formidable revolver. For comparison, the .455 Webley revolver was designed with no such requirement in place and could not compete with the Colt for power or precision. The .45 Colt was among the most powerful service cartridges ever fielded.

group from a solid firing position — usually a benchrest, but sometimes a barricade position — and then measuring the dispersal of the group. Measure the group from the inside of the most widely spaced bullet holes and come up with a group size. A good shot with plenty of practice can shoot the handgun with accuracy that is right up to the handgun's potential.

Accuracy Standards

I have discovered a number of interesting accuracy standards applied to handguns adopted by certain institutions and agencies over the years. Some are stringent, while others seem hopelessly lax. As an example, an early standard for the United States Army circa 1870 was that the handgun place five shots into 16 inches at 25 yards. That is simply terrible and would result in a clean miss if the soldier fired this inaccurate revolver at 50 yards. Yet, we know that many handguns of the day were capable of much better accuracy. Some, such as the Smith and Wesson American, set accuracy records

A steady firing position and attention to trigger press gave this young shooter good results at 100 yards.

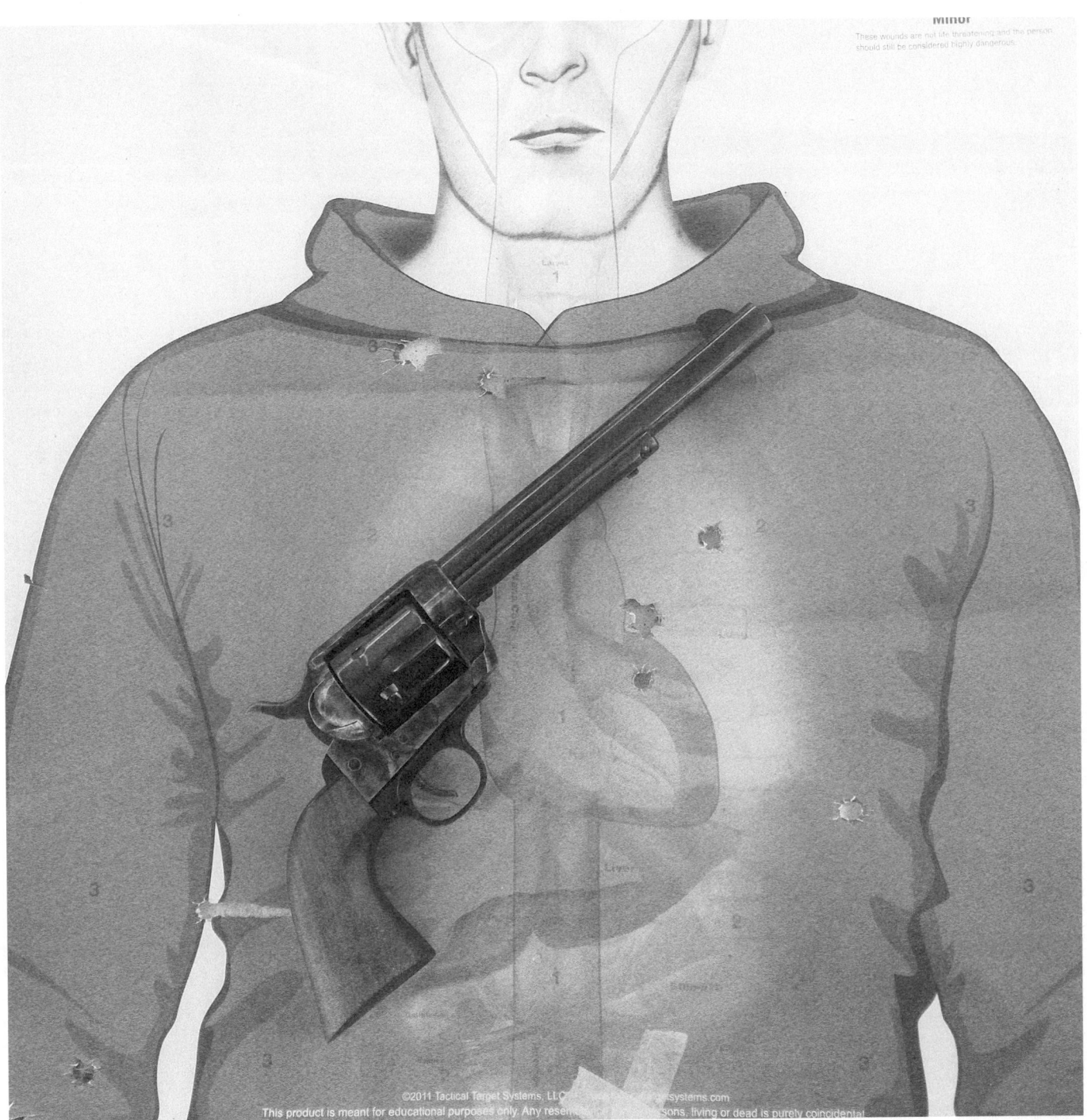

This Traditions .45 Colt revolver is plenty accurate at 100 yards for what it was designed to do. This was a formidable fighting handgun in its day, and is still useful.

Another standard for acceptance came with the Colt Government Model of 1911. Military standards called for the Colt to be capable of a five-shot, 5-inch group at 25 yards, and a five-shot, 10-inch group at 50 yards. Most 1911 handguns of the period from 1911 to 1927 are more accurate than this standard. The Army demanded accuracy and power as well. Cavalry soldiers first employed the handgun to extend their will just past saber range. The heavy horse pistol was a fixture of mounted troops for centuries. Colt Paterson .36-caliber revolvers raised the bar in accuracy. For the first time, fighting men had a weapon that they could reliably connect with at ranges at which the caliber was no longer effective. Texas Rangers used the Colt in long-range battle against Mexican troops and Indians. The Walker Colt .44 gave them the power needed and, along with this power, accuracy comparable or superior to most muskets of the day.

By 1911, the U.S. Army demanded a high standard for accuracy. Test fixtures were used to hold the handgun in place as a "standard dispersion of

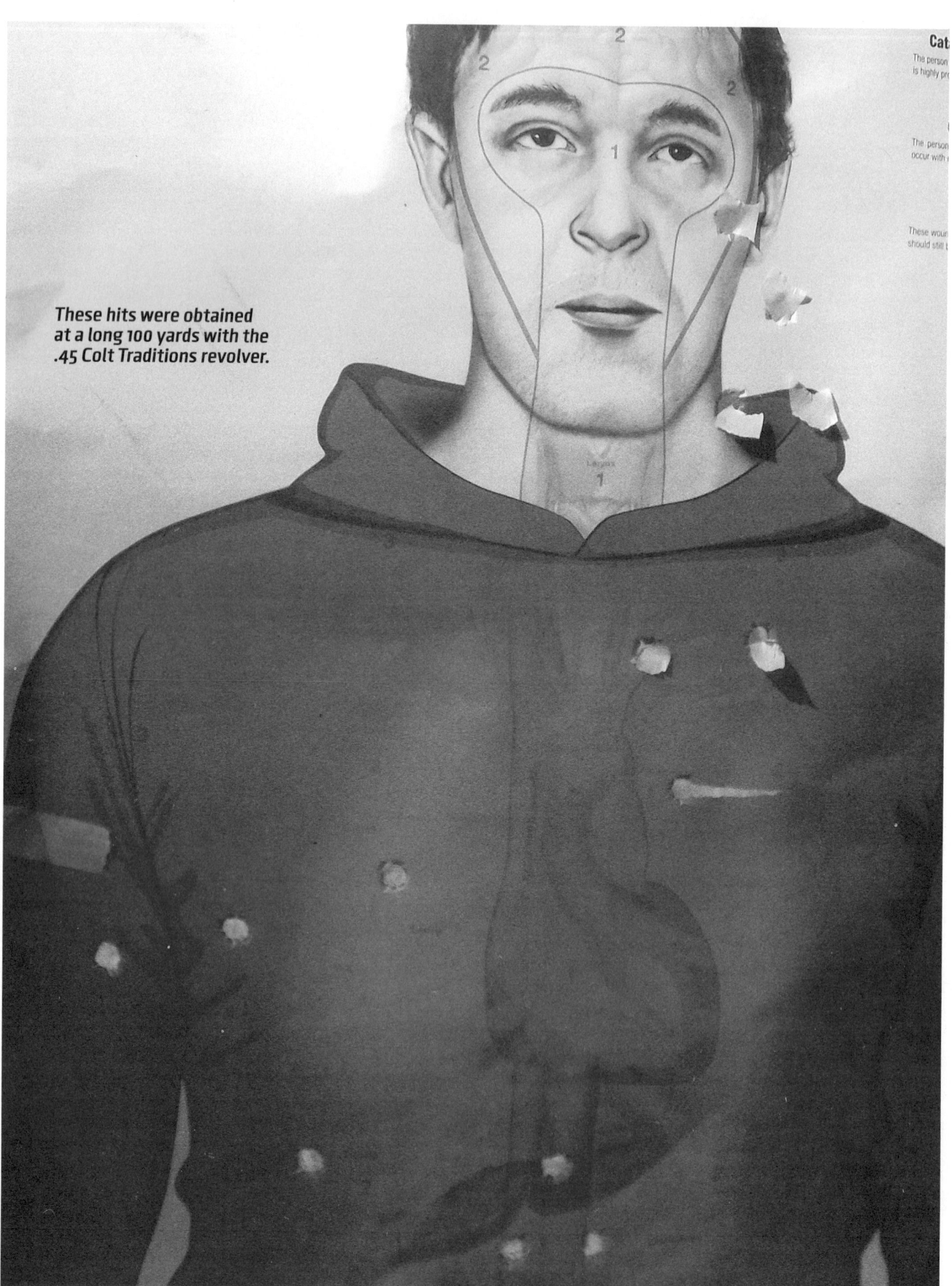

These hits were obtained at a long 100 yards with the .45 Colt Traditions revolver.

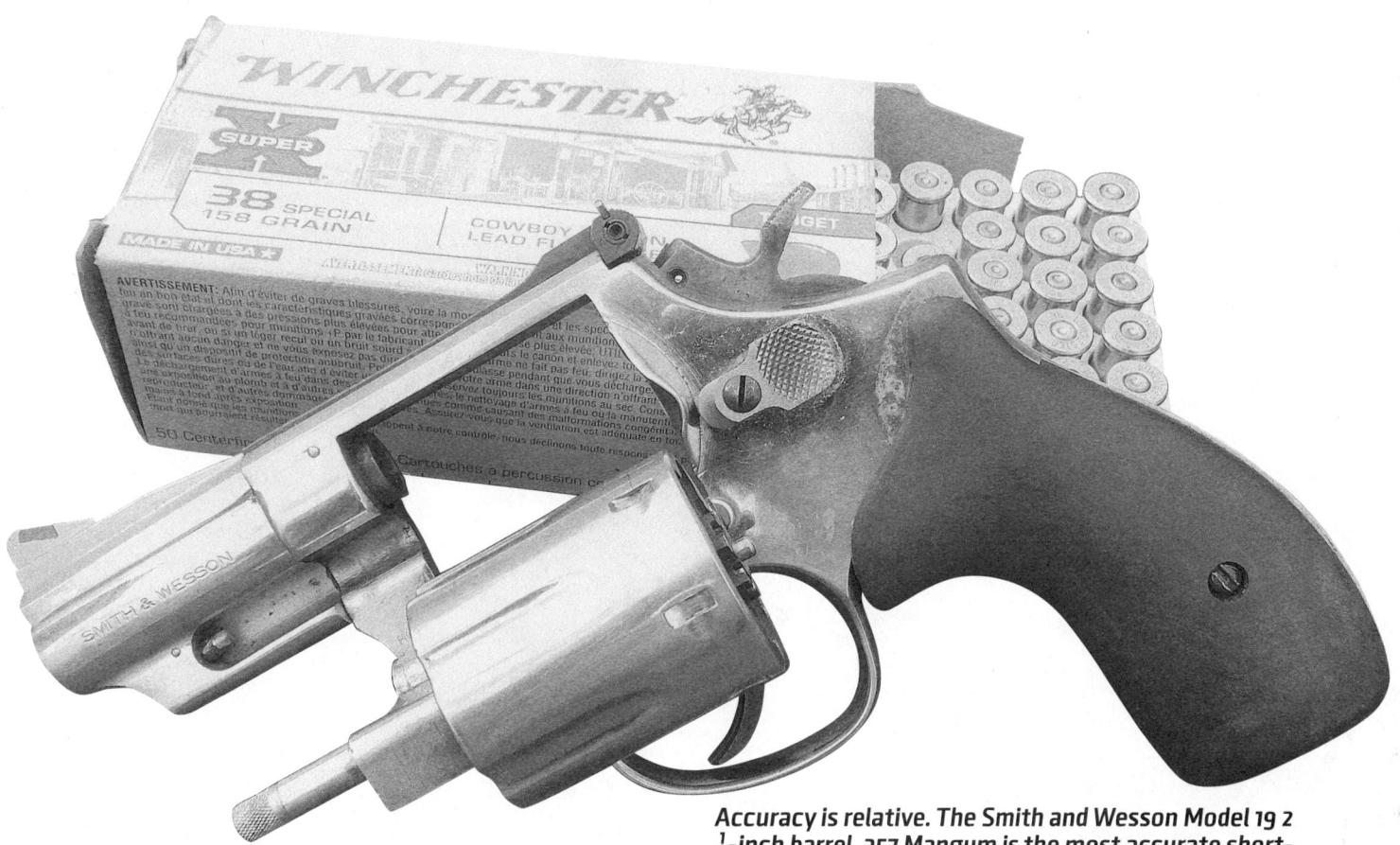

Accuracy is relative. The Smith and Wesson Model 19 2½-inch barrel .357 Mangum is the most accurate short-barrel revolver in the author's experience.

accuracy," the term used back in the day to describe accuracy testing. Ammunition was also tested. A well-documented test of wartime ammunition in .45 ACP exhibited considerable differences in average accuracy. Conducted in 1927, this test showed some ammunition as accurate as 4 inches at 100 yards. Other lots from the same maker were much less accurate (fired in a Thompson submachine gun at semi-auto). In modern times, the West German police demanded a superior handgun in order to meet accuracy standards for dealing with the new wave of terrorism and for use in hostage rescue. The SIG P220 handgun was among a very few sufficiently accurate for this demanding mission. It eventually evolved into the SIG P226 9mm, the pistol that killed Osama Bin Laden. Accuracy demands in the war on terror are high.

Accuracy demands rose to previously unheard of standards, results that would have seemed unobtainable in factory handguns and ammunition just a few generations before. The FBI demanded stringent accuracy when testing 1911 .45 ACP handguns that would arm their SWAT team and SWAT-trained officers. The standard of a five-shot, 1.25-inch group would not only have to be met by the handguns, it would have to be sustained after the handgun fired 25,000 rounds of ammunition. Incredibly, the

Springfield Armory Bureau Model met this standard with factory Remington 230-grain Golden Saber ammunition.

Accuracy of modern high-quality handguns and ammunition is extraordinary. Yet, we also live in an age of mediocrity when just good enough is good enough for most shooters. Police agencies have eliminated 50-yard handgun qualification. In the days of the Smith and Wesson Model 15 Combat Masterpiece .38 Special and the Smith and Wesson Model 19 Combat Magnum, excellent 50-yard scores were often posted. There have been a number of modern incidents in which peace officers have been practically helpless before long-range rifle fire or unable to connect at long distances with their double-action only, or DAO 9mm or .40 handguns. The Magnum revolver would have been a comfort and an aid in public safety in those cases.

The discriminating shooter demanding good accuracy seems to represent but a fraction of the gun buying public. Manufacturing has changed a great deal, and while there are still some handguns with excellent accuracy, they can be very expensive. There are a few bargain guns that are accurate beyond expectation but, by and large, you get what you pay for. A century ago, ostentatious machinery relied upon a pool of highly skilled craftsmen who took

Quality means a great deal. SIG handguns and ammunition make an excellent combination.

great pride in their work. Eventually, production techniques were developed that eliminated most human error. Much of this work was done in America. Reliability was stressed, I believe, more so in America than in Europe. The public could not be expected to go out and test new production handguns for the gun makers, the product had to be reliable. Comparing the Colt 1911 .45 auto and the Colt 1903 .32 ACP to most European handguns finds America taking the lead in reliability against firearms that were often over-engineered or beautifully machined, but prone to tie-ups.

The pendulum turned against us during the 1970s as the dismal Smith and Wesson Model 59 was compared unfavorably against the SIG P226 and Beretta 92. As for the modern handgun — sophisticated and powerful as it may be — the modern pistol operates on principles dating back over one-hundred years. The main changes are incremental technical improvements. This is a new development in old grease. Gun design has always been heavy on engineering. But there is also an important shaping of the handgun and styling, balancing the needs of function and form. A marquee identity is often based on this form as much as performance. The dichotomy of design is interesting and even fascinat-

ing. The handgun may not be designed along modern lines to the same extent as rifles. The handgun is a one-hand firearm and must be held in one hand — even if supported by the other hand. The controls and safety must be easily manipulated by one hand. Recoil cannot be uncontrollable. The sights must be accessible to the eye and quickly picked up as you aim the pistol.

Handgun Evolution

As the demand for greater accuracy became apparent at the turn of the previous century we began to see handguns with high-visibility and adjustable target sights. These were specialized versions of service pistols. There were target sighted Single Action Army .45s and very soon the Smith and Wesson Military and Police, or M&P was offered in a target sight version. Even 'tactical handguns' of the day were given better sights on special order. Both Bat Masterson and Tom Threepersons, noted lawmen

Colt's Gold Cup .45 has set the standard in accuracy for many years.

The SIG P220 .45 is easily the most accurate production grade .45-caliber self-loader the author has fired.

and gunfighters, had special high-visibility front sights added to their Peacemaker .45s. So much for the myth of unsighted fire!

Between World Wars I and II a great deal of development was done with handguns to improve accuracy. The Camp Perry National Matches were the main reason behind this development in self-loading pistols. The desire for long-range accuracy and killing power on game was the main concern among revolver developers. If there is anything those of us who love the 1911 appreciate, it is a sense of history. Emotional attachment is also important, but history is a beckoning call. I would have been bored long ago with firearms if the technical aspects were the only part of the equation. The men who designed the aforementioned match pistols are immensely interesting and so are the men and women who have used the firearms in competition and to save lives. If anyone involved receives far too little admiration it is the craftsmen that manufacture the firearms. Furthermore, those who take the 1911 in hand and win a pistol match are athletes that deserve our respect. In working this book up, I was able to borrow a superlative example of the 1911 bullseye gun. You do not need a lot of power in a target gun. With suitable modifications, the 1911 is a great all-around handgun for many roles. Over the years, a number of target features have slipped into the 1911. Among them are a long, target-grade trigger and flat mainspring housing.

As mentioned, target-grade 1911 handguns were developed shortly after World War I in order to compete in the national matches. These matches involved long-range fire at small targets. The Colt 1911 had not been designed for accuracy and needed considerable work to provide competitive results out to 50 yards — its heavy trigger and small sights had to be reworked. The trigger action, with its rapid reset, was practically ideal for defensive work. But firing at an 8-inch bullseye at 50 yards was another matter. Trigger compression had to be lightened. The 1911 had been designed for reliability above all else. As long as the locking lugs and barrel bushing were properly fitted, it didn't matter if the thing rattled and shook like a Ford Pinto with a bent crankshaft — it would place five rounds of service ammunition into a 5-inch group or better at 25 yards.

The original military accuracy standards were for the 1911 to group five bullets into 5 inches at 25 yards and 10 inches at 50 yards using mass-produced service grade ammunition. Most would perform slightly better. This is generous by modern standards, but the 1911 was a comparatively accurate handgun of the day. For competition, the 1911 needed to be roughly twice as accurate. A 4-inch 50-yard group was needed — or even smaller. Army gunsmiths went to work. They polished and

relieved the trigger action, fabricating lightweight triggers as they went along. Trigger compression was reduced from 8 to 6 pounds, then to 4 pounds or lighter. The barrel was welded up until it would not fit the slide, then the contact points carefully filed and polished into a tight fit. Target-grade sights were fabricated. These sights were not adjustable

at first, but they were large and easily acquired by the eye. They had to be filed to zero. The expense of such a handgun was prohibitive for civilian shooters. An Army gunsmith might work on the handgun for months, devoting his time to the team. Thankfully, Colt took notice and introduced the first National Match handguns.

The Springfield Operator 1911 features excellent control and good practical accuracy.

The Colt Gold Cup National Match 1911

The factory Colt National Match handguns received special treatment in fitting and trigger work as well as good, high-visibility sights. The original was a great pistol. Over the years, various fully adjustable sight combinations were used, including the Stevens, Elliason and Bomar. The Gold Cup became more of a target gun than an all-around shooter. The slide was lightened sometime around 1957. Many shooters did not like this, as they preferred the balance of the original 39-oz. slide. Ostensibly, it was lightened to facilitate function with lightly loaded target ammunition. The rear sight was attached to the slide by a pin that sometimes worked loose. Later, the Colt Gold Cup's weight was returned to standard. A rib was cut along the top of the slide for a flat top look. Many of these modifications meant that the Colt Gold Cup was a pure breed target gun, but not necessarily a good general service pistol. This has changed in recent years. The new Colt Gold Cup is a great all-around 1911, well-suited to serious duty with its round top slide and dovetailed rear sight — but also makes a very capable target gun.

During this time, many shooters preferred to build up their own 1911s, particularly in the day of the poorly attached Colt sights. If memory and research are accurate, when the Colt Gold Cup retailed for about $135, a good, used 1911A1 could be had for $50. That is a lot of room to choose your own sights and grips and pay a decent pistolsmith. The process I have outlined by which the GI gun became a target-grade 1911 was clear and certain with no detours. The picture of a Camp Perry-class pistol gradually developed as the pistolsmith plied his trade. Too often, speculative ideas are given the same footing as well as tested ones, and you cannot do that in producing a bullseye gun. The guns were similar, and it was a combination of skill and luck that made the winner.

Remington 1911 Accuracy

I do not wish to obscure the fact that a pistol like the Remington 1911 was intended for combat use. Nothing has been done to make it less reliable, but the work has made the handgun more accurate and more useful. There is much evidence that tightly fitted handguns with less looseness and motion of internal parts are more reliable and long lasting. The Remington 1911 began life as a service grade handgun during World War II. Inspectors traveled in production plants with gauges to ensure mil-spec compliance. The ideas behind the Camp Perry gun did not occur in a vacuum. They came up as a result of the demand by marksmen for a gun that would shoot well. There is no circuitous path — it was straight to the workbench to tighten the pistol, add

a national match bushing, weld the lugs up and adjust the trigger. I have known such gunsmiths and they think in terms of solid mechanical and mathematical footing. The performance of the pistol is derived from the application of these fundamentals. Yet, it is a subtle revision of the old warhorse.

The 1911 has been called Old Slabsides or Old Ugly. The beauty of such a piece is more in the firing than the viewing, but the aesthetics of the 1911 is cold and austere. It is like a metal sculpture. The 1911 is nearly perfect as a fighting handgun, and the spirit of delight and exhilaration in firing a target model is certainly evident. The exhilaration comes from hitting the target. Lately, we have become accustomed to elevated, highly modified 1911 handguns and take high performance for granted. Progress in the intervening years since the Remington Rand was manufactured is evident, but the symmetry of progress owes much to such metal as the Remington Rand/Camp Perry gun. The pistol is fitted with a micro-adjustable sight, what appears to be a handmade front sight, and a national match barrel bushing. While the trigger has been replaced, the action remains heavy at 7 pounds. Perhaps the individual shooter liked this trigger weight. This was all that was needed to make a GI gun a target gun.

Firing the Remington is a joy and a revelation. Observing the pistol from the rear, it is the same rugged 1911 but the well-worn surface isn't visible. Line the sights up and you see an excellent sight picture. Press the trigger correctly and you have a hit. I am not a trained bullseye shooter, but have fired PPC, IDPA and Pin matches, so I know a little about the game. The pistol was well-lubricated and loaded with Federal American Eagle 230-grain loads. Steel plates were addressed as well as silhouette targets at 10, 15 and 25 yards. The pistol feels solid in the hand and demonstrates good function. In testing for absolute accuracy, I fired a number of five-shot groups off of a solid benchrest at 25 yards with the Federal 230-grain match load. Average groups were 2 to 2 ½ inches. The pistol is a joy to shoot and use. Both history and practical use are elements of pride of ownership and this handgun has both. There are more expensive handguns, better finished and more accurate, but none more pleasing to shoot and own. Overall, a pleasing handgun and a great piece of history. This handgun gives you an idea of the work that went into such a pistol and how lucky we are to have factory versions today.

Revolvers and Others

The Smith and Wesson .357 Magnum was introduced in 1935. The highly accurate .38/44 Outdoorsman, a .38 Special on a .44 frame, well-suited to heavy loads, was the forerunner of the mighty .357 Magnum revolvers. At the time, perhaps one hun-

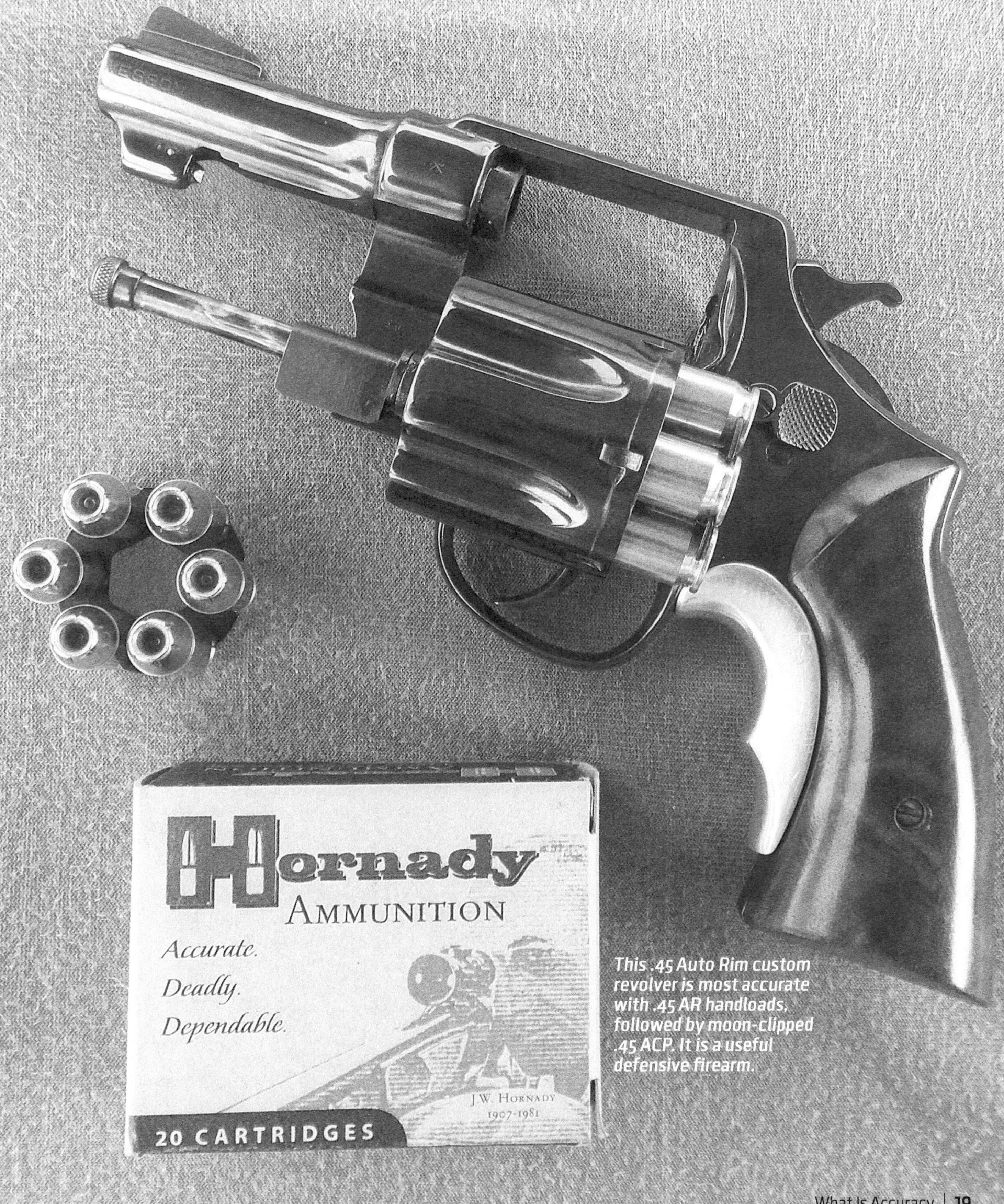

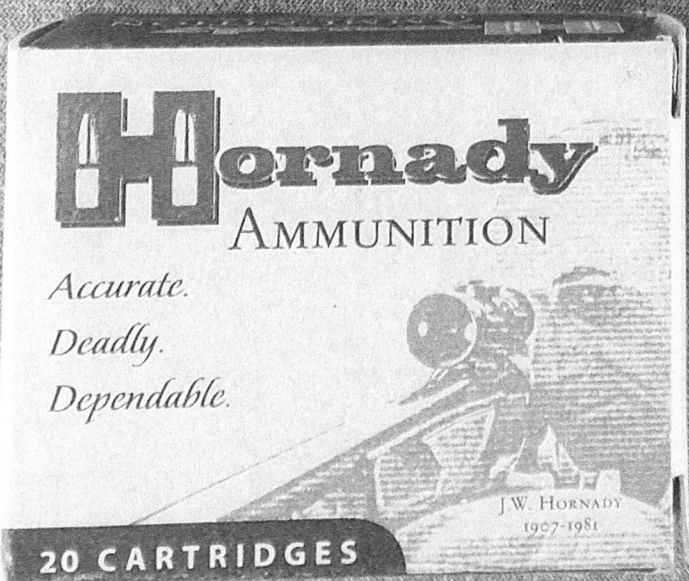

This .45 Auto Rim custom revolver is most accurate with .45 AR handloads, followed by moon-clipped .45 ACP. It is a useful defensive firearm.

The big Ruger double-action revolvers are possibly the strongest wheelguns ever built – and are plenty accurate.

.44 MAGNUM CAL.

The Beretta 92 9mm may not be the most accurate service grade handgun, but it gives up little to any other pistol. It is a useful and reliable pistol for general use.

ASSY. 9346487-65490

U.S. 9mm M9-BERETTA U.S.A.-65490

dred or more ordinary revolvers were sold for each .357 Magnum — but the magnum was a sensation. The Smith and Wesson Model 28 offered cheap accuracy with a handgun not as well finished as the original premium-grade .357; later, the lightweight Model 19 offered a compromise on size, weight, and longevity. A period of traumatic change came in the 1980s with the police and civilian move to autoloaders and the popularity of the Glock handgun.

Today most handguns are manufactured by a similar process. Individual components are produced of polymer, steel or aluminum. The order of manufacture is defined by absolute parameters. The modern day standard for service pistol accuracy is a 4-inch, five-shot group at 25 yards. Most easily meet this. Some, such as the SIG P226 will do much better under controlled conditions. Service pistols are a field of great compromise. The universal police pistol is a double-action only design in 9mm or .40 caliber. It is simple to use well, requires little maintenance, and is above all reliable. It is combat accurate but not pinpoint accurate. The compromise is inherent in modern requirements. The Glock is an outstanding handgun for short-range use by shooters who practice once a year or so. But practical accuracy limitations are reflected in police qualifications. There are more accurate handguns and many just as reliable as the Glock, but few with such an attractive mix of

low cost and reliability. Some handguns have both combat capability and superb long-range accuracy. The SIG P220 is among these and so is the modern Colt Combat Elite, Springfield Operator and a few others. The CZ 75 offers affordable excellence.

The revolver in its current form has tighter tolerances than ever, in quality examples from Ruger and Smith and Wesson. Bore and throat dimensions are tight, resulting in excellent accuracy potential. The Ruger GP100 locks up tight. It's among the most accurate revolvers ever produced. Accuracy comes from the repeatability of CNC machine tools and superior quality control. The sights and trigger action are excellent.

While I enjoy the great handguns of the past — they were indeed great in their day — the modern handgun is preferable, it simply performs better. If you are an old hand and own a brace of classic revolvers, then you are in good shape for accuracy, hunting and all-around packing use. The Colt Series 70 Gold Cup .45 or Smith and Wesson Model 27 is a great handgun. But a new shooter should not rush out to the gun show cash in hand to purchase a classic handgun at a premium. If pride of ownership, emotional attachment and a sense of history are important, then indulge yourself. If you are going to engage in a demanding practice regimen and you want your handgun to be all it can be, then a new piece is the wise choice. Purchase the best quality handgun you can afford. Unless you need a defensive handgun right now, a quality .22 is relatively inexpensive and makes a perfect marksmanship trainer. If you need the defensive handgun quickly there are good choices. In the following pages you will find a focus on accuracy, marksmanship and the most precise handguns and ammunition. The handguns and ammunition outlined will carry you through competition, hunting, personal defense and simple recreational shooting. The pursuit of accuracy is worthwhile, interesting and rewarding. By the time you get done reading — and shooting — I hope you are as fascinated by it as I am.

CHAPTER 2

THE HANDGUN MARKSMAN

As of this writing, I have been shooting handguns for 49 years, having started with a good .22 as a pre-teen. My grandfather knew I was very interested in firearms, and that I was mature and trustworthy. He was patient with my interest. My father taught me mechanics and how to be a man. After all of this time I am still learning new things concerning the handgun. The handgun is difficult to shoot well compared to a rifle. Yet, much of what we learn is simple. The command to 'don't flinch when you press the trigger' is simple enough, but difficult in practice. When a .357 Magnum goes off a few inches in front of your nose it isn't a natural thing. You have to overcome the mental reluctance to fire accurately and the natural inclination to jerk away from such a loud noise, like flinching after touching a hot match. To add to the problem, there is less stabiliz-

This shooter has small hands, but finds the CZ P01 to be a good fit.

Note the proper finger position: The pad of the first finger on the trigger.

(below) The grip is important to accurate fire and must be practiced to perfection before a shooter can proceed in marksmanship.

ing area with the handgun. The rifle and shotgun allow a three-point grip with both hands and cheek weld. The handgun offers only room for two hands and is sometimes fired with just one. The handgun's shorter sight radius — the length between the front and rear sights — allows for greater human error. The trigger can be heavy, causing you to move the gun and the sights with each press. No wonder some regard the handgun as useless beyond a few feet. The bottom line is, you will hit the target if you hold the pistol correctly, align the sights properly and do not let sight picture to be disturbed when the handgun fires. It is all quite simple. It is the path you take to that perfectly executed shot that is interesting.

There are cornerstones of marksmanship that are vital. A strong stance is a good place to begin. The stance may be a Weaver, Isosceles or a personal blend. As long as it works there is room for personal comfort and adaptation to your size and build. How you grip the handgun is less open to discussion. The grip must be strong and the handgun controlled. Sight alignment must be understood. There are com-

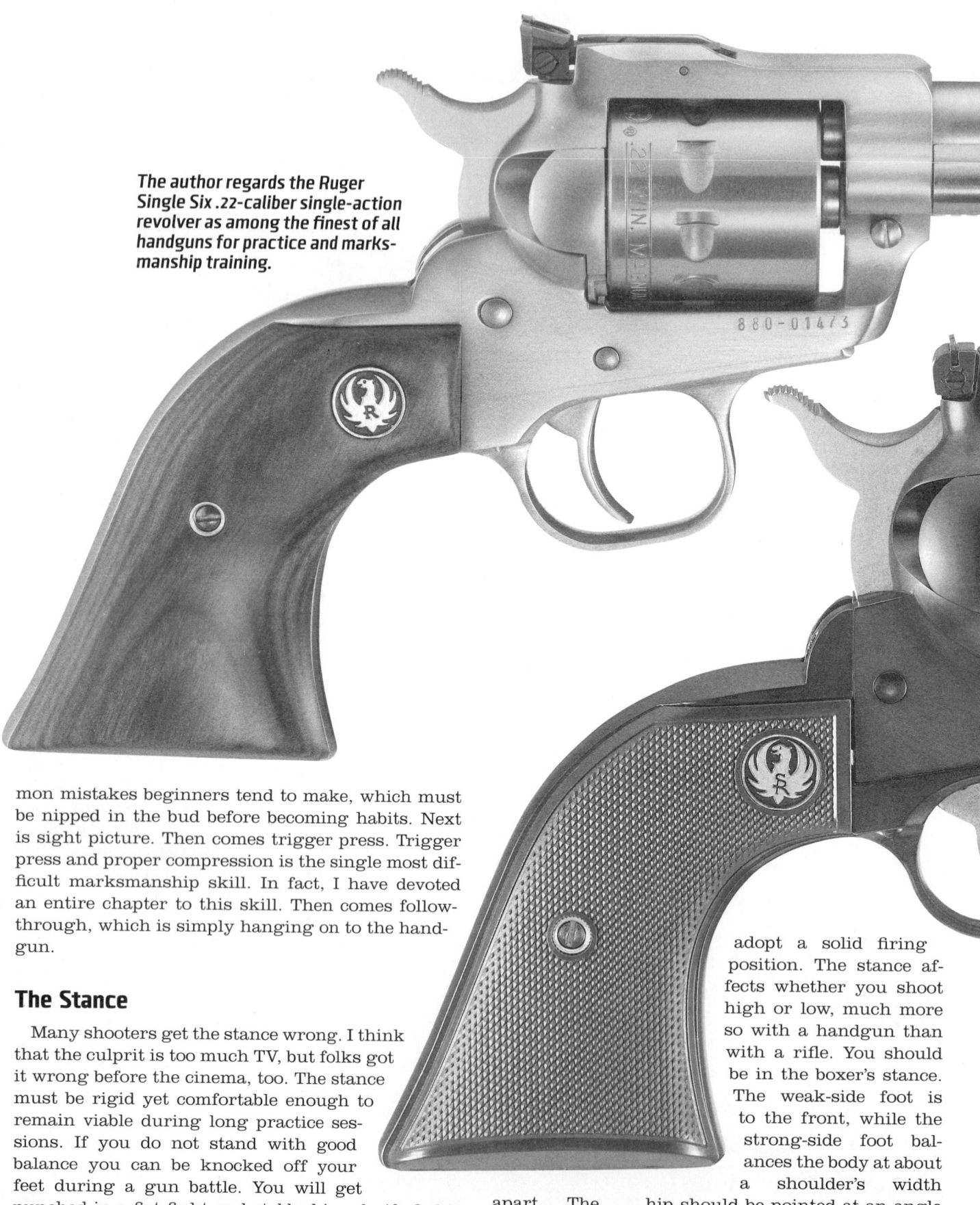

The author regards the Ruger Single Six .22-caliber single-action revolver as among the finest of all handguns for practice and marksmanship training.

mon mistakes beginners tend to make, which must be nipped in the bud before becoming habits. Next is sight picture. Then comes trigger press. Trigger press and proper compression is the single most difficult marksmanship skill. In fact, I have devoted an entire chapter to this skill. Then comes follow-through, which is simply hanging on to the handgun.

The Stance

Many shooters get the stance wrong. I think that the culprit is too much TV, but folks got it wrong before the cinema, too. The stance must be rigid yet comfortable enough to remain viable during long practice sessions. If you do not stand with good balance you can be knocked off your feet during a gun battle. You will get punched in a fist fight and stabbed in a knife fight. Chances are you will be shot in a gunfight. In competition, you will tilt from side to side if you do not

adopt a solid firing position. The stance affects whether you shoot high or low, much more so with a handgun than with a rifle. You should be in the boxer's stance. The weak-side foot is to the front, while the strong-side foot balances the body at about a shoulder's width apart. The hip should be pointed at an angle to the target. If you are firing a .22-caliber handgun or a centerfire .38 with light loads, such a stance is

The Ruger Blackhawk in the magnum calibers is not only very accurate but unbelievably rugged.

(below) The proper grip, stance, trigger press and sight picture come together to make hits with the handgun at close and long range.

adequate. If you are firing heavier handguns, your shoulders should be rolled forward to place more mass behind the handgun, which will better control recoil. A heavier handgun kicks less than a light one of the same power. Adding body weight compensates for a light handgun. Do not lean to the rear. The higher the handgun in relation to the shoulders the greater the pistol will rise during recoil. Use a solid stance and adopt the same stance for all types of practice.

Get a Grip

I am going to cover the grip more thoroughly in another chapter, but in simple terms make your grip high and solid. Too many shooters leave a portion of the rear grip strap above the hand when they grasp the pistol. This gives the handgun plenty of leverage to rise in recoil. The trigger reach will be compromised by this type of grip and the improper hold will not provide a strong base for the automatic pistol to recoil against, resulting in a short cycle (jam). The grip should be consistent. To achieve that, hold the handgun as tightly as possible until your hand trembles. Then back off until the hand ceases to tremble — there is the proper grip.

Firing from the benchrest demands concentration on the basics of marksmanship and remains a good test method of a firearm's accuracy.

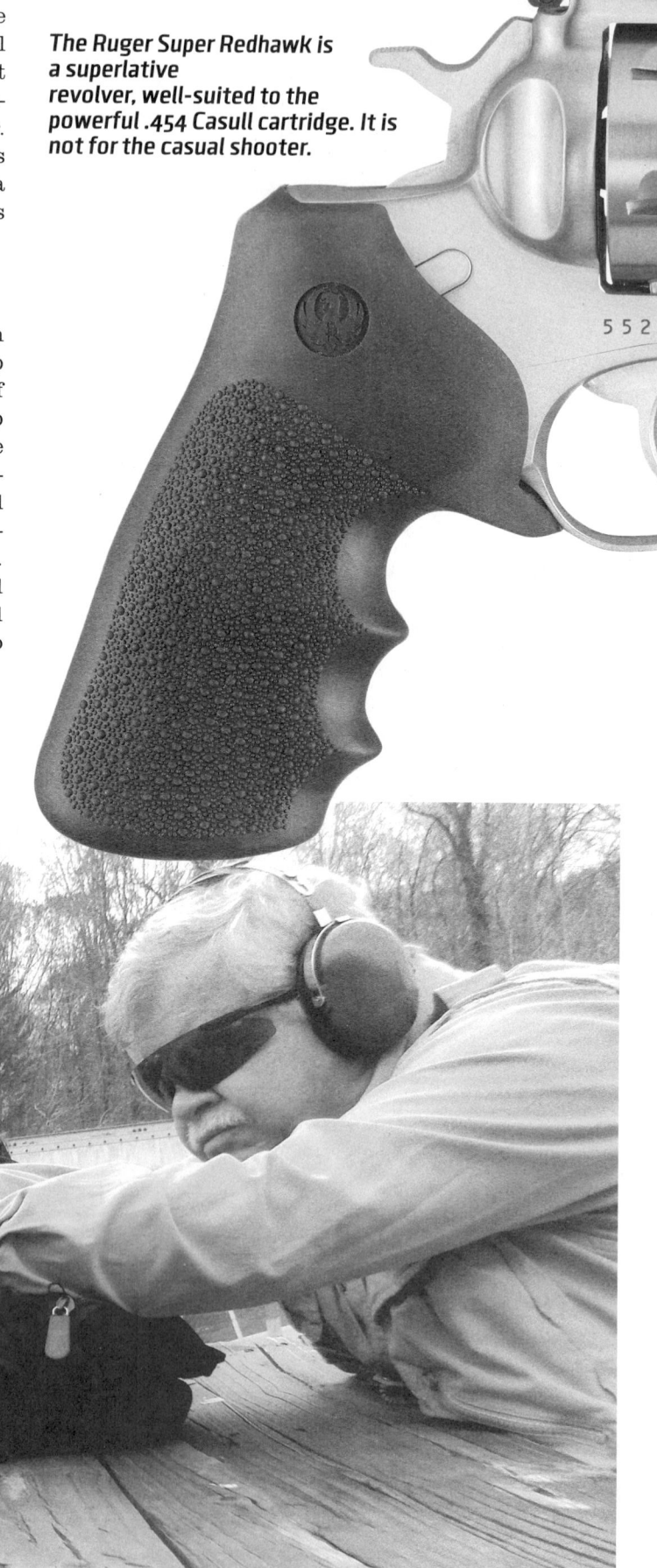

The Ruger Super Redhawk is a superlative revolver, well-suited to the powerful .454 Casull cartridge. It is not for the casual shooter.

552-71

The author practices the Weaver stance for accurate fire.

Do not engage in an awkward pantomime to find the sights. Keep the sights properly aligned and your eyes on them.

When shooting in competition, it is possible to hold the handgun in a tight grip for every shot, but to do so you will need to build hand muscles through much exercise. When in a life-saving situation, the action will not last long and the hand will not have time to become tired. Adrenaline will dump. In fact, adrenaline probably will dump in a high-pressure competition, as well. When holding the handgun, a problem that isn't readily apparent until firing is milking the grip. Humans have two sides; we are bi-laterally symmetrical. Movement in one hand results in movement in the other. By the same token when you are pressing the trigger, there is sometimes sympathetic motion in the lower digits. The trigger is pressed and the other digits move with the trigger finger. You have to smash this problem early on.

A competitor must concentrate on accuracy. Carefully analyze your performance on target and get to the root of a miss or the reason you are not getting center hits. If you have progressed to the point where you are getting good groups on the target, but they are not centered, then there is a good chance there is simply one thing off in your shooting technique. You may be mashing the trigger or lack good follow-through. Reading the target is as important as calling the shot. Calling the shot simply means that you know you have hit the target or you call a miss.

Even though the handgun is in recoil, the author has his eyes on the sights and his firing grip is controlling the handgun.

Pushing Back – Controlling Recoil

Do you recall your early experiences with a hand-gun? The first time I fired a .45 auto I am pretty certain I closed my eyes! (I was perhaps 14, no more than 15 years old.) After I took that first shot, I told my grandfather, 'It wasn't that bad.' I was hooked after years of firing the .38 Special and many bricks of .22-caliber ammunition. It goes without saying I was an exceptionally responsible young man and I had a wonderful grandfather who enjoyed the shooting sports. I had worked my way up the ladder from the .22 to the .38, to the .45, which is ideal but not always possible. Sometimes you need a handgun right now, for self-defense. Even so, I was more concerned with painful recoil than hitting the target. Unfortunately, this is a common issue. After all of these years of shooting I still fight flinch with hard-kicking handguns such as the lightweight .357 Magnum or .40-caliber compact. I try to use standard calibers such as the .38 Special and .45 ACP for my own use. Professional demands include firing many firearms. I shoot poorly designed handguns and others that are overbore for the cartridge. It isn't pretty and I find recoil control problems are cumulative. You miss because of flinch or because the gun hurts and the result is that each subsequent shot becomes less accurate. Accuracy falls apart. Recoil is real, but controllable. You must learn to control it with the proper grip.

When speed shooting with one hand the proper sight picture must still be obtained. The firing grip is always as firm as possible.

The Weaver stance provides a solid firing platform and excellent recoil control.

Firing offhand the author demonstrates a proper grip and trigger finger placement.

The firing grip is the platform for all other shooting skills.

Tool Selection

For beginning and experienced shooters alike, a handgun with less recoil is beneficial. A service grade handgun chambered for the 9mm Luger or .38 Special-class cartridges is easier to control than a compact handgun or one chambered for the .40 Smith and Wesson or .357 Magnum. While larger handguns are difficult to conceal they are easier to use well. Even in the compact frame size there

(right) Controlling the handgun is important. Note this Commander .45 has fired, the spent cartridge case is in the air, and the pistol is back on target.

(below) The .22 is a wonderful training tool. The author is practicing double taps with the Smith and Wesson Victory.

are handguns that have a reputation for good control and easy shooting. These include the Glock 19 in 9mm and the Ruger SP101 revolver firing .38 Special. No matter what handgun and caliber you choose, good control is accomplished with the proper technique and practice. Attention to detail is vital. I feel confident in controlling light but powerful handguns such as the K frame .357 Magnum revolver and the Commander .45 but only after years of practice with the proper technique. These handguns would be hopeless without recoil management. Control comes with a combination of range work and dry fire practice.

More Grip Details

A solid two-handed grip with the support hand wrapped around the gun hand and the support hand forefinger pressing up on the trigger guard is the mark of a good shot. Lock the hands with the thumbs down. Make a fist with the thumb open. Next, lock the thumb down. See how much stronger the lock thumb is? An important component of the grip is using the best stance. The Weaver stance is a steady platform that makes good shooting easier. Press forward with the firing hand, then pull back with the support hand and you have the proper grip.

The Glock trigger differs from most and must be mastered through a significant amount of practice.

(below) Despite light recoil from this .22, the author maintains a firm grip in order to control the handgun. Note trigger finger placement.

As mentioned earlier, grip the handgun as forcefully as possible and when your hand begins to shake, ease off and you have the proper grip. The thumbs should be pointed forward aimed at the threat or target. After some practice, you should be able to place both heels of the hand against the grip as you fire. The thumb of the firing hand may interfere with the slide lock if you are not careful in placing the hand, particularly when using small self-loading pistols. You do not have to raise the thumb to accom-

If all is well with the grip and sight alignment at the moment of firing you have a hit.

modate the firing grip, only point it forward. You now have excellent adhesion with the finger pointing forward and the heel of the support hand against the grip. You do not want the hands rising off of the grip. If the firing hand thumb is bent incorrectly then a cup will form under the thumb and the support hand grip will not properly lay flat — heel to grip — on the handgun. Keep your hands touching as many square inches of the handgun as possible. When there is a cup, or hollow in the grip, the handgun is allowed to recoil inconsistently. Control and accuracy are adversely affected. The grip must be consistent.

When engaging in tactical movement, the stance or firing position is important; however, it can change as you move. The firing grip, however, does not change and must be consistent. If you are able to get into the Weaver stance with the firing-side foot slightly back and the support arm low-

For the isosceles stance, the arms are thrust out and the handgun is supported in a natural position.

(left) The isosceles is a good technique that works well for most shooting chores.

(below) The .45 ACP in full recoil as the shooter controls the piece with the proper technique.

(opposite) With the handgun held using both hands, and the feet solidly planted, the isosceles stance works well enough for most uses.

(left) With a good, strong tension between the hands and one arm dropped slightly, the Weaver stance is the superior shooting stance for accuracy.

(below) The Weaver stance entails keeping one foot forward and the shooting foot to the rear for best stability.

ered to act as shock absorber, you should. If you cannot assume a good Weaver position, using the Isosceles by simply thrusting the arms forward works well. The arms should not be locked into place, but flex at the elbows to cushion rather than absorb recoil. The wrists, however, must be locked. Locking the elbows unnecessarily stresses the joints and makes movement stiff. There are other issues that must be considered when discussing recoil control. The competitors' grip is often mentioned. I use this grip from time to time. The majority of the force exerted is from the support hand. Long firing sessions with this grip work well. However, when engaging in personal defense, the idea is to get the strongest grip possible and maintain it. The grip must be as strong as possible without trembling, so practice keeping the handgun under control.

Standing Tall

As I have stressed, the stance can be important but the grip must be consistent. Keep your head erect, bring the gun to the eyes, do not bring the eyes down to the gun. Keep your thumbs clear of the slide lock. It is common for the thumbs to ride the slide and sometimes cause the lock to rise, locking the slide open. The support hand thumb is the culprit; the firing-hand thumb sometimes rides the SIG pistol slide lock, causing it to fail to lock the slide open on the last shot. When shooting, be certain to practice trigger control. Fire, allow reset, and fire again. Control the handgun and the trigger. Many of these techniques can be practiced with a triple-checked unloaded handgun. It is mandatory to practice getting a proper grip and hold with an unloaded firearm. Dry fire isn't the whole picture; you have to get the grip correct before progressing to controlling the trigger.

The Beretta Neo provides good trigger reach. It does not overstretch the average hand.

Evaluating Marksmanship

As you progress with shooting, have a means to gauge your progress. Ask yourself where you are in marksmanship. The answer is found at the firing range. There are any number of measures and sliding scales to gauge shooting ability. Most, such as police qualification, are measures of the common denominator. You pass or fail. The beginner may have exerted everything he has to pass, while the expert shooter will slide by. Both receive equal recognition. It is interesting that debates over handguns, sighting systems, action type and caliber flourish while marksmanship isn't often discussed. Let's look at what marksmanship entails, and how to rate yourself a marksman. I think that most of us have a broad idea of who the marksman is. He may be working with a special team or shooting in competition. Another is a salty old dog who thinks his 1911 or .357 Magnum is the only handgun worth carrying. Then there are those who are trusted with the low bid double-action only pistol and do the best they can. Are these perceptions fair and accurate?

Performance is gauged by the percentage of bullets on the target versus cartridges fired. A ten ring hit is valued highest. The Army specifies certain performance standards and issues badges to marksmen, sharpshooters and experts, respectively. These men and women earned their badge. This type of recognition isn't as common among police agencies these days, where pass or fail is the norm. Many

Hold the pistol firmly with no pockets between the hand and the gun. The forefinger of the support hand presses upward against the trigger guard.

tests in civil service are graded the same way. We could devise a system of gauging shooters ranging from student to grand master, given sufficient time. This would include shooters who perform on demand with service grade handguns. Civilians tend

The isosceles stance is very fast to assume and, while not as stable as the Weaver, is easily learned.

(above) The firing hand must be pressed firmly against the backstrap and not lower than the tang.

(right) Shooting champion Jessie Duff gets it right every time.

(below) Note Jessie Duff's grip and trigger finger position – she gets it right and wins the big money!

to be interested in skills that are mission-specific. Those in uniform may be called upon to perform on demand far beyond the conflict expectations of most shooters. I divide my students into categories, partly to determine how much individual instruction each will need. This gives me a good idea of where they are and how quickly they are going to arrive at where they wish to be. The four categories are: novice, beginner/proficient, specialist and professional. Let's look at each category.

Novice

The novice may be able to safely load, unload and handle his or her personal sidearm with a minimal amount of fumbling. Their level of competence is more broad than deep. This is the beginning level for each of us. While indeed minimal, it is the common skill level of quite a few non-dedicated service personnel. Shooters at this level may not survive gunfights. It really depends upon their mindset. At short range, marksmanship problems are not severe, but the combat mindset is questionable. Shooters in this class are likely recreational shooters on the civilian side. Peace officers at this level maintain their marginal skill by yearly qualification. Many look forward to these qualifications as much as they looked forward to high school fire drills. Their tactical mindset is influenced more by the media than reality. Among this group you will find many that rely upon skills they cannot demonstrate. The single greatest shortcoming among this group is a lack of complete familiarity with their sidearm.

Beginner/Proficient

The beginner may be a product of a personal training program or an agency with quarterly qualifications. Their training is likely to be relatively narrow but perceived as adequate. Some within this group realize there is room for improvement. It is important to note that this is the highest level of skill sustainable by many with job and family demands. A homeowner who keeps a firearm primarily for home defense has done well to reach this level. A peace officer trained to this level who combines his skill with streetwise tactics will be a formidable shooter. This is the highest level of skill to which administrative qualifications will lead. While common street thug adversaries are often at the duffer level, some criminals reach the beginner-proficient level. In my experience, very few of our protein-fed, ex-con criminal class rise past the novice level. The proficient class of shooters is common among those who shoot in IDPA matches. The proficient level of skill is sustainable with monthly practice and not out of the reach of anyone of normal strength and dexterity.

Specialist

This level isn't one that you arrive at by accident. Hard work is needed. The specialist is good at a number of skills. He or she will deploy a top-grade handgun and be able to use it well. This person knows the likely threat profile and practices diligently to address this threat. Well-versed in the tactics and skills likely to be needed in a personal protection scenario, they are able to handle unexpected problems. The specialist is often deeply opinioned, has formal training and often gravitates to training others.

Professional

The professional has a lot of answers dependent upon the situation. He is conversant in marksmanship and gun handling as well as advanced tactics. He is familiar with a number of firearms. While he has opinions concerning firearms, he regards each as a tool. The professional does not consider training the goal but a means to an end. His marksmanship skills are well-honed and consistent. He has fewer bad days and brilliant moments than the rest of us,

Colt's Maggie Reese demonstrates an excellent all-around firing grip and trigger finger placement.

but rather his skill is consistent. He is responsible for his actions and strives to learn new tactics while respecting the tactics and skills that saved his life in the past. His skills are demonstrably superior to most of those he trains but they are hard-won. While the specialist is a product of official training, the professional may only be produced by diligent effort on his own time — and his own dime. His training time is measured in thousands of hours. I know such men. Three have run my training classes and two were United States Marines. I also attended a class as a student with such a marksman (the only one in his class at the course), and he too was a Marine. I have no military experience and I can only state that the Marines are doing something right. As for the third I met, he was a U.S. Army veteran that had been injured overseas. Despite muscle tremors that challenged his considerable skill he aced the course and demonstrated extraordinary ability. Very few instructors have the privilege of training such men.

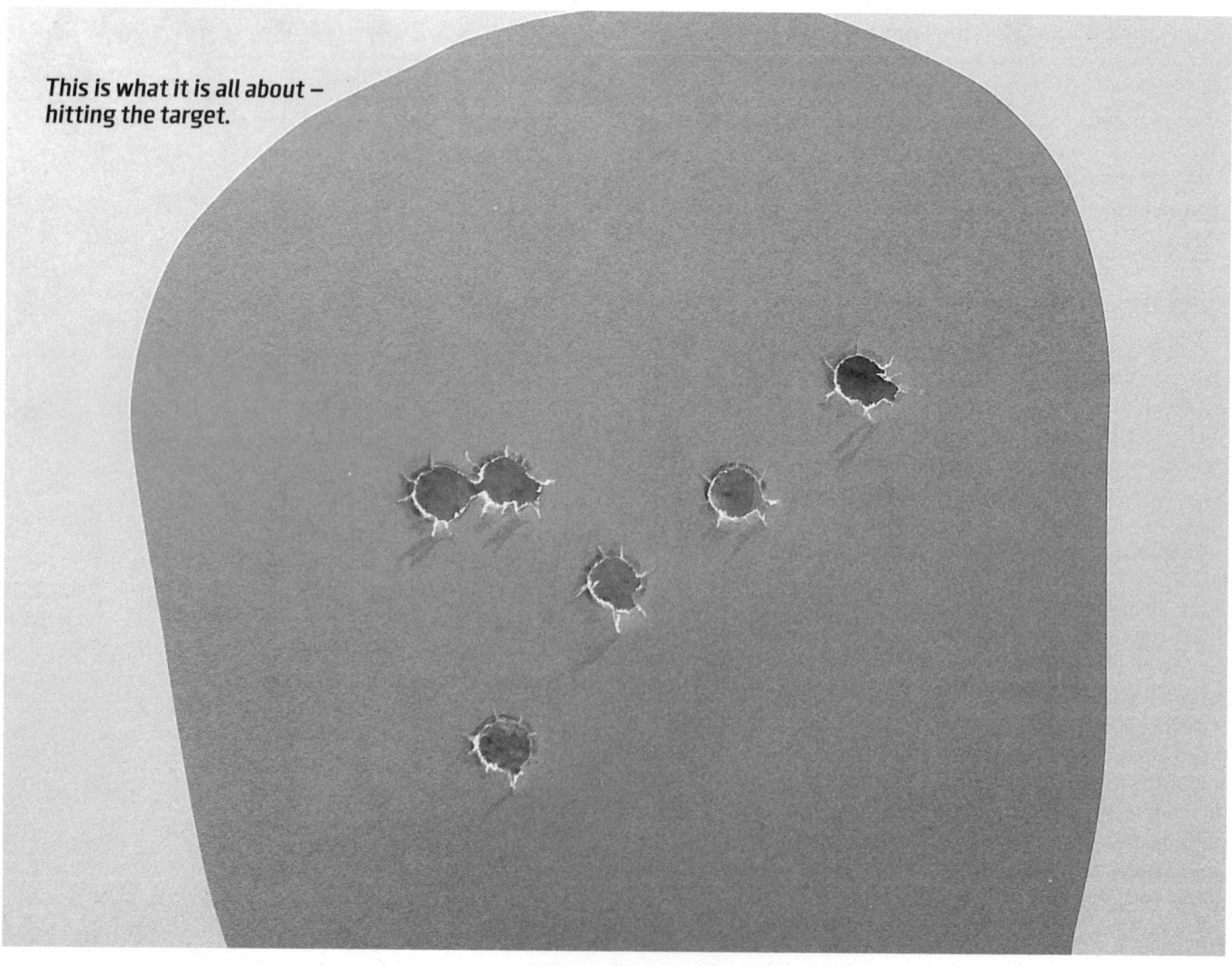

The Kel-Tec PMR 30 is a fairly large handgun in the grip, but average-sized hands can grasp the pistol and reach the trigger properly.

What is the Defining Difference in Shooters?

Are some people born with above average skills? When it comes to handgun skills, the single greatest predictor of performance is prior training. The more casual the training, the less impressive the shooter's performance. In a critical incident, the result may be death or injury to the person involved if their skills

This is what it is all about — hitting the target.

are not up to snuff. Skills take practice to acquire. You cannot simply keep practicing the skills you are good at. You must address your shortcomings as well. A great defining difference in shooters is mindset. While we all begin as novices, some stay at the level where their skills are more aspirational than operational. The next step up is training for the average encounter on your home turf. At this stage, many believe (falsely) that a basic level of training is good enough. I have seen this type helpless on two occasions when confronted with gunfire because they were unable to deliver accurate return fire past ten yards. A step up is the shooter who has trained to deal with multiple assailants at different ranges and varying distances. Those who attend regular IDPA matches are often much better shots than the institutional shooter.

The more advanced shooter has some preparation for a malfunction or a failure to stop. The professional keeps at it until his skills are evenly balanced. He doesn't hammer away in pointless drills that simply allow him to demonstrate what he is good at. He meets the challenge of weak-hand fire or other shortcomings he recognizes. He is familiar with various weapons not only by general type but specifics. The professional realizes that greater training means less risk in a critical incident.

Where Are You?

You need to give your own skills an honest appraisal. You would like to move up a rung on the ladder. Like Jacob's ladder, every rung just makes you stronger. The problem is, many who are stuck at a certain level are working below their apparent need. They really need to do better by profession and threat profile. Two real problems exist in training: time and money. Unfortunately, most agencies operate in the panic mode, training only when forced to do so. Civilians train at leisure. Both groups have more time than money. The motivation to train is internal. The external motivation comes from an attack. You will be motivated to respond, but you may lack the skills. Some of my friends and acquaintances are so busy in high demand jobs they seldom have time to progress beyond state-mandated courses that are not very challenging. The primary reason I have set forth my standards is to encourage the average shooter to excel and to present a basis for procedure. You know who you are and where you are in ability. A good self-study combined with the right range exercises will show you where you are and where you need to be.

Take a hard look at yourself and where you want to be. Always strive to be better than you were, realizing you're but a long way from where you need to be.

NOVICE

Must understand safe handling, loading and unloading. Will be able to hold a 6-inch group, offhand, at 10 yards.

BEGINNER/PROFICIENT

Has advanced gun handling skills including rapid reloads. Is conscious of tactical movement and cover. Will be able to hold a 6-inch group offhand at 15 yards.

SPECIALIST

Has skills in quickly clearing malfunctions and in addressing multiple targets. He will be able to shoot up to the gun's accuracy at 10 yards and hold a 4-inch group offhand at 15 yards.

The author demonstrating a good, solid grip with the thumbs forward and proper trigger finger placement.

PROFESSIONAL

Is able to quickly clear a malfunction, field strip and maintain his sidearm, address multiple targets, address moving targets, and move fluidly on the range and address situational problems. He is able to hold a 3-inch group at 10 yards in rapid fire and a 6-inch group offhand at 25 yards with a service pistol. He is able to strike a man-sized target at 50 yards from a solid braced position using a service pistol.

SIGHTS AND SIGHT PICTURE

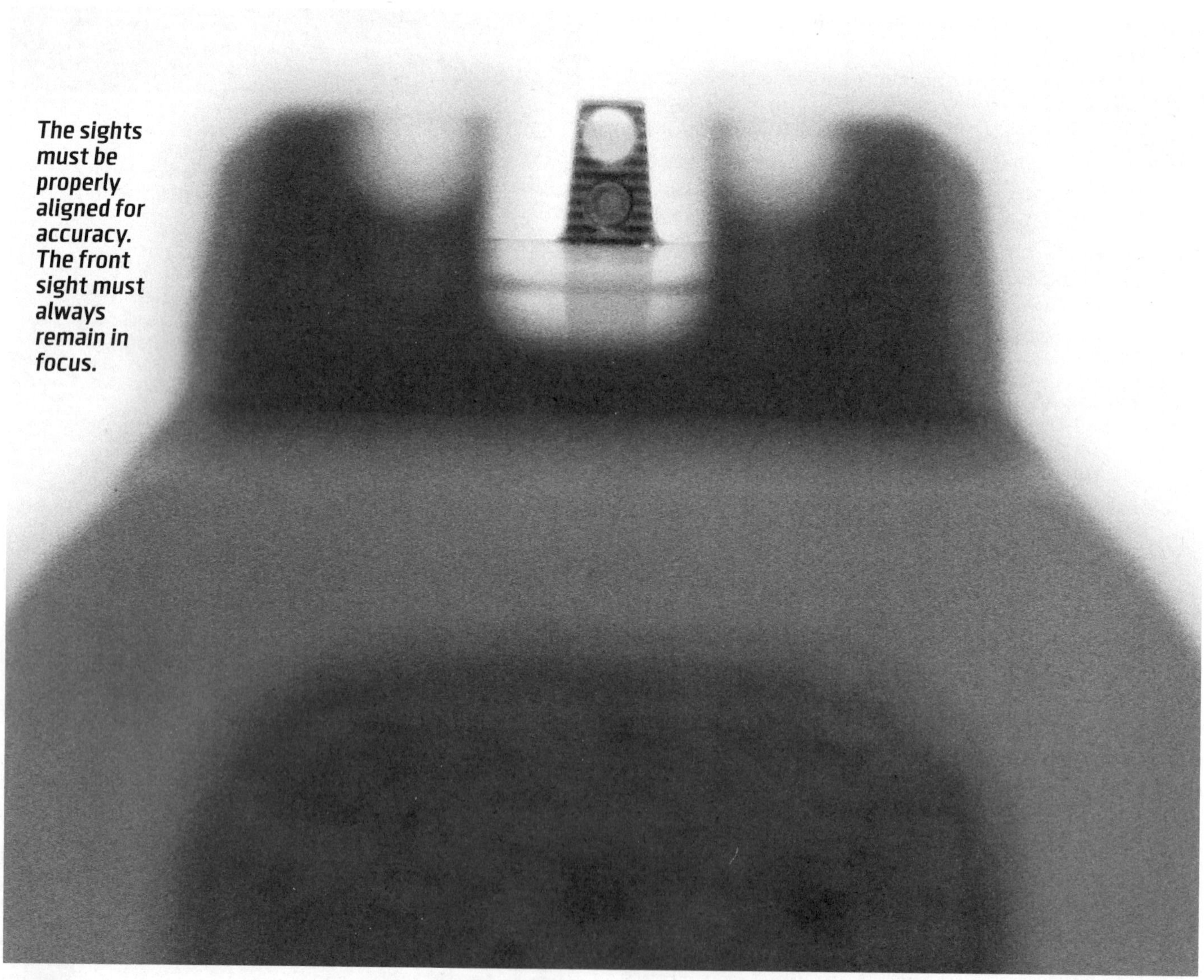

The sights must be properly aligned for accuracy. The front sight must always remain in focus.

In order to hit the target, the sights must be aligned properly on the target. This is known as sight alignment and sight picture. The top of the front sight must be level across the top of the rear sight. This is the reason modern sights have been developed that are flat across the top of the front sight. The early half moon-type front sight begged the question, where is the top of the sight? Elevation is an important consideration. The front sight held over the top of the rear sight will result in a high shot. The front sight held under the top of the rear sight will result in a low shot. The proper centering of the sight is vital.

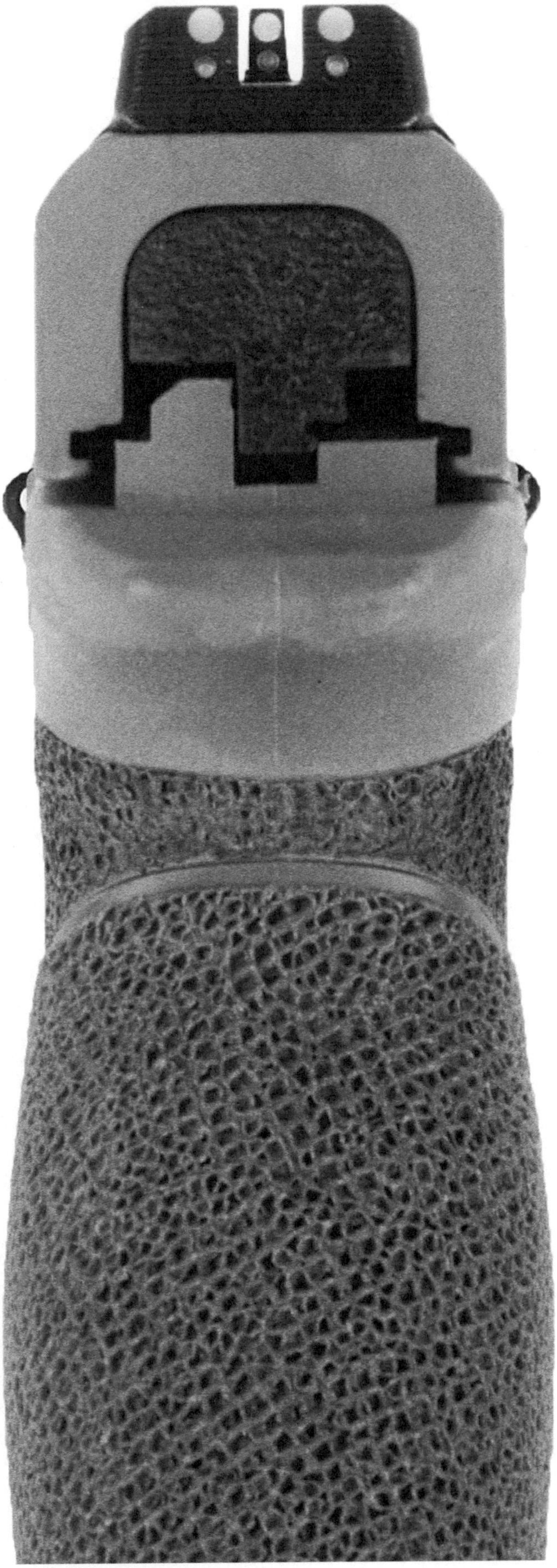

(left) This is the proper sight alignment.

(below) Bright fiber optic sights are a boon to most shooters.

(bottom) A bold, bright front sight makes for rapid sight acquisition in all conditions.

*l*Next, we study horizontal alignment. Depending upon the type of sight used, this may be the more difficult to properly align. Some sights simply do not have enough light between the rear sight posts for a fine sight picture. There must be an equal distance between each side of the rear sight notch. More or less on either side results in a pistol that isn't aimed properly at the target. The shots will be to one side or the other, often missing the

Good sights and a competent shooter will give excellent results.

when learning accurate fire is getting in too big of a hurry. This is true with the trigger press and aligning of the sights. There is plenty of time to move to faster shooting after you have mastered the basics of accurate shooting. (I am more concerned with accurate shooting than combat shooting in these pages.) When you are learning proper sight alignment, place the handgun at arm's length in the normal firing position. Acquire the sight alignment and hold it for a minute or so. Your arms may become tired of holding the pistol but you will have a good idea of what proper sight alignment looks like.

These old notch sights were adequate at best back in the day, but there are better choices today.

target completely at 25 yards or more. Some blocky service grade sights are the worst offenders in this regard. In short, you are guiding the bullet to the target. If you have not properly aligned the guidance system, the sights, then the bullet, cannot hit the target even if the grips and trigger press are properly addressed. Good results at short range may give you false confidence. If you find that you are homing the bullets in on target at 7 yards, a reasonable starting point, you may feel smug. Just address the basics and you will get the shot in at 25 yards, you may think. Not so. If the shot is off at 7 yards by only a sixteenth of an inch, the shot will be off the bullseye by 5 inches or so at 25 yards! Without delving too deeply into the mathematical formula, simply understand that errors are magnified by range.

It is true that the pistol's zero may be off. Double check and confirm the zero and be certain of your performance with other handguns. Go back to the .22. If you are drifting off of zero with all handguns, then you need to work on your technique. The sights may be misaligned, or the handgun may not be stable in your hand. You must look at the whole picture — grip, stance, sight alignment, sight picture and also the trigger press. One common problem

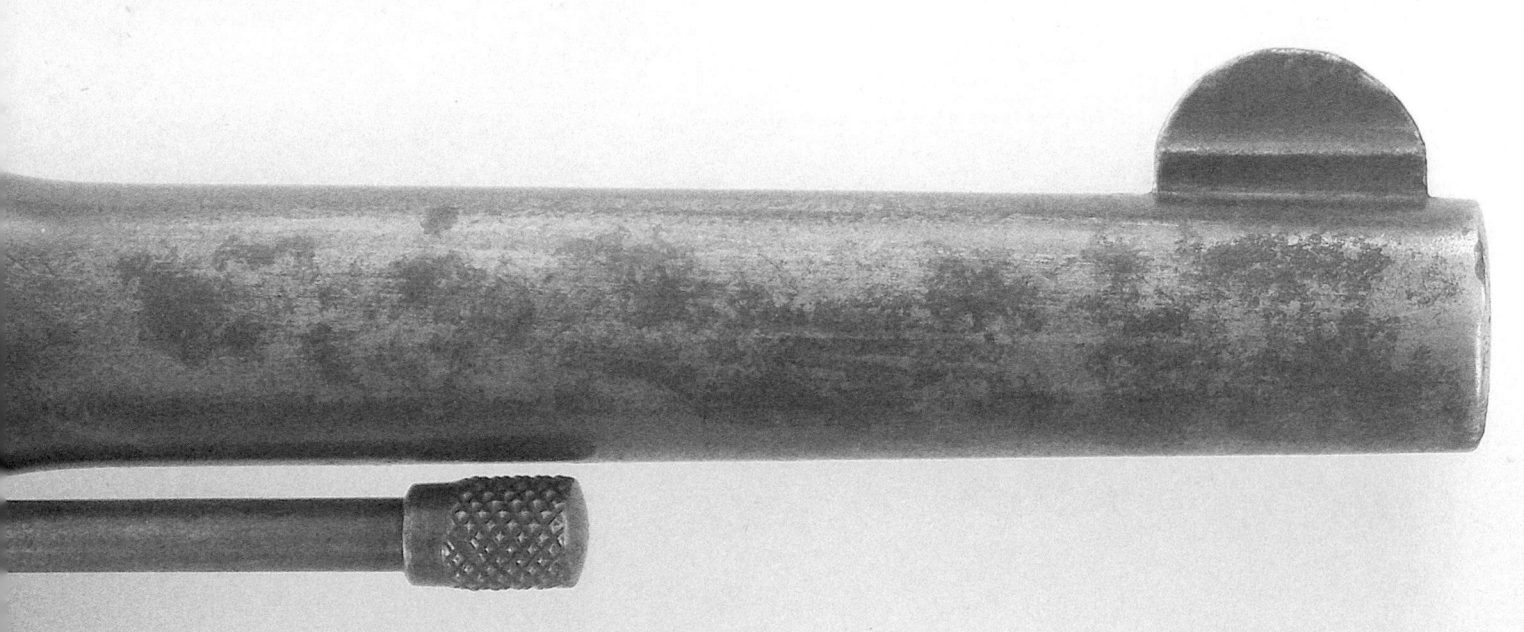

(top) This type of sight leaves the shooter wondering, where is the top?

(above) The target-grade AT84 9mm features excellent sights.

(right) A bold front post is an aid in marksmanship.

(opposite) GI sights sometimes work loose in low-end 1911 handguns. It is best to choose another sight system.

(top left) When firing for accuracy, a good set of sights is invaluable and takes some of the work out of shooting.

(top right) A high-profile sight is needed for accurate shooting.

(bottom) The Walther P38, in the author's opinion, was ahead of its time for sight design and profile.

Practice for a half minute to a minute in dry fire with a triple-checked unloaded firearm. Practice on a single problem — sight alignment. Just as the proper trigger press is built into muscle memory, your goal is to imprint proper sight alignment, too. You will find that when you are shooting on the range, you will pick up the proper sight alignment much more quickly after this type of indoctrination. The front sight should be sharply in focus. The eye cannot focus on three objects simultaneously — front sight, rear sight and the target. The front sight must be in sharp focus, leaving the rear sight and target slightly blurred.

The ability to quickly line the sights up and get hits is important in both personal defense and competition shooting.

The sight picture is the superimposition of the sights over the target. The target focus must be finite. Avoid area aiming. In competition, you do not aim at a whole target but a finite spot on the target. When hunting game you do not aim at the whole deer but the small vitals area. When engaged in personal defense practice — or God forbid the real thing — aim at a small area. Keep the sights aligned properly and the sight picture on the target. When the combination of sight alignment and sight picture is properly addressed, you have aimed your handgun properly.

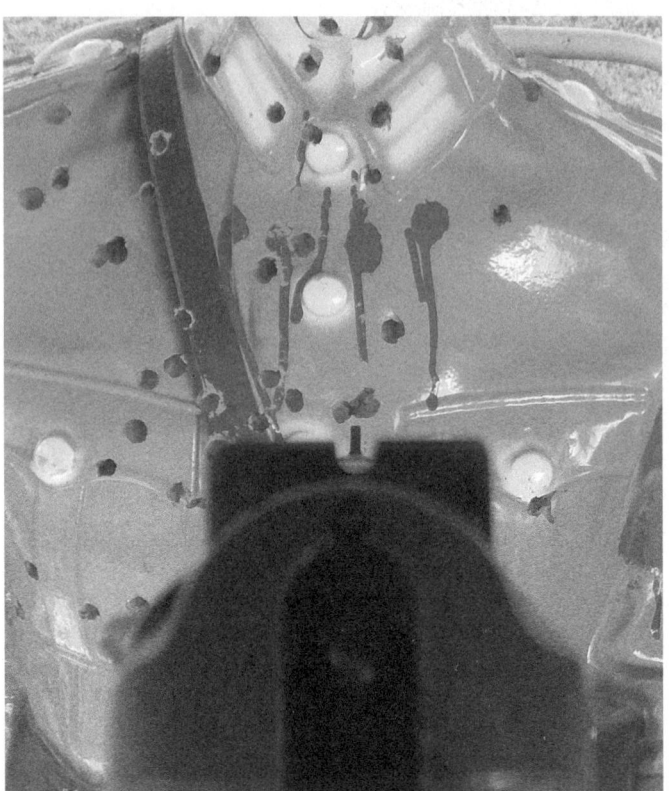

It is vital to have a bold front sight design that allows rapid acquisition with your eyes.

Now you must master pressing the trigger and maintaining the grip. When you read the target, you will understand if you are pressing the trigger right or left instead of straight to the rear, or if you are misaligning the sights. The front sight is the most important focus point. You must focus intently on it; by doing so, there is a natural tendency to properly align the sights. I like a sight with some type of contrast. My son uses a gold bead insert in his Novak Custom 1911. I like the three dot inserts, and on revolvers the orange insert front post is a great choice. (The Honor Defense handguns also have an orange insert.) Others want black sights and nothing else. The bright fiber optic has some appeal. The bottom line is, if the sights make the front sight appear as a blob they are not ideal for accuracy. If the insert draws attention to a small area of the handgun's front sight for aiming purposes, then you have an advantage.

An important consideration is the sight picture on the target. Some refer to the "bullseye hold," the "six o'clock hold" or holding "dead on." You can let a fixed-sight handgun dictate the hold — compensating hold for where the gun hits. Then there is the question of where the handgun maker zeros the firearm. There are different types of zeros and, thankfully, modern fixed-sight handguns seem to be properly zeroed more often than not. Then you have to wonder if some makers even test fire their handguns

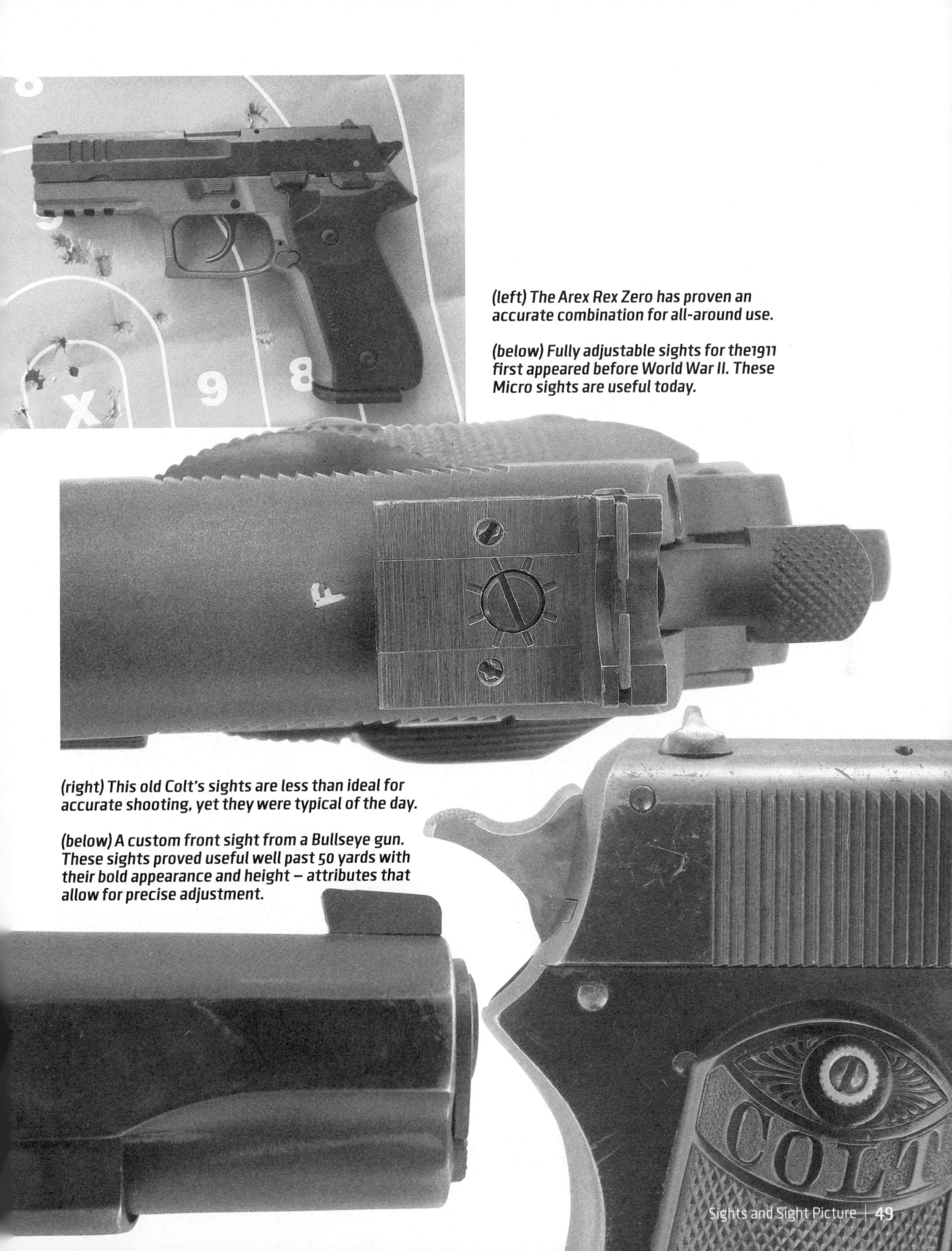

(left) The Arex Rex Zero has proven an accurate combination for all-around use.

(below) Fully adjustable sights for the 1911 first appeared before World War II. These Micro sights are useful today.

(right) This old Colt's sights are less than ideal for accurate shooting, yet they were typical of the day.

(below) A custom front sight from a Bullseye gun. These sights proved useful well past 50 yards with their bold appearance and height — attributes that allow for precise adjustment.

at all. As amazing as it may seem, some gems are not always fired for reliability and point of aim/point of impact correlation. That is up to the end user. The six o' clock hold simply means holding the sights under the target. The front sight is at six o' clock on the target and the bullet will strike the center of the bullseye.

Some shooters prefer a sight picture in which the front sight is directly below the object to be struck. The dead-on hold is one in which the front sight covers about half the object to be struck. I have used this hold for most of my shooting life when I have

a choice. For fast work and getting good hits quickly, this is the preferred hold. While the traditional bullseye hold works well for paper targets and slow fire, life isn't always paper targets and slow fire. The six o' clock hold has the greatest value when you understand how the pistol hits at long range. From there, you can use two different holds depending upon the distance. The six o' clock hold can be used with a Colt 1911 automatic at 25 yards. However, at 50 yards the drop of the bullet is such that the dead-on hold will be chosen. Even if you have adjustable sights, understanding the difference between these

Springfield's Range Officer is among the best buys in a modern 1911. Note the fully adjustable rear sight and post front sight.

(above) Possibly the best combat sights ever found on a handgun belong on this British Enfield .38-caliber revolver.

(right) Note the bold, front sight found on the British Enfield. It's not only a good combat sight, but changeable as well.

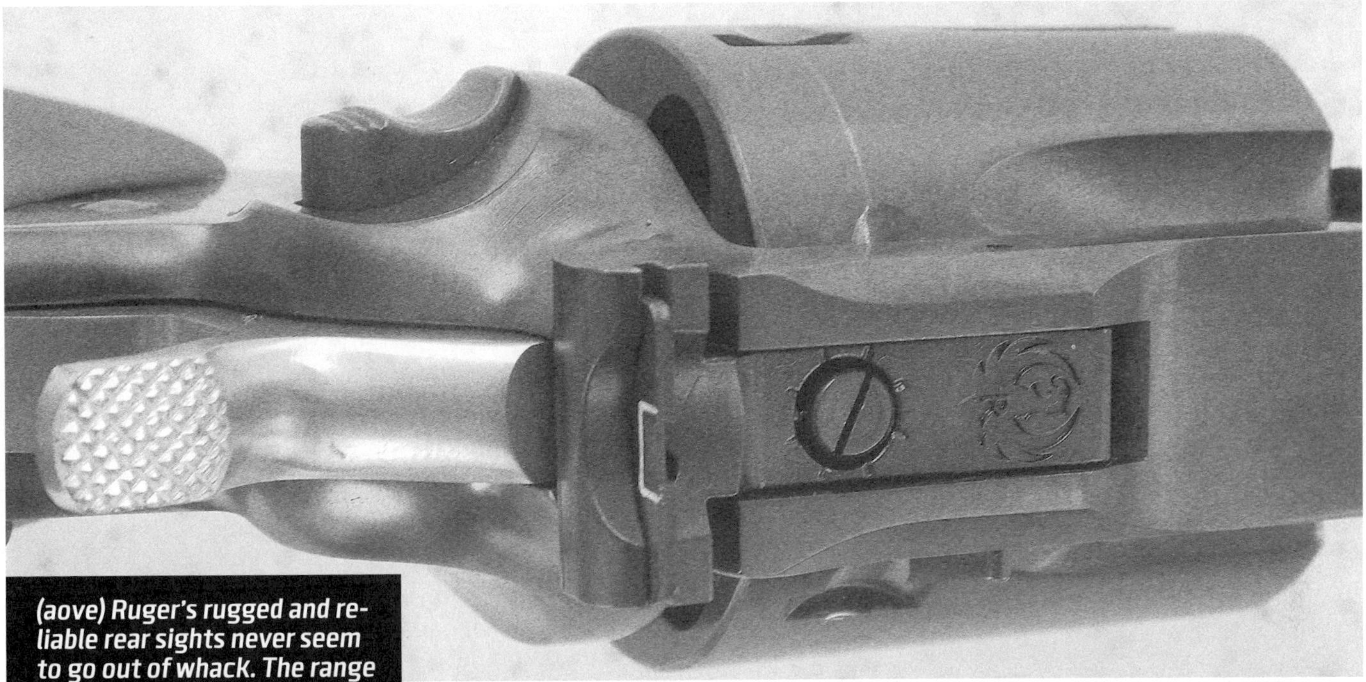

two holds at different ranges will be beneficial.

Perfect sight alignment is important, but so is getting a perfect sight picture on the target. To reiterate again: never aim at the whole target. Aim at a finite spot on the target. Aiming at the whole target is called area aiming and is a major cause of missing the target. You would not aim at a whole deer when hunting, you aim at the vitals. This is a small area about 8 inches wide on most game animals; you need to superimpose the sights on this area and aim for the exact center. By the same token, in a personal defense situation you should aim for a finite area on the threat. A front shirt button or the arterial region is preferred as an aiming point.

The superiority of the modern ramped front sight, left, to the traditional half moon front sight, right, is obvious. The ramped sight allows much greater precision.

Factory adjusted, fixed revolver sights, right, never go out of adjustment. For hard service they work well. The fully adjustable sight, left, is a great boon to handloaders and anyone using different loads and striving for accuracy.

Types of Handgun Sights

The types of handgun sights are many. The ideal choice for accurate shooting is some type of fully adjustable pistol sight. The best overall choice will be geared toward general purpose use. Specialized use includes long-range varmint shooting that requires a thin, front sight blade for acceptable accuracy or self-luminous irons for personal defense use in dim light conditions. With few exceptions, early handgun sights were no more than notches in the rear strap and bumps on the front of the barrel. They were a vague aiming point and probably the reason that so many shooters felt they had to rely upon unaimed fire or point shooting. Yet, excellent long-range shooting was done at times during the Indian Wars with the simple notch in the hammer (later in the top strap) and bead front sight of Colt revolvers. Improved sights began to appear incrementally by 1900. Some Colt and Smith and Wesson revolvers featured good-quality, high-visibility sights that work well even

The red dot sight is useful for target shooting and even small game and can be a great deal of fun on the right handgun.

today. For the most part, service grade revolver sights used a groove cut into the top strap and simple notch rear sight. Over time, the rear notch was widened and the front sight became a ramp. This is pretty much where fixed revolver sights remain today.

The nature of the automatic pistol slide demanded a sight that was mounted above the slide. Early examples were quite small and no better than revolver sights. Development of competition-oriented sights led to larger high-visibility options. The revolver developed more quickly than the automatic pistol. During the period directly following World War I, useful and effective fully adjustable revolver sights were developed and are still in general use, although the modern types are more rugged and reliable. Modern fully adjustable automatic pistol sights are, finally, rugged and reliable enough for

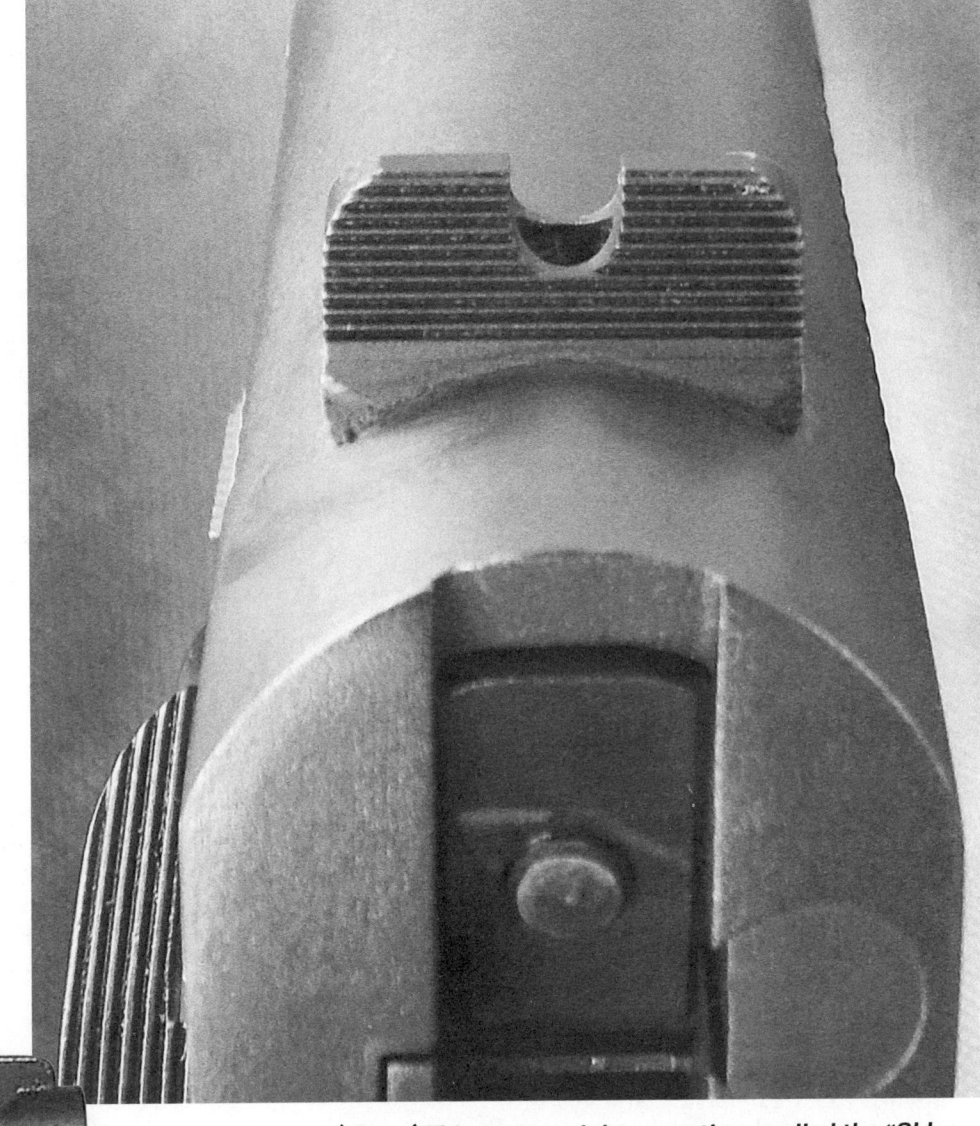

(above) This custom sight, sometimes called the "Old Man's" sight, as it is easily picked up visually by those with fading vision, is a viable option that offers surprisingly good accuracy.

(left) These sights are properly lined up for precision shooting. While termed a "fixed sight," some adjustment is possible by drifting the sight in the dovetailed sight groove in the slide.

service use. During World War II, the old types of sights were in abundance but there were standouts in modern sight innovation. The Enfield .38-caliber service revolver isn't very powerful but sports the best combat sights of the day — and they are by no means outdated today. The Walther P38 features a set of high-visibility sights well-suited to long-range or precision fire. During this time, the development of fully adjustable rear sights for revolvers coupled with ramped front sights solved the problems associated with revolver sights. The Colt Python, Smith

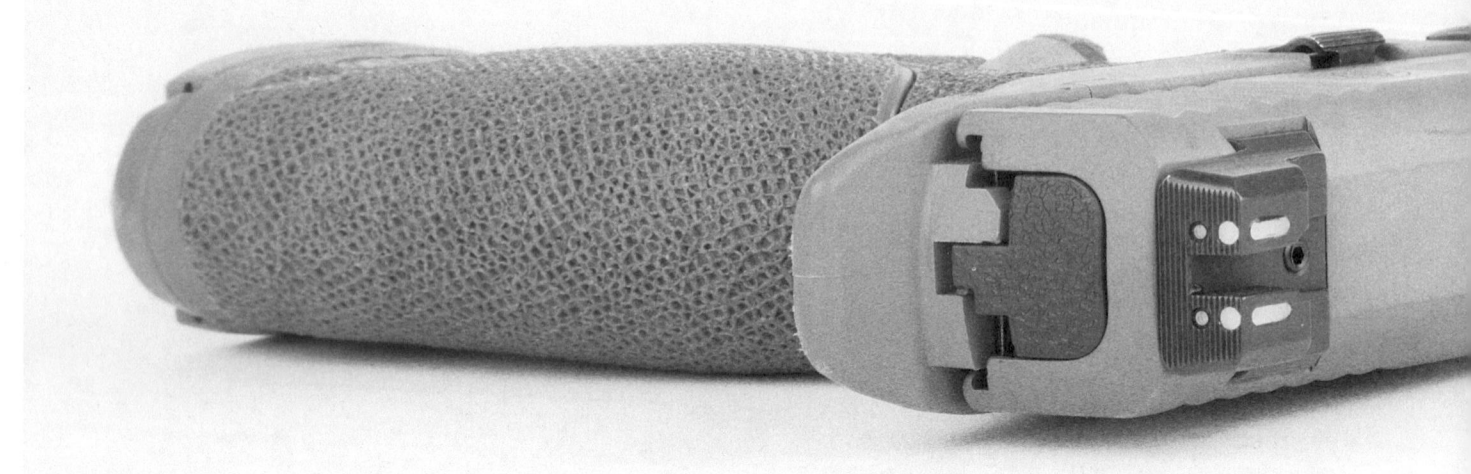

Viking Tactical sights offer excellent all-around night and day utility.

This Smith and Wesson features a Novak front and a fully adjustable rear sight.

and Wesson Combat Magnum and other revolvers featured excellent adjustable sights.

Colt's National Match pistols also featured adjustable sights, but the attachment by a hollow pin wasn't the sturdiest and neither were the sights. Aftermarket Bomar sights gave the person wishing a target-grade 1911 suitable for field use a formidable combination. A generation of fixed sights were developed for the 1911. These included the King's Hardballer and Micro-type fixed sights. They were good examples of general use fixed sights. These were relatively inexpensive and offered a good option for the 1911. Colt did not improve the GI sight picture with the Series 70 but offered modestly improved sights with the Series 80. As for the real difference between these improved sights and GI sights, it is slight in firing from the benchrest. The GI sights are small but precise when properly aligned. The larger sights are easier to see and are picked up more quickly when firing offhand. For accuracy, it is best to choose at least an improved fixed sight with the 1911 handgun. It is relatively easy to upgrade to some types of 1911 sights, while others will require the services of a machinist/gunsmith.

While you can upgrade, the more economical course is to purchase a handgun with credible sights in the first place. The sights should be chosen for quality, practical accuracy, non-snag construction, and durability. This is a tall order, but one that modern sights fulfill well. Among the first practical high-visibility sights was the Novak Lo Mount. This featured a pyramid-like rear sight that provided an excellent sight picture. The Novak sights are standard issue on many of the Springfield 1911 handguns and provide great utility. Kimber night sights

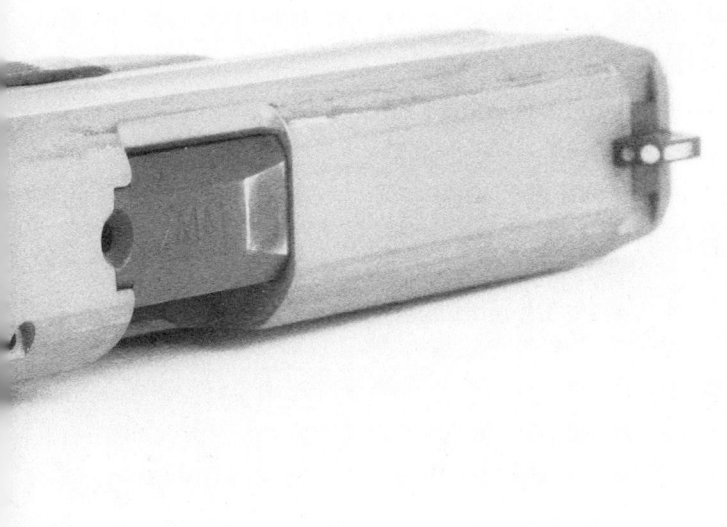

are available as an option and should be ordered on every personal defense pistol from Kimber. The sight will not catch on clothing during the draw and offers a virtually snag-free contour. The Kimber front sight is a bold post that may be from .200- to .249-inches high, depending on the application. Reducing the vertical profile of a pistol sight is important because the sights rub on all manner of things, including the holster and clothing.

There are a number of considerations including short-, medium-, and long-range fire and snag-free presentation. Testing something as subjective as handgun sights is difficult. It is easy to make a qualified statement that Novak sights are superior to mil spec ones, but to compare those from Novak to Kimber is more difficult. The rear sight should have a bold profile that is easily picked up quickly. The pyramid-style sights now available offer a good sight picture and do not trap shadows. When all is said and done, the Novak and Kimber-style combat sights are at the top of the heap and offer excellent usability.

An excellent shooter firing the Smith and Wesson SW1911 target model at 50 yards.

There are choices in sight types as well. Plain black, white three dot and tritium night inserts are the most common. Novak also offers a gold bead front sight, which is among the very best. This bead gives an excellent all-around sight picture, can be seen in the dark with a minimum of ambient light and is immune to oil and solvent. Self-luminous iron sights are a good option, too, but they are not without drawbacks. For example, during daytime or bright light shooting, tritium can reflect sunlight. The same is true of nickel-plated sights, but the tritium insert is not as reflective as nickel.

Depending upon how deeply the shock-mounted insert is buried, sunlight may play on the tritium. Tritium inserts will work loose. Typically, the front sight is the one to take flight. I have only had this happen once, and it was at the 10,000-round mark. Note that light glinting on the left side of a brightly reflective sight will cause the pistol to fire right due to a non-standard sight picture, and vice versa.

I once strongly preferred black over white three dot sights. With the coming of age and a loss in visual acuity, I now find the white dot sights work well for me. With unaided vision, blurred sights are

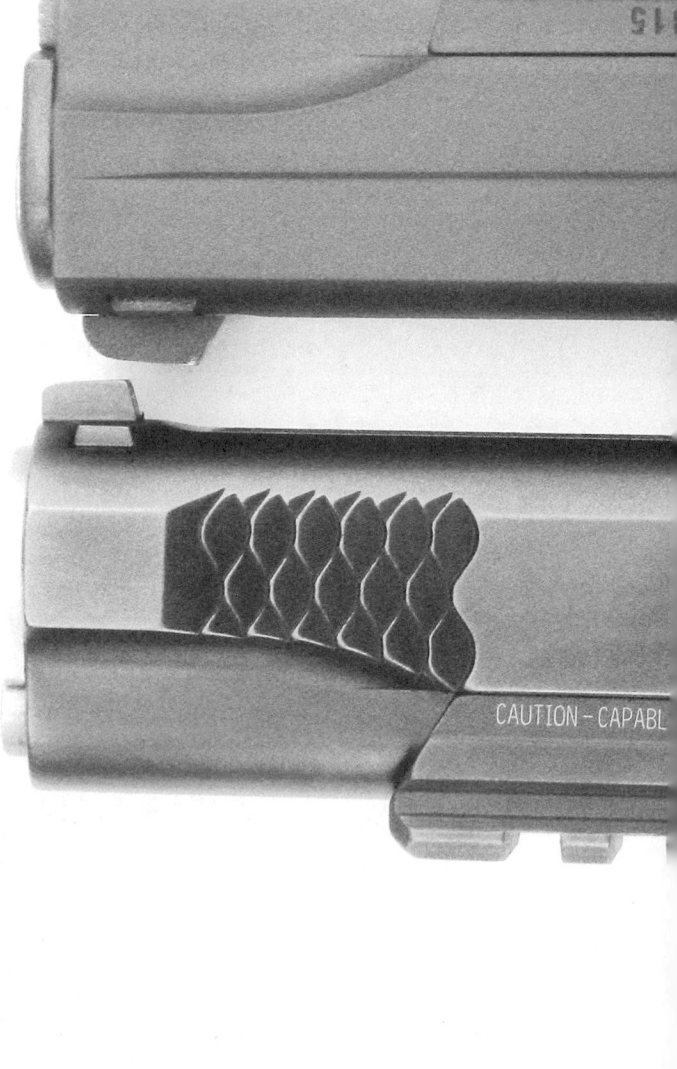

These 1911 handguns feature Novak sights of slightly different configuration.

The Novak rear sight is snag-free for concealed carry but gives you a perfect sight picture for accuracy. It is good for both speed and precision.

SIG SAUER INC.
EXETER-NH-USA

54A 0

Smith&Wesson
SW1911TA

...RING WITH MAGAZINE REMOVED

The author has seen mixed results with fiber optic sights. Some stay mounted while others work loose with time.

The Springfield TRP features Novak sights with tritium inserts. It doesn't get any better.

a real problem. Fiber optic or white dots help a great deal. I can recommend Novak with the fiber optic option, but in the past I have suffered the loss of the fiber optic component with relatively light use of sights of other makes. The Novak is quite robust. Perhaps they did not introduce their version until it was perfected. An elegant option I find useful is the Novak Gold Bead front sight. All who use this sight appreciate the gold bead. It shows up in most dim conditions and provides an excellent visual aiming point. Kel-Tec offers easily changeable options for their PMR 30 pistol.

There is more to the equation than how the sights look and how well you are able to quickly acquire them. Some are too sharp for efficient holster use. They need to be snag-free when carried in tight-fitting concealment holsters. The Novak rear sight will not grab tender skin. That is efficiency by design. The original Novak Lo Mount is the king of concealment, but Wilson Combat sights also do a good job. The sights that absolutely must be avoided are the add-on adjustable ones that hang over the rear of the slide. These are lousy for service use and are not my favorites for target applications, either. A proper target sight should be low riding, properly set into a machined dovetail, and rugged enough for duty use. The inexpensive add-ons are not very robust and, when they protrude from the rear of the slide, you are asking for them to be knocked off on a door jam. They are poor examples and should be avoided. If you want the good stuff, look at the factory adjustable sights used by Les Baer, Springfield and Kimber — they are all very desirable. Each are dirt tough adjustable sights well worth their price.

We have come a long way from fragile adjustable sights for automatic pistols. The Bomar was an excellent sight in its day, but now many factories offer first-class options for 1911 handguns. When you address hand fit and trigger press in the shop before purchasing a new handgun, add a new dimension. Consider the sight picture as well. It is among the most important choices you will make.

ALL IN THE TRIGGER

*Proper sight alignment and trigger control
coupled with a firm grip results in accurate hits.
A good set of sights is a big help.*

Controlling the trigger is the single most difficult part of handgunning. Yet, the process is simply explained: The trigger is pressed to the rear without disturbing the sight alignment or sight picture. There can be no disturbance as the trigger is carefully pressed and the shot breaks. I am not certain that calling it a trigger pull is ever correct. The way a beginner addresses the trigger is often called a "jerk." They slap, or jerk the trigger until the sear breaks and the striker or hammer releases to fire the handgun. Pressing the trigger is a controlled movement.

The notion of squeezing the trigger has some merit to describe the action, but it seems to denote for

This is the proper grip and trigger position. It should be practiced on a daily basis.

Jerking or clutching the trigger as a result of sympathetic movement in the hand is often the result of anticipating recoil. Recoil impulse is strong with some handguns. I believe that muzzle blast is as likely to cause flinch as is recoil. Muzzle blast isn't something we are used to and it can have an effect on your concentration. That is why it is best to begin shooting with a .22-caliber handgun. Once you have mastered the basics, then you can add becoming acclimated to recoil and blast separately.

many the act of compression in portion. You do compress the trigger; the proper action is best expressed by the term "trigger press." The trigger is pressed to the rear and fires the pistol. This movement of the trigger finger must be clean and free of hitches, jerks and hesitation. The trigger must ride smoothly to the rear and the handgun must remain steady. The beginning shooter often finds the other fingers moving in a sympathetic action as the trigger is pressed. This is sometimes called milking the trigger as the hand moves in a manner similar to milking a cow. The trigger finger must always move independently from the rest of the hand and fingers. Another reason that shooters miss is due to jerking the trigger.

The proper finger position for controlling a pistol trigger.

Note excellent control by Jessie Duff as she fires the 1911 in rapid fire.

When you anticipate recoil there are several indicators on the target. If you are a reasonably good shot and have been controlling the .22 and begin scattering the shots on the target with a 9mm, then you are having a problem with recoil. If you are shooting the 1911 .45 and the groups are reasonably cohesive but the shots are low, then you are probably jerking the trigger and pulling shots downward. This is where dry fire practice pays off. Dry fire is safe manipulation of the trigger with a triple-checked unloaded handgun. When you press the trigger, the hammer should fall without disturbing the sights. You will be surprised how much wobble is evident in the hold even when practicing in dry fire. Practice the hold and sight picture while executing the trigger press until you cannot get it wrong. Milking the trigger is also a cause of missing the point of aim. It may take many forms as both the trigger action and the grip are affected. As the trigger is jerked, the pistol will be off aim, but the hands move and this results in missing as the handgun cannot recoil into the same place time after time without a tight grip. During the press, the pad of the trigger finger should be on the trigger face while the handgun is held with the proper high grip. The bore of the handgun — the centerline of the barrel — is ideally lined up with the bone in the forearm. This affords stability, direction and control.

(below) This competition shooter exhibits good form as she homes in on the 50-yard bullseye. (Courtesy CMP)

(bottom) This shooter's form is ideal. Note the web of the hand is hard against the grip tang. (Courtesy CMP)

There are handguns that are a challenge to properly control in this manner. The Beretta 92 9mm is fat for my hands, but an easy shooter due to the 9mm cartridge. The Glock 21 .45 is an easy-kicking .45 with much to recommend, and the long-slide Model 41 even better. Even so, I cannot control this size handgun well. The same goes for the Glock 20 10mm which, in my experience, is the single most accurate Glock handgun. I can control these handguns off of the benchrest and when firing on the range. However, in a true tactical situation or a high-speed drill, they are not controllable by this shooter. So, while the human element is most important, be certain that you have not overstressed your hand with a pistol that is too large.

If you have done everything but trigger action correctly you will miss the target. If the sight picture is just a little off, chances off you will hit the target. Jerk the trigger — and you will miss. A common error is laying too much of the trigger finger on the handgun (over-extending the finger). The trigger finger may even contact the trigger guard and the frame. Not having proper contact with the trigger face will result in your shots landing to one side or the other. Even worse is laying the body of the trigger finger against the frame when shooting. When you do this, part of your effort is absorbed in moving against the frame, the effect making the trigger press seem much heavier. It is very important that you regard every shot as an individual effort. Never consider the shots fired as a string of shots. Each trigger pull is an individual event and must be delivered with accuracy.

The action cycles after firing and the trigger resets. This is true even of revolver triggers that are reset by means of a trigger return spring. If the trigger finger is on the trigger face when it resets, you will feel it — a signal that it's ready for another press. Being in complete control includes being in control of trigger reset. If you ride the trigger with your finger then you are in control for subsequent shots. Take-up is

shorter and you will not have to ride the long take-up of actions such as those found in the Glock. When firing a revolver, the trigger will reset completely forward and you must allow this. However, many double-action revolver shooters have adopted the successful technique of allowing as much time for the trigger to reset as is involved in the trigger press. Press the trigger, the revolver fires, then you allow the trigger to reset and it is on the target again. When firing a double-action first-shot handgun such as the CZ 75, control the first round and keep the trigger in contact with your finger as it

(top) The shooting stance must be comfortable to allow long practice sessions, but also strong and rigid enough to control recoil and maintain accuracy.

(middle) Practice, practice and more practice is demanded. The proper firing grip must be firm and the handgun must be controlled.

(bottom) Revolvers and self-loaders require you to modify your grip to fit the individual handgun. Each must be practiced to master the type.

The LaserMax green laser is a great aid in marksmanship training.

resets; then follow with controlled single-action fire. These skills are learned in dry fire. Fire, keep the finger on the trigger, and rack the slide of an automatic pistol to reset the trigger. Dry fire again, etc.

Catching the Link

Catching the link is an expression related to proper management of the trigger. I have used the trigger properly and made quite a few brilliant shots, won competitions, and awed myself. When I have not used the trigger properly, I have missed at ridiculously close range. Consistency is what counts. A consistent shooter that gives it all he has will beat a better shooter that has doubts and does not practice. The steady student is more impressive than the student who occasionally gets it right. We all reach a plateau at which we seem not to advance. We struggle to get to the next level. Just stay on course and be certain your shots are controlled until you get there. I often fire in personal practice until I can fire faster than I can control the shots, then I fire at my controlled cadence to remind myself that I can shoot well. You have to push yourself and work hard to grow as a shooter.

There are rules that pertain to trigger management. Like all good rules there are exceptions to their implementation. The rule of using only the tip of the trigger finger to press the trigger is one that simply cannot always be applied. Different hand sizes, trigger

reach and finger placement required for the various action types make perfect finger placement difficult to define. There are single action, double action, double-action only, and two-stage military triggers. Some break remarkably clean. Others are as rough as the parking brake of a Ford Pinto. Triggers are like taking a step. Each is paced and the event should be natural and under your control. If you address the trigger improperly, the action is like a fall or misstep that leaves you off balance.

If you anticipate firing from behind cover or from less-than-ideal shooting positions, these firing positions should be practiced.

When addressing a good, smooth trigger action — like the one found on the Springfield TRP — use the first pad of the trigger finger. That action breaks at less than five pounds and is clean as a whistle. Conversely, the long double-action trigger of the Beretta 92, at some 14 pounds compression, demands greater control, so use the second pad of your finger on the face of the trigger for greater leverage. The first position with tip of the finger is for a gradual application of pressure and a break that is invariably smooth. The double action is longer, heavier and not nearly as smooth or crisp, but good shooting can be done with either type given adequate practice, the proper mindset and

(left) Firing when moving from one shooting position to another can be mastered when the basics of proper grip and sight picture are ingrained.

With practice, powerful handguns such as the .45 ACP can be controlled in rapid fire. Note cartridge case in the air and the handgun is back on target.

Draw, fire, and the left-hand plate swings from a solid hit. Steel plates are an excellent training resource.

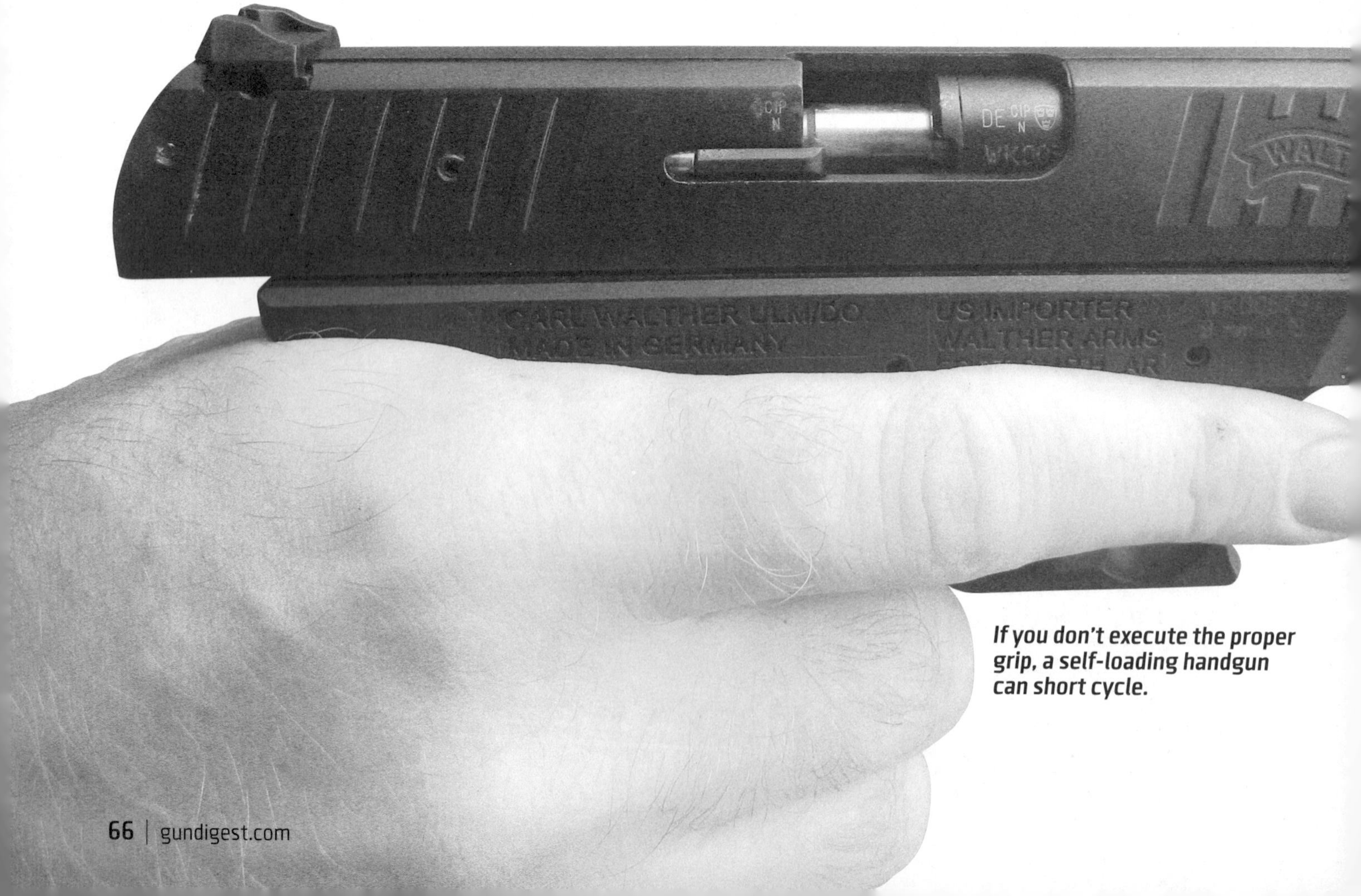

If you don't execute the proper grip, a self-loading handgun can short cycle.

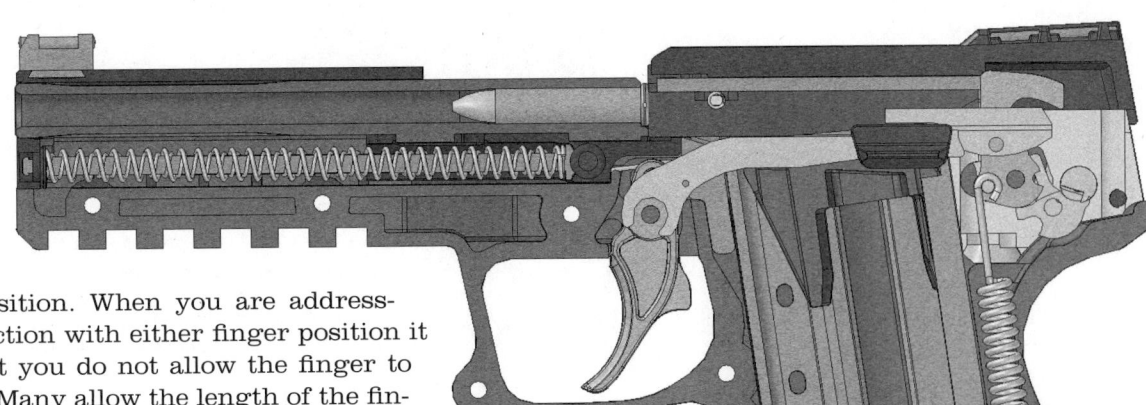

trigger-finger position. When you are addressing the trigger action with either finger position it is imperative that you do not allow the finger to touch the frame. Many allow the length of the finger to ride against the frame when a certain offset and a crooked finger is needed. Touching or 'riding' the frame or receiver adds unwanted pounds to the trigger action and throws consistency out the window. (Trigger finger drag on the frame is one of the reasons the original Colt 1911 was given the now-standard 1911A1 finger slots in the frame. Particularly short fingers often contacted the frame in the original design. The 1911A1 became a more shootable handgun.)

By the same token, when the Smith and Wesson Model 39 was morphed into the high capacity M59, the larger grip and trigger reach made for a handgun more difficult to use well. A professional manages the trigger issued and doesn't complain, but we recognize the relative difficulty of the types. Even with well-shaped grips and frames the novice will sometimes drag the finger on the frame. Catch this problem, observe and eliminate it.

I routinely teach students who have chosen a double-action revolver or a double-action, first-shot autoloader for concealed carry. These shooters will tire quickly when shooting the handgun if they attempt to maintain the first pad on the trigger. When you have the luxury of choosing the handgun upon which you will bet your life, the smoothness of the trigger mechanism should influence your purchase. (In service, personnel persevere with what is issued.) After checking the chamber and the magazine well to be certain the firearm is not loaded, you can test the trigger action. Check it twice to be certain again that it isn't loaded. Cock it and aim at a safe backstop. Press the trigger. Give attention to the sight picture and sight alignment but concentration most on the trigger press. Form a mental image of the trigger action as it is engaged and as the trigger is compressed. As you press the trigger, does it begin to stack? Is there any creep felt as you take up the slack, or free movement before engagement? Do you feel grit in the action? The pistol

may have a defect from the factory or it might simply need lubrication. Some very good trigger actions have characteristics that take time to understand. Even the tightest CZ 75 pistols often exhibit a modest backlash in the single-action trigger after firing.

As you break the trigger you will feel the striker or hammer disconnect from the sear. When you are able to discern this break, then you are becoming acquainted with the firearm. Keep trying to detect this subtle disengagement. Rack the slide with your finger on the trigger. Do you feel the action as the trigger resets? A good rhythm or cadence is to allow the same time to press the trigger as the reset. The cadence of fire is not set by how quickly you are able to press the trigger but by how quickly you are able to reacquire the sight picture. I am pretty certain you could teach a monkey to press the trigger quickly. Controlling the trigger and making hits is another matter.

Dry fire is the cornerstone of proficiency. As you dry fire your handgun and control it without moving the sights, attempt different finger positions. Try the first pad, and alternate with the tip to see how trigger control is affected. You will find that one position for every trigger size and trigger pull weight simply cannot be applied to every firearm or action. The trigger is simply a mechanical device that must be handled. It is somewhere between a charcoal lighter and a Geiger counter in complexity, and is a critical step in mastering the firearm.

When mastering the trigger it is good to understand how the trigger, sear, transfer bar and disconnect operate.

THE INVALUABLE .22

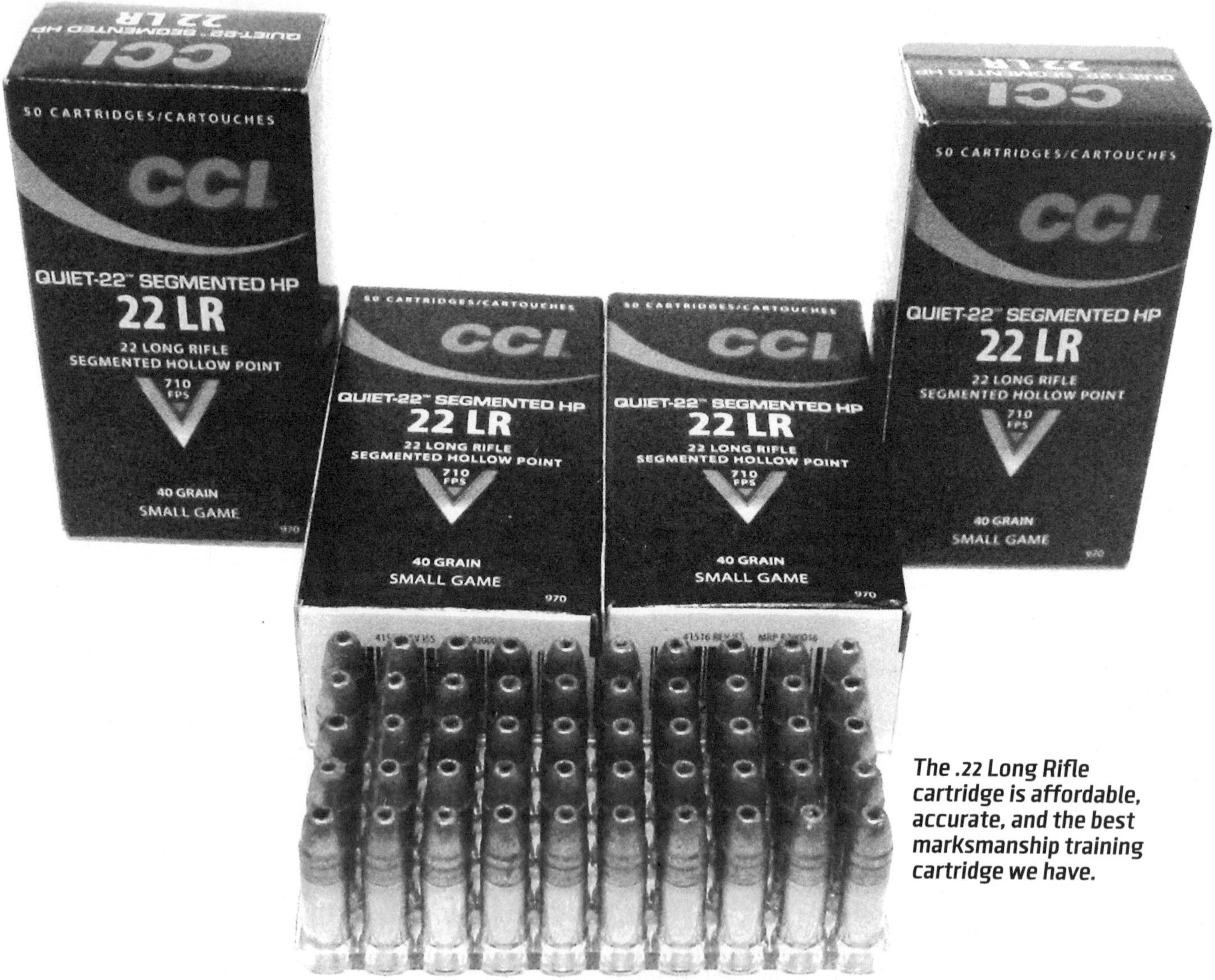

The .22 Long Rifle cartridge is affordable, accurate, and the best marksmanship training cartridge we have.

A proven resource in creating a marksman is the use of inexpensive .22-caliber ammunition and firearms. The rimfire offers little or no recoil, minimal report, and good accuracy. It is recognized as a foundational training aid for pure marksmanship, that is, trigger control and learning sight alignment and sight picture. In today's tight economy we see both .22-caliber conversions and dedicated firearms of the diminutive caliber pressed into service in training. With the high and increasing costs of training, .22 conversion units and purpose-built rimfire guns are a good buy. Any way you slice it, the difference in price between rimfire and centerfire ammunition allows you to fire many more rounds of rimfire than is possible in a single service cartridge of centerfire.

on this rim. When the firing pin strikes the case rim and crushes it against the firing chamber, the priming compound creates a flame that ignites the powder in the cartridge case. This type of ignition is not as reliable as centerfire technology. Rimfire cartridges are reliable in general but not as dependable as the modern centerfire cartridge. For this reason, the .22 isn't recommended for personal defense, although many have a .22 on

The humble .22's construction is 1840s style with a heel-based bullet and rimfire inside priming. It isn't as reliable as centerfire cartridges.

The .22 can be used in ranges that would not be safe with high-powered firearms. It is a different design from a different era, and this must be understood. It isn't a miniature centerfire, far from it. Let's look at the construction of a .22-caliber rimfire cartridge.

The .22 bullet is of soft lead and heel-based, which simply means that the projectile is the same diameter as the cartridge case. A heel or rebated rim on the base of the bullet allows it to be pinched into the cartridge case. This construction is not as robust as the centerfire, which typically features a bullet crimped into the case. The rimfire gets its name from the type of priming compound it uses. The .22 Long Rifle is the last survivor of the rimfire cartridges, primarily because it is not used for critical duty. The service size .38 and .44 rimfire cartridges have long been obsolete. The inside of the cartridge case is primed around the cartridge case rim. The .22 headspaces

hand that they have pressed into this role. Change ammunition in the gun often if you have a .22 dedicated to critical duty.

Due to their rimfire construction, .22-caliber firearms can be damaged if they are dry fired. The firing pin will strike the firing chamber and it goes without saying that steel on steel isn't good. Something has to give — either you will peck up the chamber or break the firing pin. The heel-based bullet is also not as sturdy as the crimped centerfire. (The modern .22 Rimfire Magnum uses a crimped, jacketed bullet.) The bullet is easily bent away from the cartridge case during cycling. When the rimfire fails to properly feed due to a bullet shifting in the case, an immediate action drill ramming the bolt forward often makes the jam worse. The powder used in rimfire cartridges is intended to maximize the cartridge in a rifle barrel. This powder often fails to burn completely in a short handgun barrel. As a result, the .22 is dirtier-loading than any properly loaded centerfire cartridge. Powder ash builds up more quickly.

Due to its heel-based construction, the .22 LR is more prone to damage and misfeeds than centerfire ammunition. This is simply a trade-off, and a modest one at that.

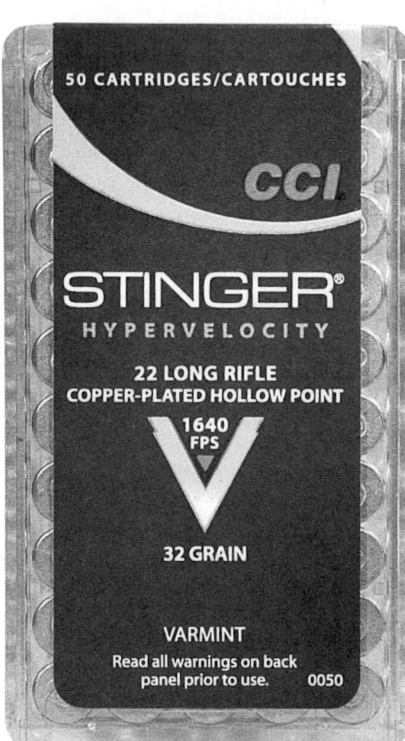

While hyper-velocity cartridges are most efficient in rifles, the author has found that they function well in self-loading handguns, too.

All of these drawbacks are apparent to sportsmen and shooters who grew up on the .22. A tactical shooter practicing with the rimfire may be disappointed. They will find that the little pipsqueak begins to malfunction at around the 300-round mark. Cleaning is needed more often. The bullet is less robust in handling than a centerfire. When shooting thousands of rounds, more often than not there will be several misfeeds and even a failure to fire of the inside primed rimfire cartridge. These malfunctions are recognized by those who grew up with the .22, but may prove unsettling to a shooter who knows that the centerfire Beretta, Glock or SIG will go thousands of rounds without any sort of issue.

While the value of the rimfire is unquestioned, those who adopt it for training must understand the nature of the cartridge. When using modern .22

Centerfire cartridges (outside) are more reliable than rimfire cartridges (inside).

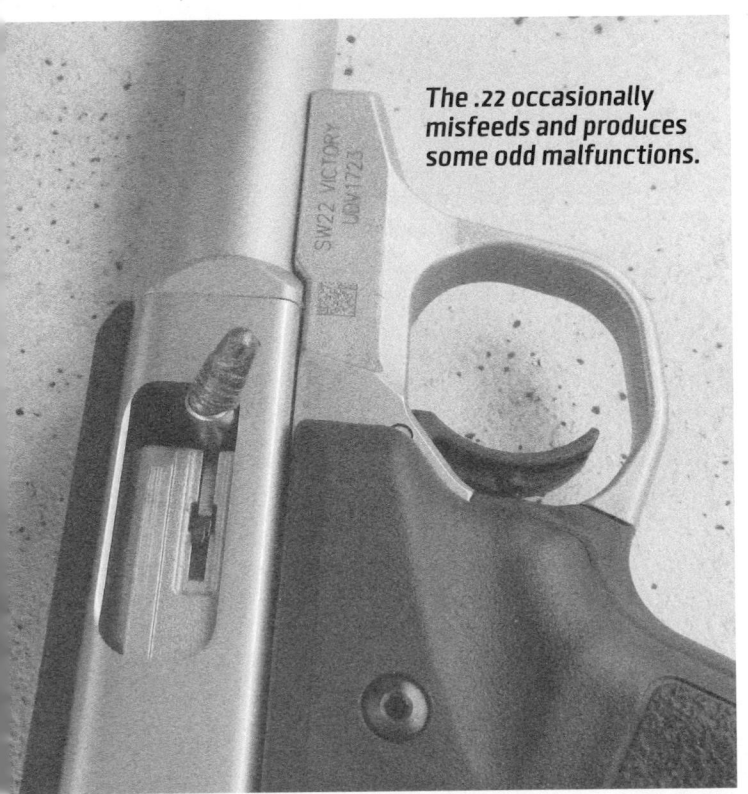

The .22 occasionally misfeeds and produces some odd malfunctions.

ammo, such as the CCI Mini-Mag, malfunctions are very low. If you use a revolver, you may never notice malfunctions. That being said, the .22 is a wonderful training cartridge and a fine small game round. Even so, the shooter moving from larger calibers like the 9mm to the .22 needs to understand the cartridge.

.22 Training Considerations

We have discussed the characteristics of the .22-caliber cartridge. The need to clean the firearm often is indicated as well as the acceptance of less cartridge reliability. The .22's light recoil and low muzzle blast are ideal for marksmanship training. There is no distraction from the fundamentals of marksmanship. This is fine for target shooting. Tactical shooting, though, demands movement and firing quickly at moving targets. These tactical drills are not the same as target shooting. The primary mistake most shooters make when using rimfire firearms for practice is failing to firmly grasp the firearm as they would when using a centerfire. They relax the grip because there is no recoil. They breeze through training and ace the course with minimal

The Tactical Solutions .22 conversion unit for the Glock is a great training tool that is reliable and accurate enough for meaningful practice.

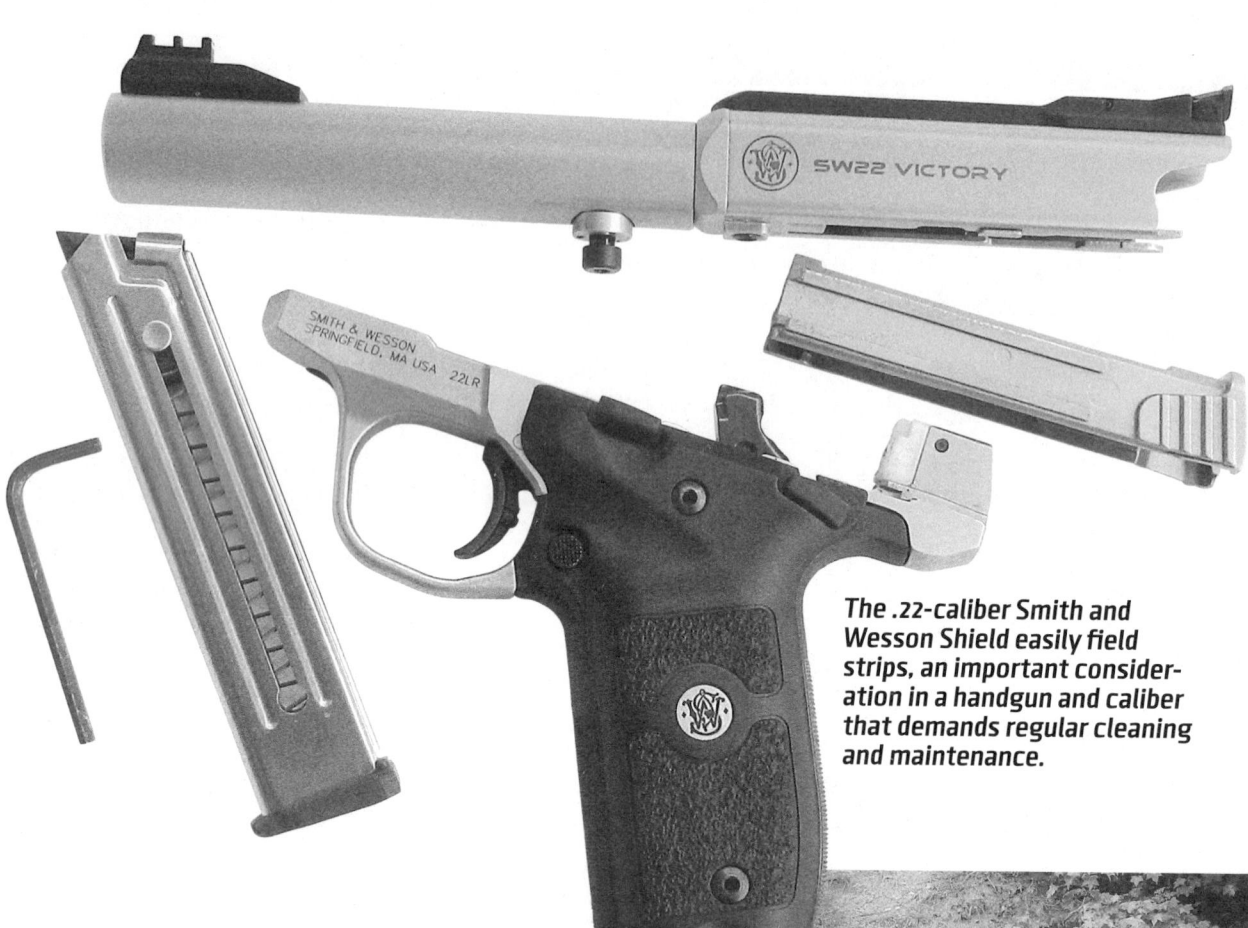

The .22-caliber Smith and Wesson Shield easily field strips, an important consideration in a handgun and caliber that demands regular cleaning and maintenance.

effort. The cadence of fire is also disrupted.

When shooting a service pistol, the cadence of fire is not set by how quickly you are able to press the trigger but by how quickly you are able to reacquire the sights and control recoil. The .22 does not present the same set of problems. You may find yourself firing much more quickly and perhaps making five hits with the .22 in the time it takes to make two good hits with the .40-caliber pistol. This is not necessarily a good thing. If this training crosses over to the centerfire handgun, you will be firing too quickly and end up missing. When shooting the .22 for tactical training, you must use the same strong grip and hold you use with the centerfire, and you should time your shots in the same manner as the centerfire as well. Fire, control recoil, reacquire the sights, and fire again. Only in this manner will rimfire training cross over to the centerfire in a profitable manner.

When it comes to rimfire training, the distance is not as important with handguns. Whether shooting rimfire or centerfire, keep your training within 25 yards. Pepper poppers and other steel reaction targets must be set for the .22 rimfire or they will fail to register hits. Often, even a light ping isn't heard despite a direct hit with the .22. There is much tinkering that must be done in order to make rimfire

Ashley Thomas fires a vintage Colt Official Police .22.

Ashley Thomas practices with her personal .22 Magnum defensive revolver.

training profitable. Such training will never take the place of live fire with the service gun and ammunition, but it is a cost-effective option that will sharpen your skills. With a few simple considerations a rimfire training program will be both profitable for your proficiency and light on your wallet.

.22 History

By far the most popular rimfire today is the .22 Long Rifle, or .22 LR. This loading has been around since 1887, originally stoked with black powder. The .22s were seen as gallery rounds for indoor target practice and for taking small game. The .22 short is … shorter and less powerful. It's also more expensive these days, but a fun little round for short-range plinking. It's still loaded primarily in the excellent CCI CB 'cap' for low-power plinking. There are also shotshells available for the .22 for ridding the garden of pests at close range. Just over three billion rounds of .22 are produced every year. Keep shooting folks!

Gauging Accuracy

The discussion of which .22 LR loading is most accurate is often asked but seldom answered. The truth of the matter is that there are several loads that may be the ne plus ultra in your personal firearm. If you own a compact Bersa or Walther P22 — good, light plinking guns — you may not be able to discern much difference in loads. A Smith and Wesson Victory or Beretta Neos will demonstrate a greater degree of precision. Velocity is also a consideration. I have tested most of the available .22 LR loads. I have found them accurate enough for targets, small game and training. However, for competition, you need to benchrest test different loads and be as steady and serious as possible. The load that delivers the best accuracy from my Beretta Neos may not be the top accuracy load in your Ruger Standard Model, but chances are it will not be a poor shooter, either. Very few shooters if any will be able to tell the difference when shooting offhand. I have tested a number of loads for accuracy. Below are the results with some of the popular loads. Groups were fired at 15 yards and are in inches for a five-shot group. Velocity is the average between the two guns, the Neos averaged about 20 fps higher velocity.

A steel reaction target is a good tool for reinforcing shooting skills. This one is from MGM.

Table 5-1

Load	Velocity	S&W Victory (in.)	Beretta Neos (in.)
CCI Blazer	992 fps	1.2	1.0
CCI Velocitor	890 fps	1.5	1.2
CCI Game Point	907 fps	1.0	1.3
CCI Mini Mag	940 fps	1.25	.9
Eley Force	932 fps	1.4	1.25
Fiocchi RNL	1,022 fps	1.45	1.4
Fiocchi HVHP	1,101 fps	.9	1.1
Remington RNL	870 fps	1.5	1.4
Winchester HP	909 fps	.9	1.25
Winchester M22	945 fps	1.25	1.2
Winchester DynaPoint	870 fps	1.4	.9

The author finds .22 practice relaxing but vital as well.

The .22 has an enduring place in my heart. I have tested every load I have been able to obtain. Some are very expensive, others are not, but most cannot be faulted on performance. With some loads you expect optimal accuracy. High price may indicate a significant promise. The fact is, with handguns and the nominal 25-yard range — 50 maximum under controlled conditions — most of the high-velocity 40-grain loads give similar results. However, after years of testing, I have seen definite differences that may lead to better performance at longer range. Remember, rifle performance does not usually cross over to handguns due to the differences in barrel length. A slower-burning powder that works well in a rifle may not be the single best choice for a pistol. You pay a premium for ammunition marked "Match" and you should receive good performance in turn. Excellent ammunition may improve a common gun but will common ammunition perform well in an excellent gun? Match-grade ammunition is de-

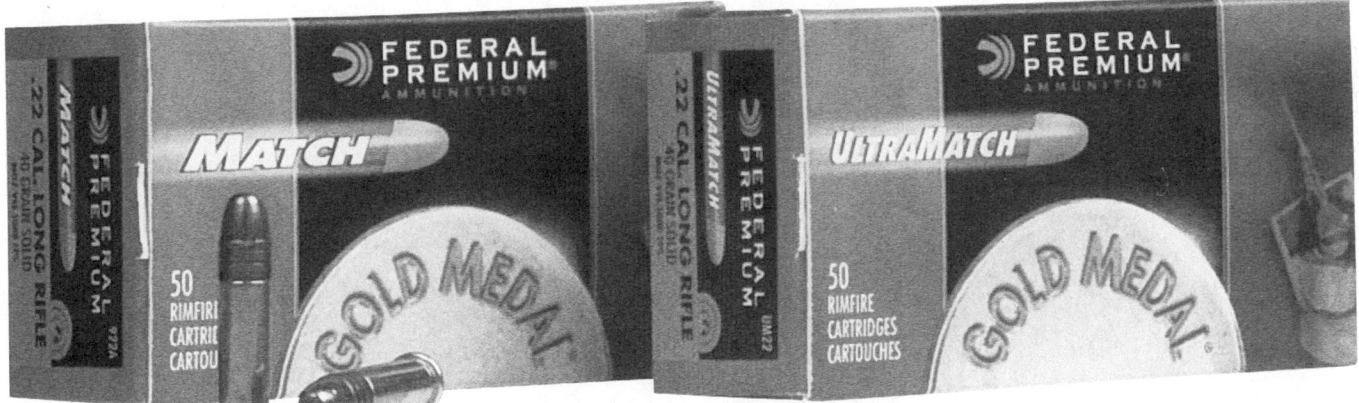

Federal's Match loads are not necessary for most practice but give the best accuracy in a variety of handguns.

signed to eliminate variables as much as possible. I have tested many of the loads available and the results are interesting. There have been many changes since I first began shooting the .22 LR handgun. As an example, almost all loads are now packaged in plastic boxes that separate the bullet noses. This prevents bumping and deforming the nose, which can affect accuracy. I have also discovered that most people do not benefit from match loads unless they are Olympic-level shooters. What follows are some of my observations on a variety of loads.

Blazer

This is an inexpensive loading that is plenty accurate for most uses. The standard deviation (SD) or velocity deviation between shots is usually about 20 fps.

CCI Copper

This is a 21-grain copper/polymer bullet load with good velocity. However, velocity deviation is often well over 25 fps and it isn't usually accurate in handguns.

CCI Mini-Mag

A surprisingly accurate number with much to recommend. As an overall good performer it cannot be bested for the price. The standard deviation of velocity between shots is usually in the teens.

CCI SGB

A blunt-nose all-lead game bullet. It works well on game but here is the kicker: after much experience in a dozen handguns I find this load more accurate than the Mini-Mag. The all-lead versus copper-clad bullet may be the difference.

CCI Quiet-22

It is OK, but too slow to function in most autoloaders. The SD is as high as 30 fps. Best used in rifles.

CCI Velocitor

A good, strong .22 with much to recommend. In my experience, this load is as accurate as the CCI Green Tag.

CCI Green Tag

This is a vaunted match load that works well in competition pistols but isn't worthwhile in most field guns. The Mini-Mag is usually as accurate in my handguns.

Eley Force

This load has a relatively low SD of 16 fps but is no more accurate overall than the CCI Mini Mag.

Eley Tenex

At well over $20 dollars a box of 50 this isn't plinking ammunition. Just the same, there are advantages in some forms of competition. The SD is around 15 fps and, as such, the load is plenty accurate.

Fiocchi HV

Like most Fiocchi loads, this .22 LR is affordable but accurate and gives good results in practically any firearm in which you fire it.

Winchester Super X

This copper-clad 37-grain hollowpoint is about as accurate as the Mini-Mag, but not quite as accurate as the CCI SGB.

The Winchester is more accurate than most of us can hold. But the Super X holds much promise for long-range consistency, with a standard deviation of as little as 10 fps. Yes, that is 10 feet per second deviation, practically unheard of with even match-grade centerfire loads.

THE ACCURATE RIMFIRE

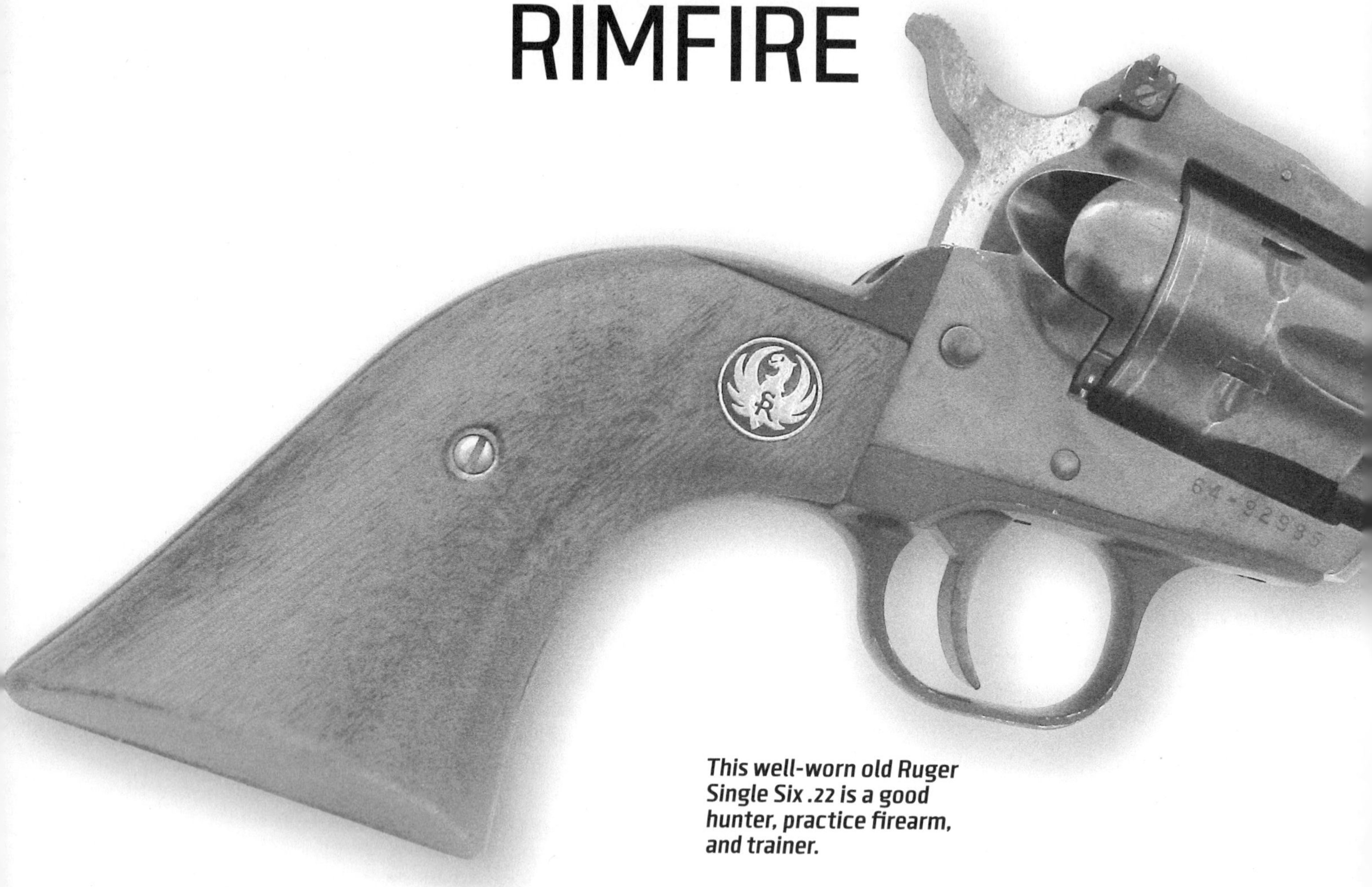

This well-worn old Ruger Single Six .22 is a good hunter, practice firearm, and trainer.

When it comes to .22-caliber handguns, there are many uses and criteria to consider depending upon the mission. No handgun is too large for range use. A long-barrel handgun with a heavy frame is wonderfully accurate and a joy to shoot. A field gun needs to be a little lighter, but heavy enough for accurate shooting when taking game. A just-in-case gun worn for the occasional game animal but mostly just for feeling protected in the field is another matter, and only needs to be reliable and not particularly accurate. Generally, a .22 should be reasonably light, accurate, and reliable. It should be useful for the intended chore or, ideally, a variety of chores. The .22 LR is a wonderful trainer, plinker, and hunter. A more powerful cartridge should be chosen for personal defense, but then again, a 40-grain bullet between wind and water has been known to anchor coyote, feral dogs and bad men. I like to have a handgun on the hip while hiking or camping and a good .22 is a comfort. A great .22 is even better!

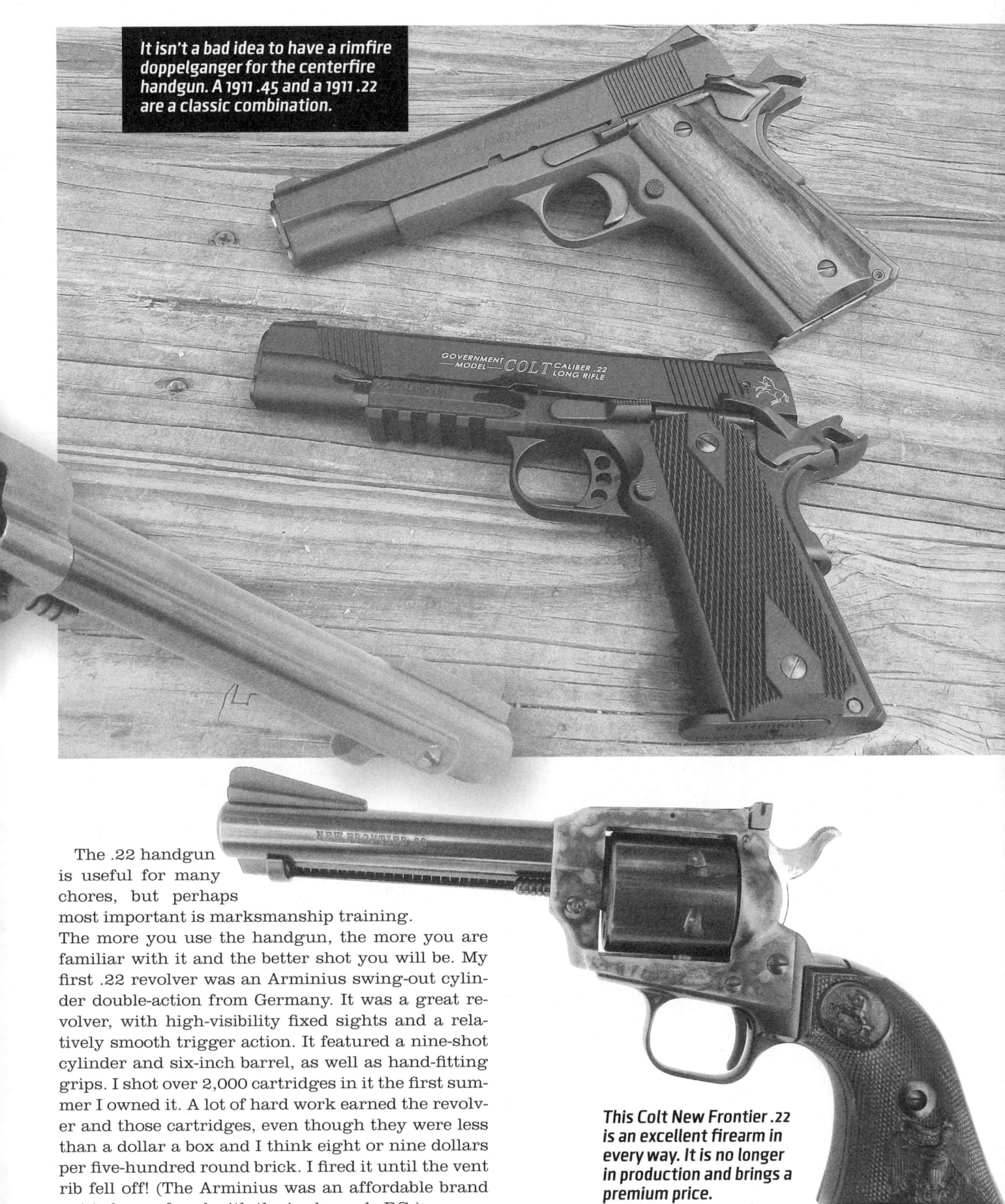

It isn't a bad idea to have a rimfire doppelganger for the centerfire handgun. A 1911 .45 and a 1911 .22 are a classic combination.

The .22 handgun is useful for many chores, but perhaps most important is marksmanship training. The more you use the handgun, the more you are familiar with it and the better shot you will be. My first .22 revolver was an Arminius swing-out cylinder double-action from Germany. It was a great revolver, with high-visibility fixed sights and a relatively smooth trigger action. It featured a nine-shot cylinder and six-inch barrel, as well as hand-fitting grips. I shot over 2,000 cartridges in it the first summer I owned it. A lot of hard work earned the revolver and those cartridges, even though they were less than a dollar a box and I think eight or nine dollars per five-hundred round brick. I fired it until the vent rib fell off! (The Arminius was an affordable brand not to be confused with the junk-grade RG.)

This Colt New Frontier .22 is an excellent firearm in every way. It is no longer in production and brings a premium price.

The Colt ACE in .22 caliber or a Colt .22 conversion kit is a worthwhile investment.

(below) The Charter Arms Pathfinder is a neat little revolver for field or tackle box use. It isn't the most accurate revolver but it is light and handy.

Winchester's M22 .22 Long Rifle loading is a relatively recent addition. This load was designed to burn clean in self-loading .22-caliber AR-15 rifles. It also works well in .22 handguns.

A short-barrel .22 makes an ideal trainer. It forces you to concentrate on aligning the sights and getting everything right.

If you own a full-caliber defensive revolver, having a .22 counterpart to it makes a fantastic understudy for training.

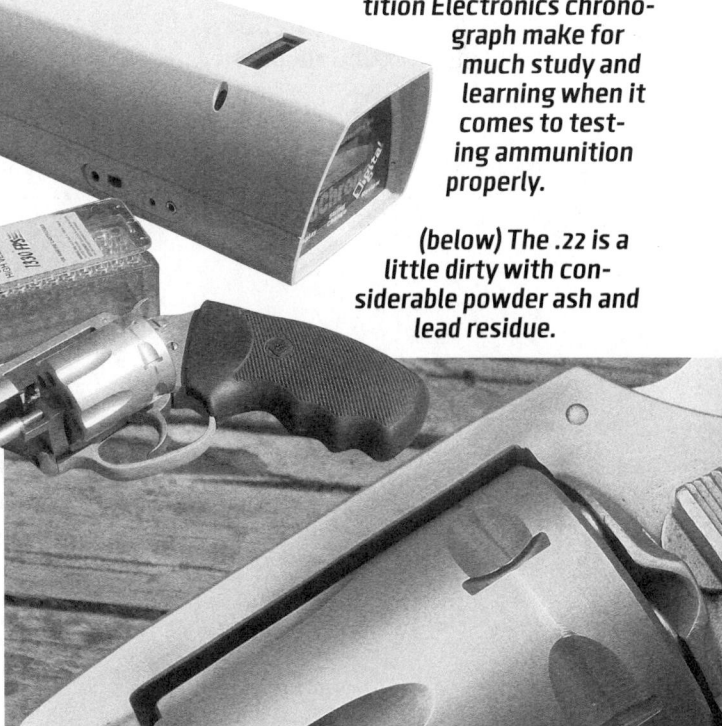

A .22, some ammo and the Competition Electronics chronograph make for much study and learning when it comes to testing ammunition properly.

(below) The .22 is a little dirty with considerable powder ash and lead residue.

I graduated to a Smith and Wesson Kit Gun, which I did not use very well, trained at college in the Criminal Justice program with a first-quality Smith and Wesson Combat Masterpiece, and later a Ruger Single Six. I shot these .22s every chance I had. They were simple to use well, accurate, affordable to shoot and friendly. By friendly, I mean no sharp edges and a decent trigger pull combined with low recoil and good, practical accuracy. I simply enjoyed shooting but, as time went by, I became a better shot. Quite a few shooters purchasing more powerful handguns such as the .357 Magnum for their first revolver had unprofitable experiences. They learned how flinch destroys accuracy and the economic reality of attempting to become a good shot with expensive factory ammunition. Some folks develop bad shooting habits and become doubtful of their own ability.

When you choose your personal .22, the field is broad and there are a number of choices that give good results. The Walther P22 and the similar Ruger SR22 are lightweight handguns, but provide respectable results in training. They are not as accurate as the Ruger Standard Model but are usually reliable and useful for training. Your first .22

should not be too small. A 2-inch barrel revolver is too light for most shooters to deal with as a first gun — its short sight radius will play against you. A reasonably light handgun, such as a 4-inch barrel revolver is a better choice, or even the Walther P22 I mentioned earlier. If you are going to use the handgun and carry it consistently in the field and on the range, then light weight and comfort are important. If the handgun is too heavy it will be at home instead of on the hip.

Accuracy should not be compromised. And the baseline for what you wish to accomplish must be considered. An all-around field gun should be accurate enough to take a squirrel in a tall tree, behead a dangerous snake at a few paces, and provide meaningful practice. Accuracy and weight must be balanced. While the ultra-lights are not accurate enough for some uses, the Ruger MK III with 4-inch barrel is light enough and offers a combination of good hand fit and excellent accuracy. The Ruger is the standard by which all others are judged, and most typically come up short. The Ruger .22/45 with polymer frame is an affordable handgun with much to recommend, as well.

Smith & Wesson Victory .22

The new Smith and Wesson Victory .22 is a solid choice that performs exceptionally well. The Victory just may become the new baseline in .22 pistols. Let's take a hard look at it and then you can judge the oth-

ers based on the performance of this handgun.

The Victory has garnered a lot of interest since its introduction. It is intended to compete with similar .22s such as the Browning Buckmark and Ruger Standard Model. As such, it has good features, is reliable, and has acceptable accuracy. The price point is also important. Smith and Wesson's previous .22 self-loaders were not in the same class as this pistol and, as such, high hopes have been pinned on the Victory, not without justification. The Victory is a modern .22 with tons of useful features and excellent performance. Known as the "SW22," it's a winner and a fun gun as well. Smith and Wesson calls the SW22 Victory a "modern, classic target pistol." Indeed, it fits the bill in that sense — a handgun intended

The Beretta Neos easily field strips and provides overall excellent service.

On the line! The author runs a class with Browning, Colt and Ruger .22-caliber handguns well represented, not to mention a few conversion units.

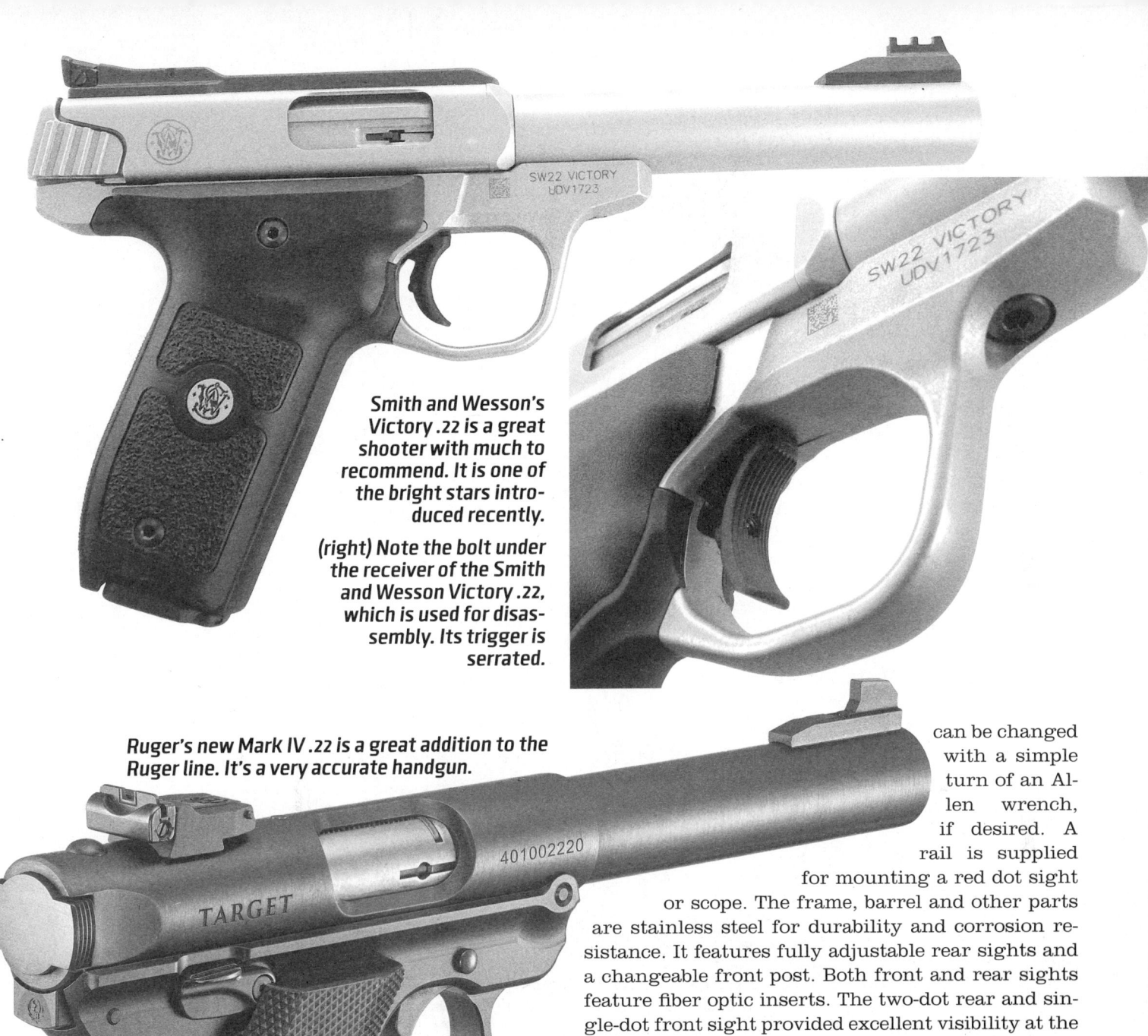

Smith and Wesson's Victory .22 is a great shooter with much to recommend. It is one of the bright stars introduced recently.

(right) Note the bolt under the receiver of the Smith and Wesson Victory .22, which is used for disassembly. Its trigger is serrated.

Ruger's new Mark IV .22 is a great addition to the Ruger line. It's a very accurate handgun.

for informal target practice, marksmanship training and small game hunting. It isn't a Smith and Wesson Model 41, but then what is?

The Victory pistol is a single-action trigger, with blowback design. It operates best with high-velocity .22 Long Rifle ammunition. The monolithic receiver remains stationary on firing and the bolt recoils out the rear of the receiver. The barrel can be changed with a simple turn of an Allen wrench, if desired. A rail is supplied for mounting a red dot sight or scope. The frame, barrel and other parts are stainless steel for durability and corrosion resistance. It features fully adjustable rear sights and a changeable front post. Both front and rear sights feature fiber optic inserts. The two-dot rear and single-dot front sight provided excellent visibility at the firing range and were among the most appreciated features of the Victory. The sights offer excellent hit probability in rapid shooting and precision accuracy in deliberate fire.

The controls are simple enough, with a push-button magazine release, slide lock, and a frame-mounted thumb-activated safety. The controls were easily manipulated with one hand. The trigger action is lovely. This is an uncommon trait among factory pistols. The Victory's trigger breaks at a perfect three pounds. As I examined the pistol, I knew accuracy potential should be high. A final touch is a set of well-designed hard plastic grips. The standard model tested sports a 5.5-inch barrel with a one-turn-in-15-inch rifling twist. The pistol is hefty at 37 ounces. This gives the trained shooter excellent control. The pistol has good balance and sits low in the hand. The width is 1.3 inches. The pistol is the ideal size for target use.

I was more excited to fire the Victory than most of the pieces I test. Certainly, it's not a personal defense piece, but a recreational handgun. Truth be told, we just do not get enough fun shooting around the homestead. I collected an assortment of .22 ammunition. This included a number of bargain basement RNL loads from Federal Cartridge, CCI's Stinger and Velocitor and Winchester M22. The Federal load represents what we find on sale with a RNL bullet, the CCI loads are hunting loads, and the M22 was designed for reliable function in the AR-15/.22. The Victory's bolt was well-lubricated and magazines loaded with the Federal RNL first. The mags were tight-fitting with strong springs, but not too difficult to load. In firing the first few magazines there were several failures to fully close the bolt, perhaps one to two a magazine. This disappeared after the first forty rounds. The pistol proved reliable with all loads tested thereafter. Yes, this was a fun gun.

The majority of the loads shot through the Smith & Wesson Victory were done so offhand. I have taken quite a few squirrels and bedded rabbit with the .22 pistol. This handgun would be well-suited to that pursuit, more so

The new Ruger MK IV breaks down much more easily than the previous pistols. This is a good all-around .22 self-loader.

The newest Ruger, the Mark IV, features a new takedown system that answers the only valid criticism of the Ruger Standard Model.

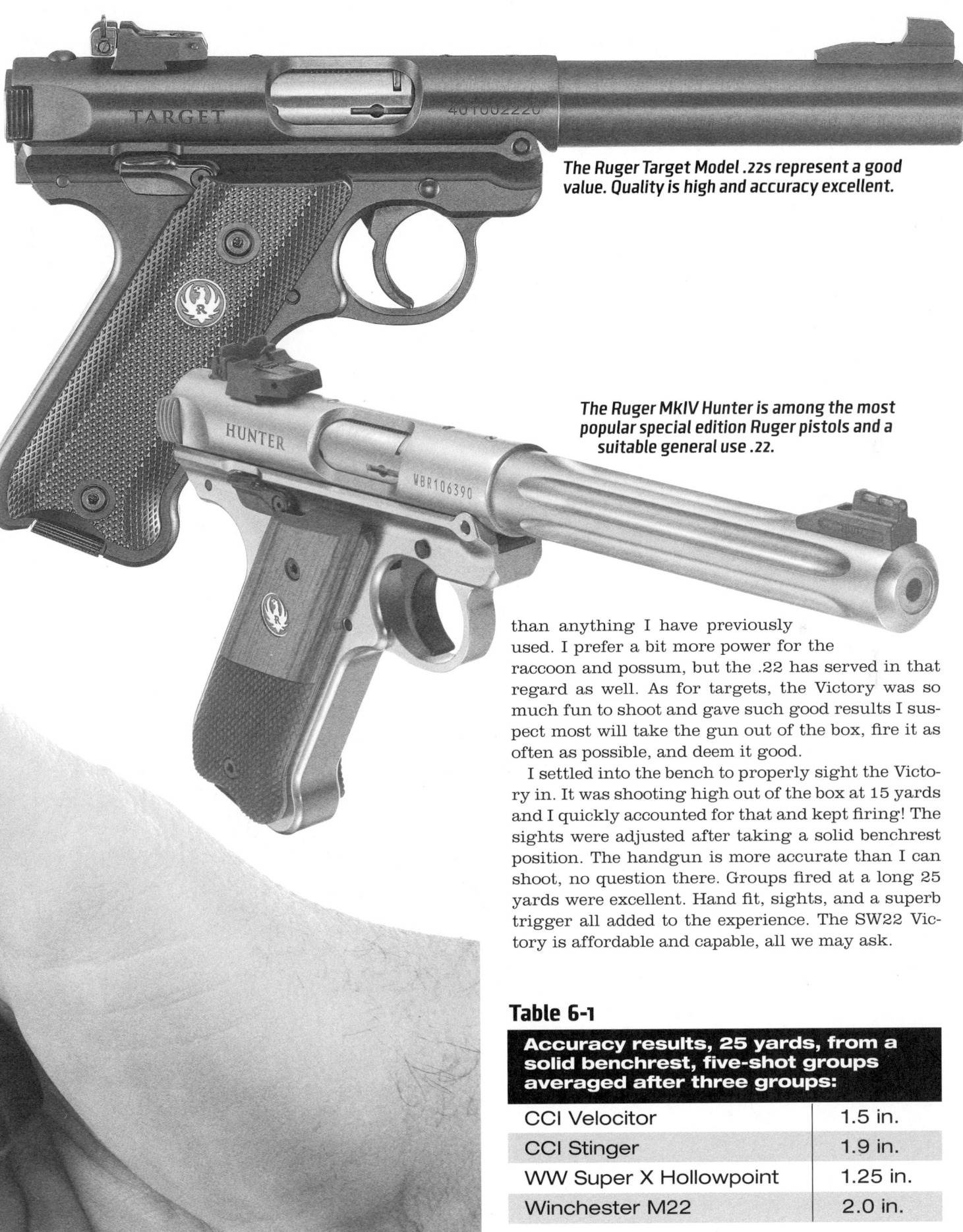

The Ruger Target Model .22s represent a good value. Quality is high and accuracy excellent.

The Ruger MkIV Hunter is among the most popular special edition Ruger pistols and a suitable general use .22.

than anything I have previously used. I prefer a bit more power for the raccoon and possum, but the .22 has served in that regard as well. As for targets, the Victory was so much fun to shoot and gave such good results I suspect most will take the gun out of the box, fire it as often as possible, and deem it good.

I settled into the bench to properly sight the Victory in. It was shooting high out of the box at 15 yards and I quickly accounted for that and kept firing! The sights were adjusted after taking a solid benchrest position. The handgun is more accurate than I can shoot, no question there. Groups fired at a long 25 yards were excellent. Hand fit, sights, and a superb trigger all added to the experience. The SW22 Victory is affordable and capable, all we may ask.

Table 6-1

Accuracy results, 25 yards, from a solid benchrest, five-shot groups averaged after three groups:	
CCI Velocitor	1.5 in.
CCI Stinger	1.9 in.
WW Super X Hollowpoint	1.25 in.
Winchester M22	2.0 in.

.22 Field Guns

When you look at the field gun, reliability is paramount. Many shooters have simply given up on the SIG Mosquito. While some have stated the pistol works fine after a break-in period, most have had poor results. It should be avoided. Other handguns will prove more reliable with one load or the other, especially with CCI Mini-Mag and Winchester Super X. Compact short-slide autoloaders are the least reliable, in my experience. Just the same, I have enjoyed good results with the Bersa compact .22. The Walther PPK .22s have proven problematic.

Since .22 ammunition is simply dirtier than centerfire — its powder burns dirtier and there is more lead and lead lubricant deposited after firing than when using a centerfire cartridge — to provide for greater reliability the pistol should be cleaned no less than every three hundred shots. Even revolvers

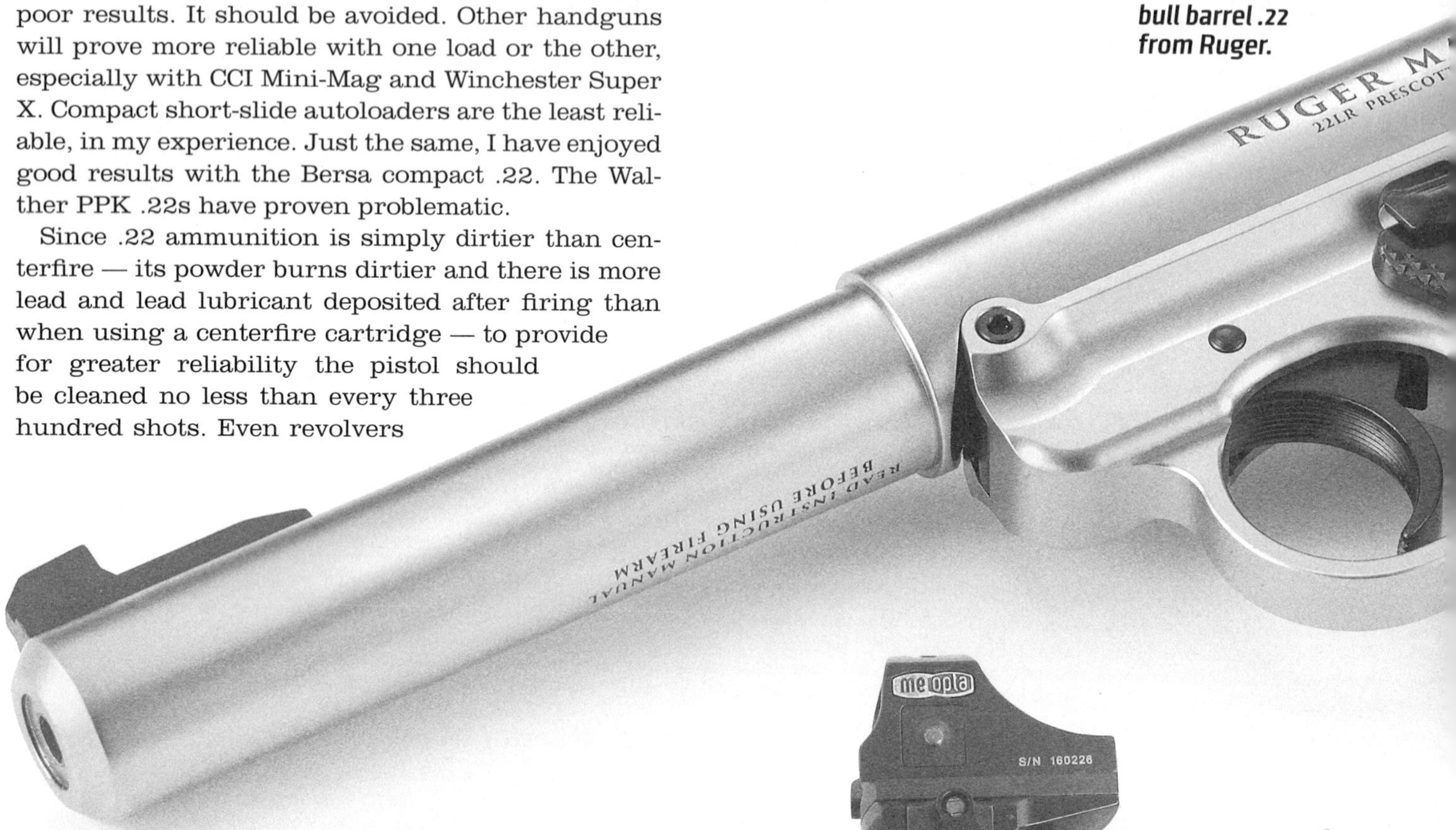

The stainless steel bull barrel .22 from Ruger.

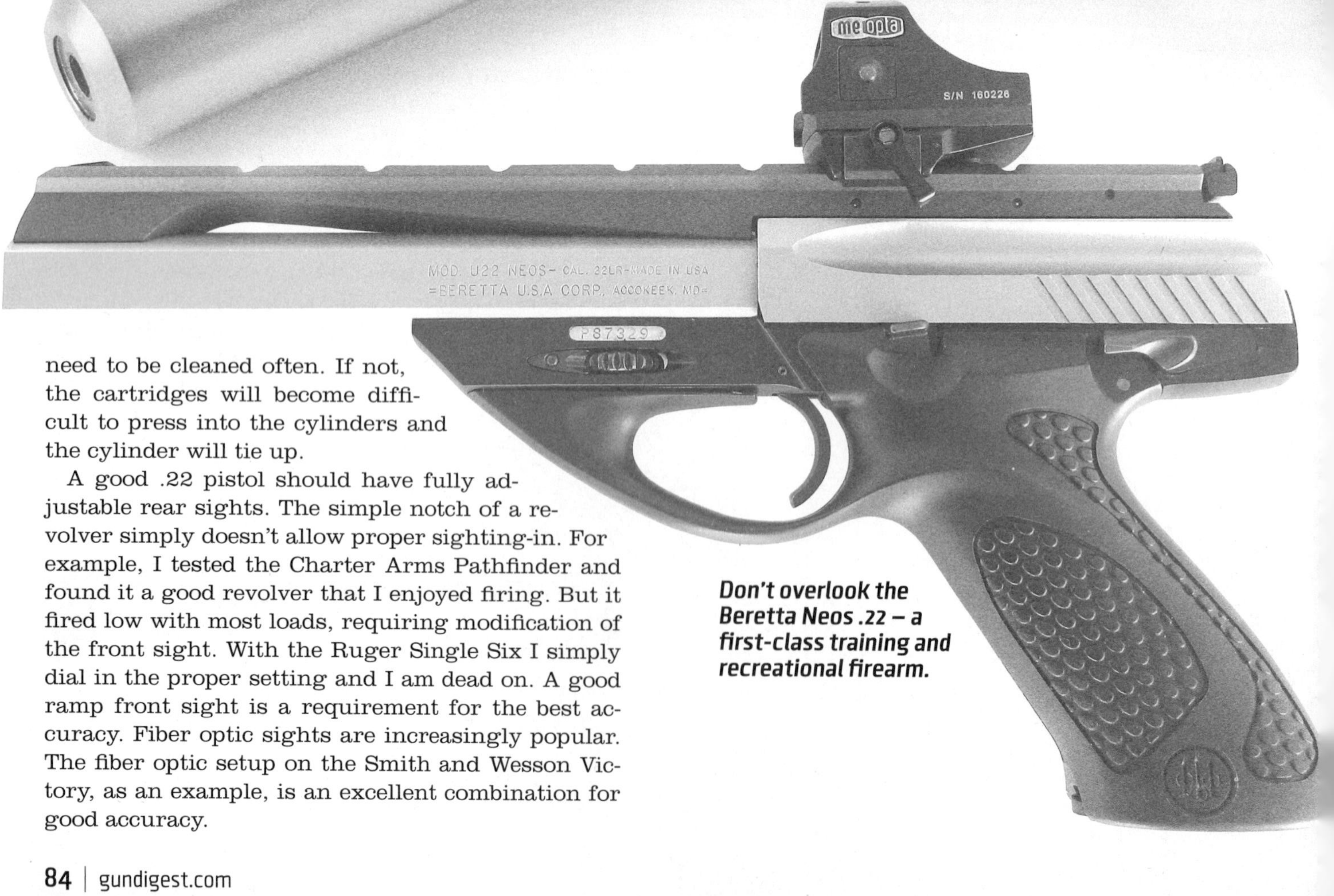

need to be cleaned often. If not, the cartridges will become difficult to press into the cylinders and the cylinder will tie up.

A good .22 pistol should have fully adjustable rear sights. The simple notch of a revolver simply doesn't allow proper sighting-in. For example, I tested the Charter Arms Pathfinder and found it a good revolver that I enjoyed firing. But it fired low with most loads, requiring modification of the front sight. With the Ruger Single Six I simply dial in the proper setting and I am dead on. A good ramp front sight is a requirement for the best accuracy. Fiber optic sights are increasingly popular. The fiber optic setup on the Smith and Wesson Victory, as an example, is an excellent combination for good accuracy.

Don't overlook the Beretta Neos .22 — a first-class training and recreational firearm.

Ruger Standard Model .22

Perhaps the most widespread .22 LR self-loader is the Ruger Standard Model, now in the Mark IV configuration — the standard by which all others are judged. Recently, Ruger redesigned the pistol with a much easier takedown for disassembly. The stainless steel models are pricey these days, but the pistol is a late-1940s design in which labor and machining are intensive. It is worth its price, but there are accurate handguns that cost less as well. Just the same, the Ruger .22 is a gold standard for reliability and accuracy. It's available in diverse models with different barrel lengths, heavy barrels, a polymer frame version and a model with stainless steel construction.

A Meopta red reflex sight mounted on the Beretta Neos .22 handgun.

When looking for a good-quality .22, be aware of the features of each handgun. The Beretta Neos features a recessed barrel crown and adjustable front sight.

Ruger offers a number of variations on the Ruger Single Six .22, including easy-packing models and long-barrel hunting revolvers.

Beretta Neos

A handgun that I came to accept a bit later than some is the Beretta Neos. Beretta just doesn't manufacture second rate pistols and the NEOS is an affordable jewel. My example is the longer barrel version and it is heavier than some but amazingly accurate when I do my part. It is well-made of good material. Once you get past its space gun looks you find excellent human engineering. The Neos is a light-packing .22 at 31 ounces in the shorter barrel version. Like all the .22 LR self-loaders, the Neos is a simple blowback action intended for high-velocity cartridges. The sight track is a little difficult to get used to. The sights are well-designed but buried in an upper rail. I like the rail but you have to concentrate on the iron sights not to be distracted. The rear sight is a standout for utility and modern design. The safety is ambidextrous and easily activated. The magazine release is ergonomically designed and easily used. It rides on the right side of the frame and is activated by the trigger finger. You never have to shift your grip to use it.

Beretta has done things with this pistol you simply cannot do with a centerfire handgun. The grip offers an excellent firing angle. The magazine is well-made of good material, a solidly engineered feeding device. While the muzzle-heavy feel of the 6-inch barrel handgun is comfortable when firing offhand, it isn't much more accurate than any other .22 fired that way, but it tracks well. A very nice 3-pound trigger aided in offhand fire. The Neo came into its own and earned the price of admission when firing off of the benchrest, too. Firing from a solid rest firing position the results were notable:

Table 6-2

Accuracy results of the Beretta Neos. 5-shot groups, 25 yards:	
CCI Mini Mag	1.1 in.
Fiocchi SV	1.2 in.
WW Super X	1.35 in.

The author favors the Ruger 4 ¾-inch barrel Single Six .22 for easy carry and all-around use.

Some prefer the cowboy revolver look of this fixed-sight Ruger Single Six. While nostalgia is good, the overall utility of the revolver is not as great as the adjustable sight revolvers.

Ruger Single Six

The .22-caliber revolver I have the most experience with is the single-action Ruger Single Six. This revolver, like all Ruger products, seems indestructible. I can honestly say I have never seen one in need of repair. Unless you fire the undersized .22 LR in the .22 Magnum cylinder you cannot damage it, and even that problem is easily addressed with the proper tools. The Single Six manages to give good service with the .22 LR and the .22 Magnum cartridge. If you intend to hunt with the revolver, the .22 Magnum raises the bar considerably in killing power. The problem is that the .22 Magnum demands a slightly larger bore diameter.

The Single Six may not be as accurate as the same revolver with the Magnum cylinder fitted. For most uses that is fine, but the Single Six isn't quite as accurate as a MK4 Ruger autoloader. On average, the revolver will turn in groups of 1.5-2.25 inches at 25 yards, certainly excellent but not as good as the better class of self-loading pistols. With the hotter and more expensive .22 Mangum cartridges, the Single Six will do 1.25 to 1.75 inches. If you plan to hunt with the revolver, purchase the long-barrel hunter version. No matter how you slice it, if you like revolvers and single-action styling, then the Single Six is a winning choice.

Final Word on .22 Accuracy

The dead-on hold used with defensive handguns may not be the best for hunting handguns. For a .22 intended to take a squirrel out of a tree or pop a bunny in the head at ranges over 15 yards, a precise sight picture and a bullseye-style hold is needed. This means considerable work off of the bench using the best technique and testing a variety of loads for top accuracy. I rest the autoloader on the frame, while revolvers are rested with the wrists on the sandbag, keeping the wheelgun free of contact with the rest. It is important to understand that the pistol will fire low at close range. After all, the bore is .75 inch or so lower than the front sight and line of sight. Compensate for this and keep the pistol sighted properly for longer range.

THE BEST HANDGUNS FOR ACCURACY

Very few handguns exhibit the inherent accuracy potential of the 1911 .45.

SPRINGFIELD ARMORY

SPRINGFIELD INC
GENESEO IL USA
NM 453005

O nce you have learned to shoot well, and know the qualities that define good handguns and ammunition, you need to determine which handguns have the greatest accuracy potential. You will not achieve the best accuracy with a second- or third-rate handgun. Even so, there are a number of handguns that tend to exhibit excellent accuracy and yet are not terribly expensive.

When you consider accuracy you must determine first the use to which the handgun will be put. A few years ago, I read an article describing how a shooter had a custom-grade Browning Hi Power put together with Novak sights and a Bar-Sto barrel — all great additions. Then the writer, obviously given the wrong assignment to cover, fired the piece at 7 yards and voiced the opinion that a defensive handgun would never be used past that distance! There are

The Browning Hi Power 9mm was the first "wonder nine" and is a very reliable handgun.

(right) The author finds the steel-frame Commander .45 to be a useful defensive and packing handgun.

competing demands on the handgun, but the worst case scenario is the one that I consider. I may limit my sure kill range when deer hunting to 35 yards with the .45 ACP, but would 50 yards be too much? The Ruger Blackhawk .44 Magnum will stretch that range to all of 100 yards if I do my part. On the other hand, if you are going to shoot at Camp Perry, the emphasis will be on accuracy and the piece must be more accurate than most any off-the-shelf handgun.

There must also be a balance of power and accuracy. The defensive handgun that isn't going to be called upon past 7 yards may be the pistol on hand when you have the opportunity to stop an active shooter. It should be accurate enough for the chore and it should fire a powerful cartridge.

Ruger's Super Blackhawk is a specialist handgun, well-suited for long-range work and hunting large animals.

The old modified Remington Rand is a classic example of the Bulls-eye competition gun. We will not see their like again, but then again there are modern guns that are more accurate.

The Ruger SP101 .357 Magnum, top, is a handy, lightweight defensive handgun, while the GP100, lower, is a dandy all-around packing and hunting gun.

sulting in a reduction of the accuracy problems that once dogged the .45 Auto Rim. Modern Smith and Wesson revolvers in all calibers are more accurate than any previous revolver from this company. Ergonomics and sights are much better than ever before in all quality handguns. Handguns with tighter tolerances simply last longer. There isn't much slip or banging of misfit parts when the pistol fires, resulting in less wear. Accuracy and reliability are better, too.

Today, we have off-the-shelf 1911 handguns that will deliver accuracy of 2 inches at 25 yards with good loads. Colt, SIG and Springfield 1911s with adjustable sights are available for the serious handgunner. While some experimentation with ammunition is necessary, these handguns are often surprisingly accurate. A modern magnum revolver may be even more accurate. My personal Ruger GP100 .357 Magnum revolver is the single most accurate handgun

A target gun need only cut a hole in paper, but it may have to do so at long range. In a defensive handgun, reliability is a million times more important than anything else. In a competition gun, reliability is less important. The occasional malfunction with a .22 is par for the course. Modern handguns have stronger, better steel than ever before and tighter tolerances. Modern Smith and Wesson revolvers have tighter throats than ever, re-

(above) The .40 S&W isn't the author's favorite caliber. Just the same, the Beretta Vertec in this popular caliber is a reasonably accurate handgun that hits hard.

(left) The author's go-to 1911 .45 is the Springfield Range Officer Operator. While an affordable handgun, it is also incredibly capable.

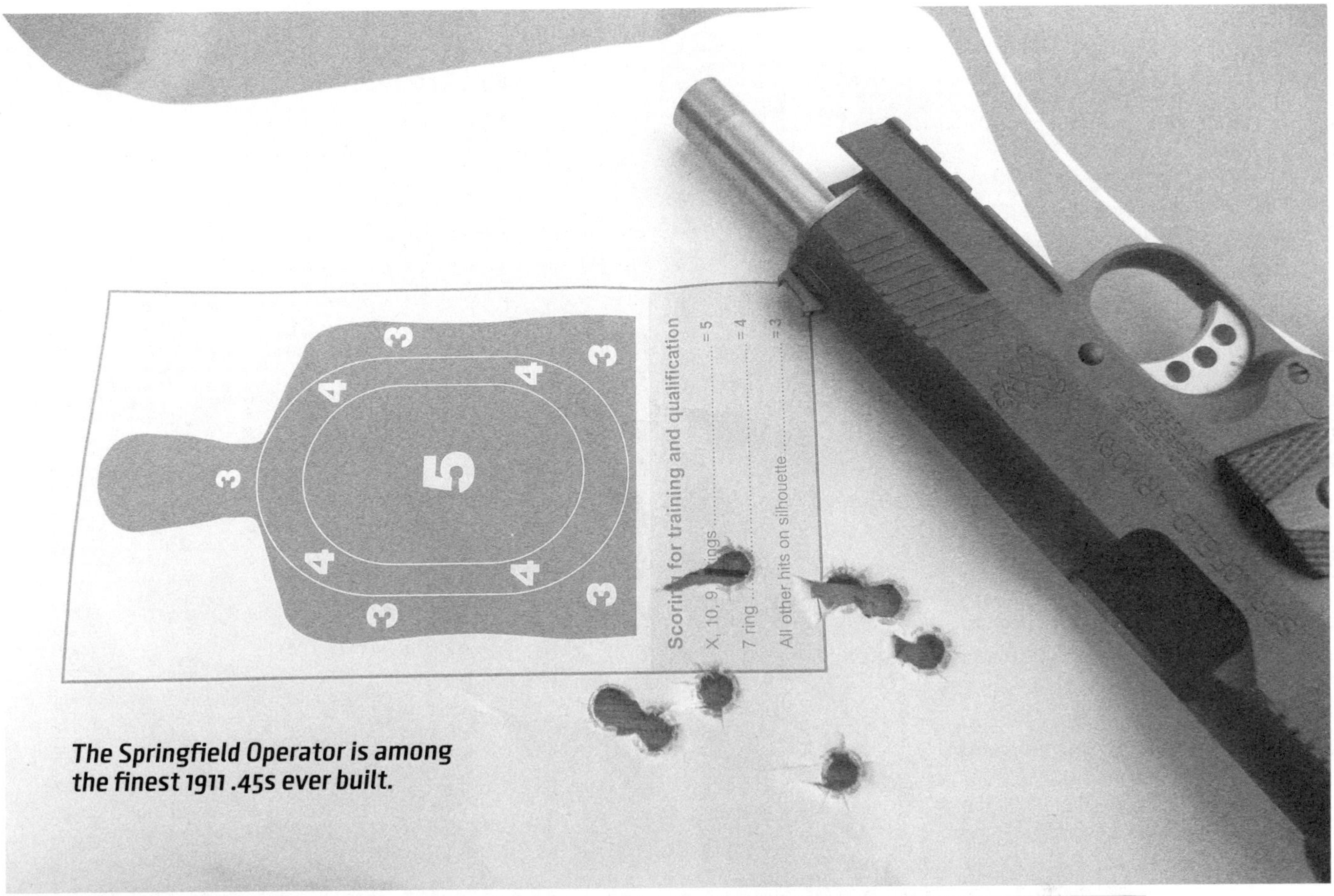

The Springfield Operator is among the finest 1911 .45s ever built.

The Browning Hi Power and its variants offer good accuracy and excellent reliability.

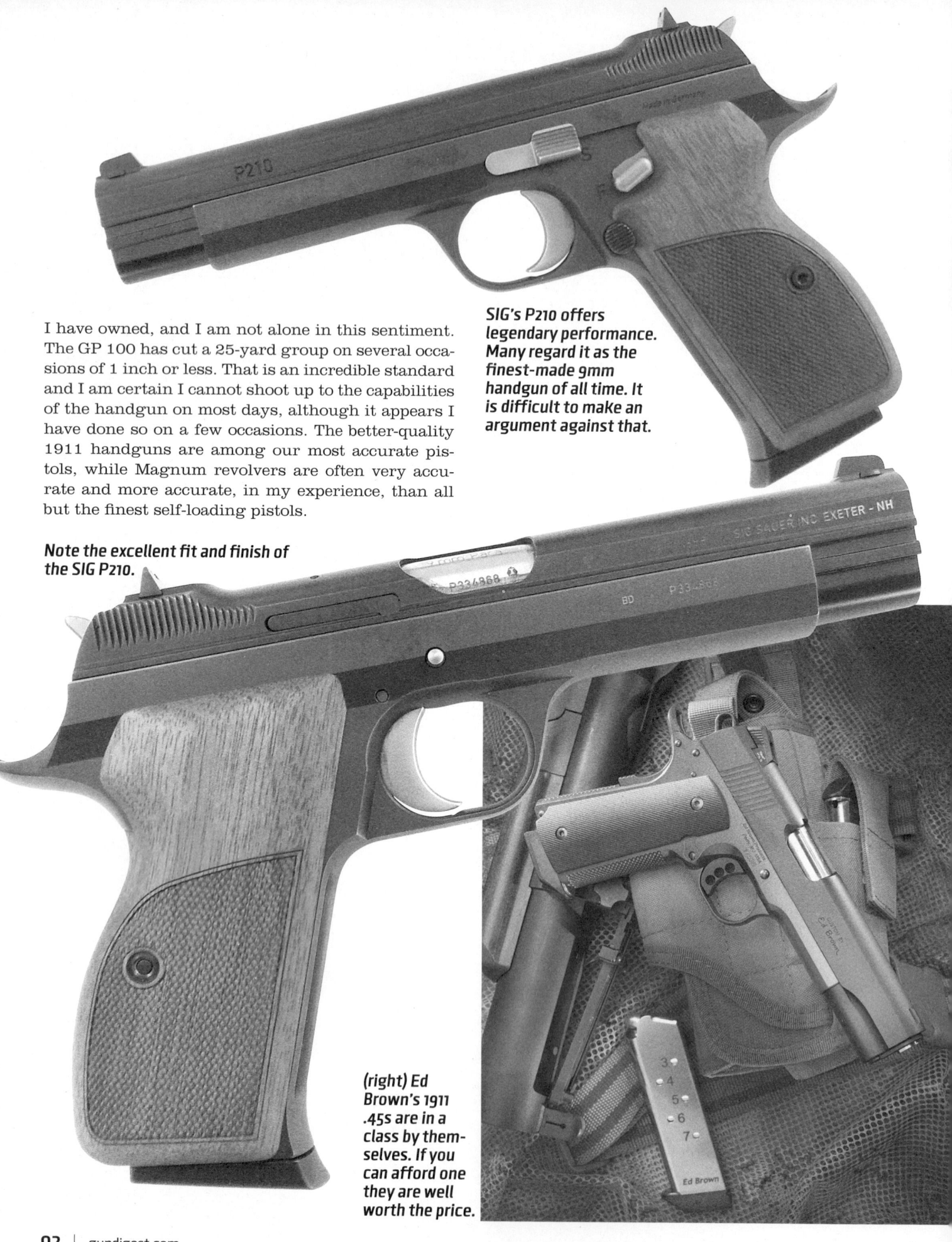

I have owned, and I am not alone in this sentiment. The GP 100 has cut a 25-yard group on several occasions of 1 inch or less. That is an incredible standard and I am certain I cannot shoot up to the capabilities of the handgun on most days, although it appears I have done so on a few occasions. The better-quality 1911 handguns are among our most accurate pistols, while Magnum revolvers are often very accurate and more accurate, in my experience, than all but the finest self-loading pistols.

SIG's P210 offers legendary performance. Many regard it as the finest-made 9mm handgun of all time. It is difficult to make an argument against that.

Note the excellent fit and finish of the SIG P210.

(right) Ed Brown's 1911 .45s are in a class by themselves. If you can afford one they are well worth the price.

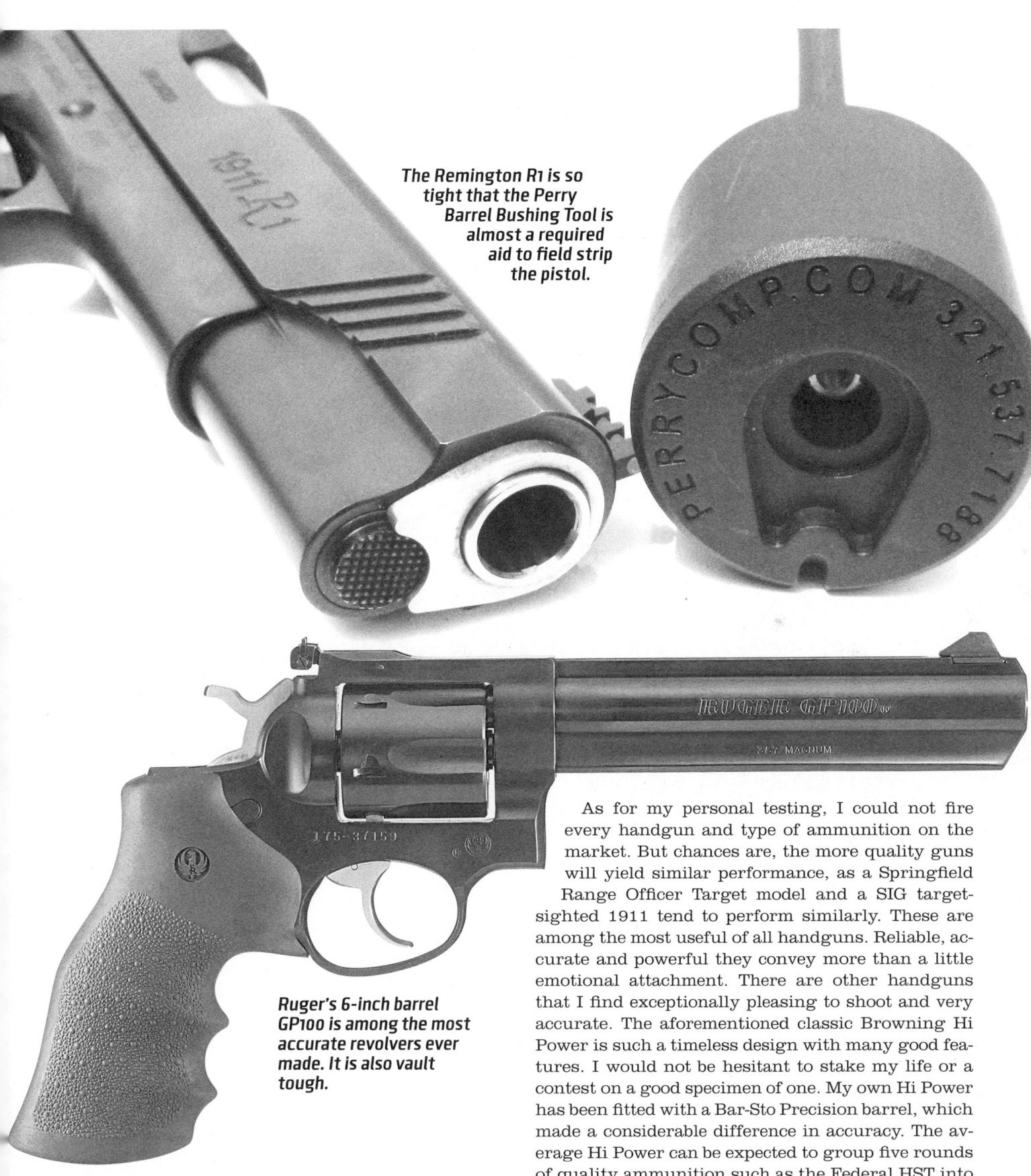

The Remington R1 is so tight that the Perry Barrel Bushing Tool is almost a required aid to field strip the pistol.

Ruger's 6-inch barrel GP100 is among the most accurate revolvers ever made. It is also vault tough.

As for my personal testing, I could not fire every handgun and type of ammunition on the market. But chances are, the more quality guns will yield similar performance, as a Springfield Range Officer Target model and a SIG target-sighted 1911 tend to perform similarly. These are among the most useful of all handguns. Reliable, accurate and powerful they convey more than a little emotional attachment. There are other handguns that I find exceptionally pleasing to shoot and very accurate. The aforementioned classic Browning Hi Power is such a timeless design with many good features. I would not be hesitant to stake my life or a contest on a good specimen of one. My own Hi Power has been fitted with a Bar-Sto Precision barrel, which made a considerable difference in accuracy. The average Hi Power can be expected to group five rounds of quality ammunition such as the Federal HST into 2.5 inches at 25 yards. The trigger on the Hi Power is notoriously heavy, although later models are better and early handguns sometimes become much smoother with age. The Bar-Sto fitted Hi Power will shave an inch off that group given proper fitting and carefully chosen ammunition. The SIG P210 is even more accurate straight from the factory, but very expensive and leaving something to be desired as for the location of its safety and general handling.

The CZ 75 is respected for ruggedness and reliability. And it has a good reputation for accuracy. Although the contest is a tight one, in general the CZ 75 will outshoot the Browning Hi Power. It takes a fine shot to demonstrate this — and benchrest accuracy is theoretical when comparing combat guns — but I had rather have the CZ 75 in a fight than any other 9mm handgun. It is that good and the combination of features is excellent.

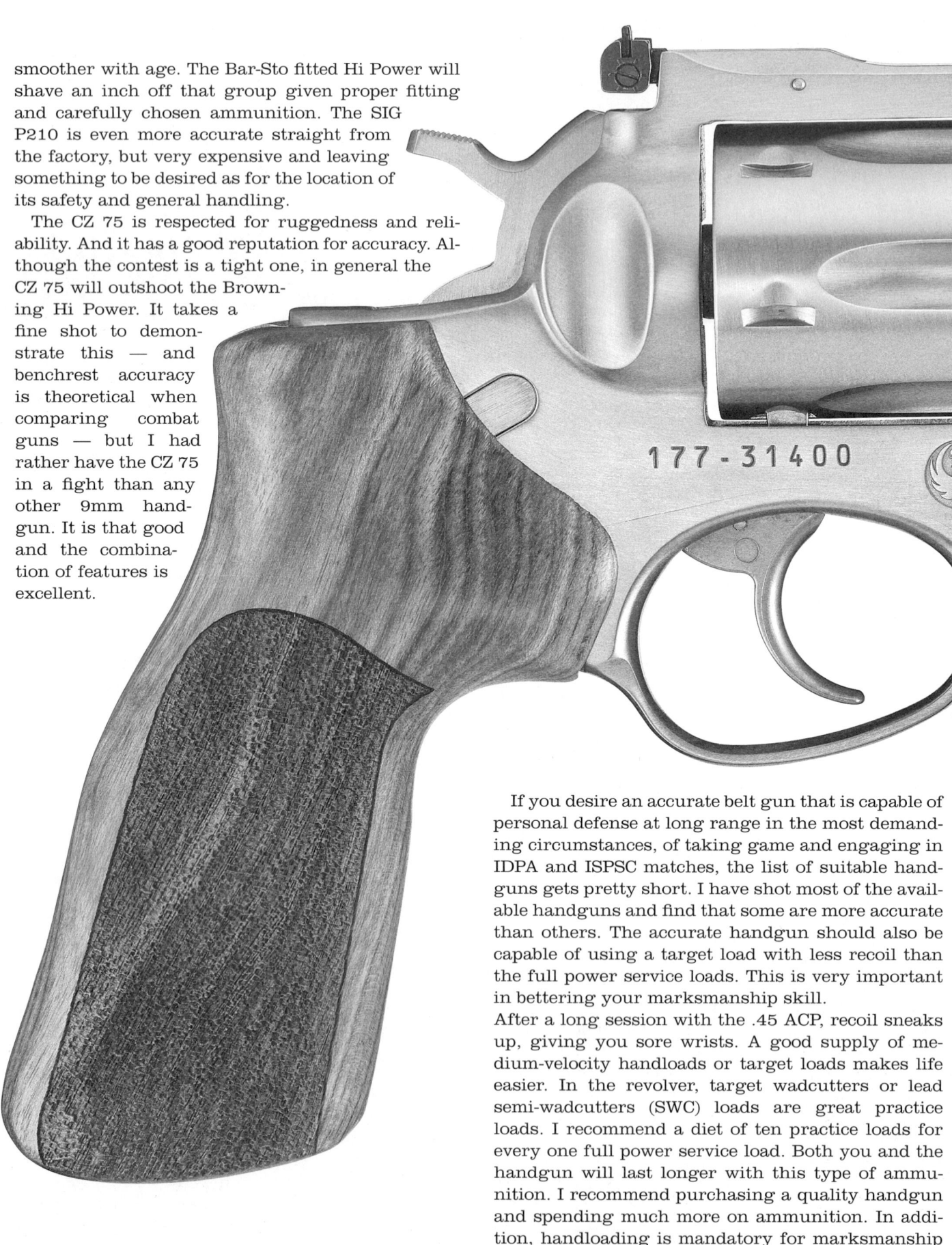

If you desire an accurate belt gun that is capable of personal defense at long range in the most demanding circumstances, of taking game and engaging in IDPA and ISPSC matches, the list of suitable handguns gets pretty short. I have shot most of the available handguns and find that some are more accurate than others. The accurate handgun should also be capable of using a target load with less recoil than the full power service loads. This is very important in bettering your marksmanship skill.

After a long session with the .45 ACP, recoil sneaks up, giving you sore wrists. A good supply of medium-velocity handloads or target loads makes life easier. In the revolver, target wadcutters or lead semi-wadcutters (SWC) loads are great practice loads. I recommend a diet of ten practice loads for every one full power service load. Both you and the handgun will last longer with this type of ammunition. I recommend purchasing a quality handgun and spending much more on ammunition. In addition, handloading is mandatory for marksmanship growth.

The new Match Target version of the GP100 has features that make it more ergonomic than the standard model. Accuracy is easier to come by with this handgun.

Considering Custom Handguns

The question often comes up of choosing a custom handgun. The 1911 is expensive enough, with quality examples often costing well over one-thousand dollars. Examples of the platform from Colt, Kimber, Springfield and SIG do very well as far as longevity, accuracy and overall performance. Purchase the best handgun you can afford from one of these makers. Of course, if you have the means, there are other makers offering hand-built customs. Ed Brown and Wilson Combat are among these. They certainly up the ante in price but is the performance worthwhile? If you need the extra edge you will know when you get there. As for myself, the Colt and Springfield pistols do the business for me. In revolvers, Smith and Wesson offers custom shop guns that will give the average shooter sticker shock! It took some time for me to wrap my mind around a thousand-dollar revolver. A counterpoint is the affordable Ruger Match Champion ver-

The CZ 75 Sport and Target models are first-class handguns, with much to recommend.

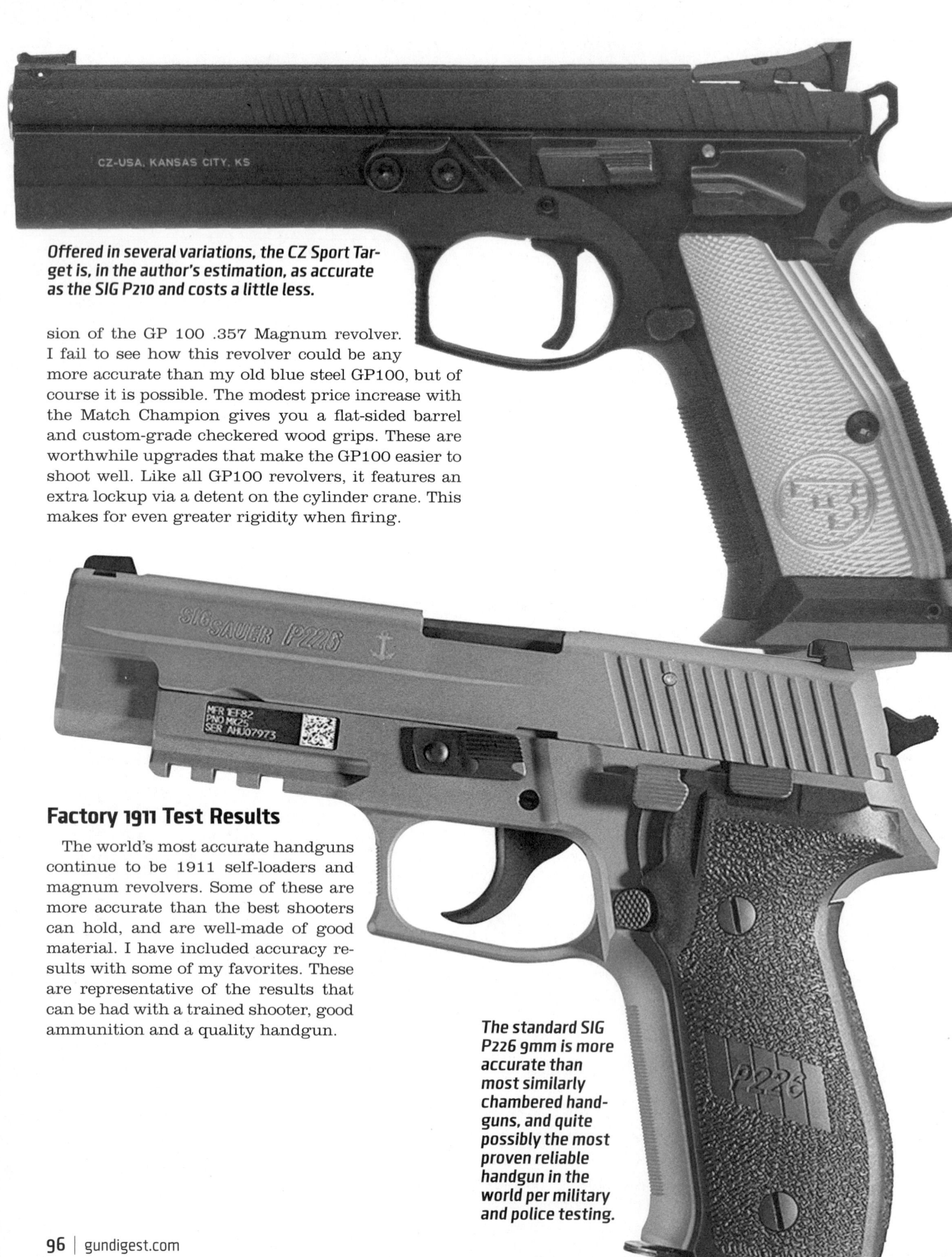

Offered in several variations, the CZ Sport Target is, in the author's estimation, as accurate as the SIG P210 and costs a little less.

sion of the GP 100 .357 Magnum revolver. I fail to see how this revolver could be any more accurate than my old blue steel GP100, but of course it is possible. The modest price increase with the Match Champion gives you a flat-sided barrel and custom-grade checkered wood grips. These are worthwhile upgrades that make the GP100 easier to shoot well. Like all GP100 revolvers, it features an extra lockup via a detent on the cylinder crane. This makes for even greater rigidity when firing.

Factory 1911 Test Results

The world's most accurate handguns continue to be 1911 self-loaders and magnum revolvers. Some of these are more accurate than the best shooters can hold, and are well-made of good material. I have included accuracy results with some of my favorites. These are representative of the results that can be had with a trained shooter, good ammunition and a quality handgun.

The standard SIG P226 9mm is more accurate than most similarly chambered handguns, and quite possibly the most proven reliable handgun in the world per military and police testing.

Table 7-1

Ruger GP100 4-inch barrel, 25-yard benchrest groups.	
Factory .357 Magnum ammunition	
Black Hills 125-gr. JHP	1.25 in.
Federal 180-gr. JHP	1.1 in.
Winchester 158-gr. JHP	1.25 in.
Handloads	
Hornady 125-gr. XTP H110/1,600 fps	1.1 in.
Matt's Bullets 175-gr. SWC H110/1,100 fps	1.0 in.

Table 7-2

Ruger Blackhawk .44 Magnum 7 ½-inch barrel, 25-yard benchrest groups.	
Fiocchi 200-gr. JHP	2.0 in.
Fiocchi 240-gr. JHP	1.75 in.
Black Hills 300-gr. JHPP	1.25 in.
Hornady 200-gr. XTP	1.4 in.
Hornady 240-gr. XTP	1.2 in.
Sig Sauer 240-gr. JHP V Crown	1.15 in.

Table 7-3

Sig Sauer 1911 25-yard benchrest groups.	
Black Hills 185-gr. TAC +P	2.0 in.
Hornady 200-gr. XTP	1.8 in.
Hornady 230-gr. XTP	2.0 in.
Remington 230-gr. Golden Saber	2.4 in.

Table 7-4

Springfield Range Officer Target Model 25-yard benchrest groups.	
Black Hills 230-gr. JHP	1.9 in.
Black Hills 185-gr. TAC +P	1.75 in.
Hornady 200-gr. XTP	1.85 in.

Table 7-5

Springfield Range Officer Operator 25-yard benchrest groups.	
Federal 230-gr. Match	1.95 in.
Black Hills 230-gr. JHP	2.0 in.
Hornady 200-gr. XTP	2.25 in.

Table 7-6

Colt Combat Elite 25-yard benchrest groups.	
Fiocchi 230-gr. Extreme JHP	2.25 in.
Black Hills 230-gr. JHP	2.4 in.
Hornady 230-gr. XTP +P	2.55 in.
Gorilla 230-gr. JHP	2.1 in.

Table 7-7

CZ 75 9mm Stainless 25-yard benchrest groups.	
Black Hills 124-gr. JHP +P	1.9 in.
Hornady 124-gr. XTP	1.8 in.
Hornady 147-gr. XTP	1.8 in.
Gorilla 115-gr. JHP	1.95 in.
Gorilla 135-gr. JHP	1.5 in.

Table 7-8

SIG P226 MKI 9mm 25-yard benchrest groups.	
Gorilla 135-gr. JHP	2.2 in.
Winchester 115-gr. Silvertip	2.45 in.
Winchester 124-gr. PDX +P	1.7 in.

ACCURACY STANDARDS

While the Honor Defense 9mm Honor Guard pistol is a compact design, it doesn't compromise on accuracy.

When we speak of accuracy standards the subject is more complex than anticipated. These standards apply to the handgun, ammunition and shooter. Accuracy standards are generally divided into three broad groups. These are personal defense, hunting, and competition. All are important to the individual marksman, but perhaps the most important is personal defense. My standards are more stringent than some, but are nonetheless shared by many professionals.

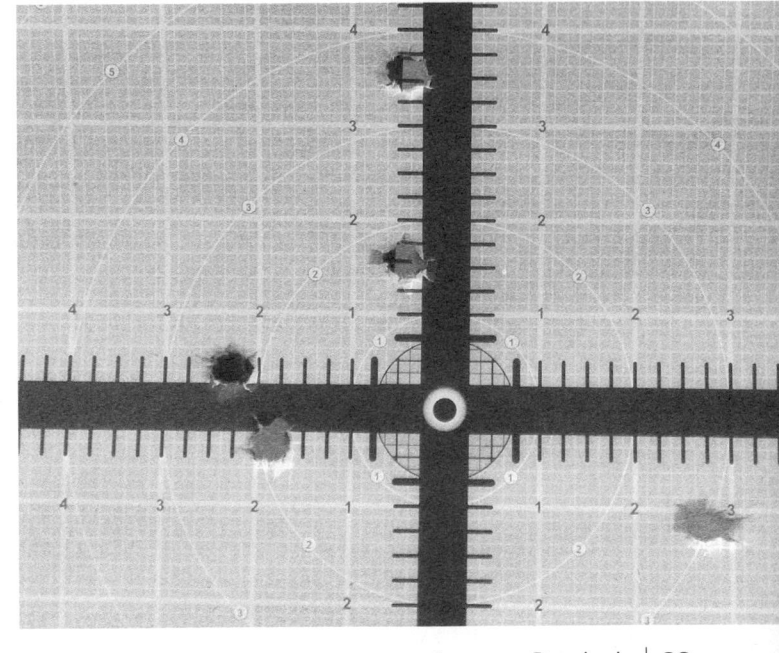

Accuracy standards vary by handgun type. The Smith and Wesson Shield in .45 ACP is more accurate than the author expected.

During the course of a number of critical incidents, the marksmanship problems I faced were not severe, although one involved a moving target at 17 yards. The real problem is controlling the sights, trigger and muscle tremor. The "tyranny of the moment," as it is often referred, constricts blood vessels and affects your vision. Fine motor skills are affected. Because motor movement and muscle control are affected, it is good to have skills in place that you have practiced relentlessly. Otherwise, you will be helpless in a personal defense situation.

This is a very decent group for most handguns at 25 yards, however, one of the five shots is off to the right. Ever present is human or mechanical error.

As for the accuracy needed, those I debriefed after a successful defense told me that they focused on the front sight. You shoot as you have trained and the mantra should be: front sight, front sight, front sight! Some post-shooting armed citizens remembered minute details like the bars on a notched front sight, while others recalled the orange dot insert of a revolver sight. I have yet to hear, "I pointed the gun and hit them." I will never be the instructor who went to court and had to tell the judge and jury that I taught a student to fire without using their sights. In addition, the proverbial innocent bystander will profit from you using your sights. The accuracy needed for personal defense is situational and based upon the scenario in which you are involved. It is true that a fast 6-inch group at 5 yards will save your life. But public safety and simple morality demand you be as well-armed and as accurate

The Traditions Single Action Army, or SAA .45 with 7 $\frac{1}{2}$-inch barrel, is among the author's favorite recreational firearms. The long-barrel .45 is more useful than most would believe.

The author conducted an experiment in which he fired the Traditions .45 Colt revolver at a long 100 yards. The results were surprisingly good.

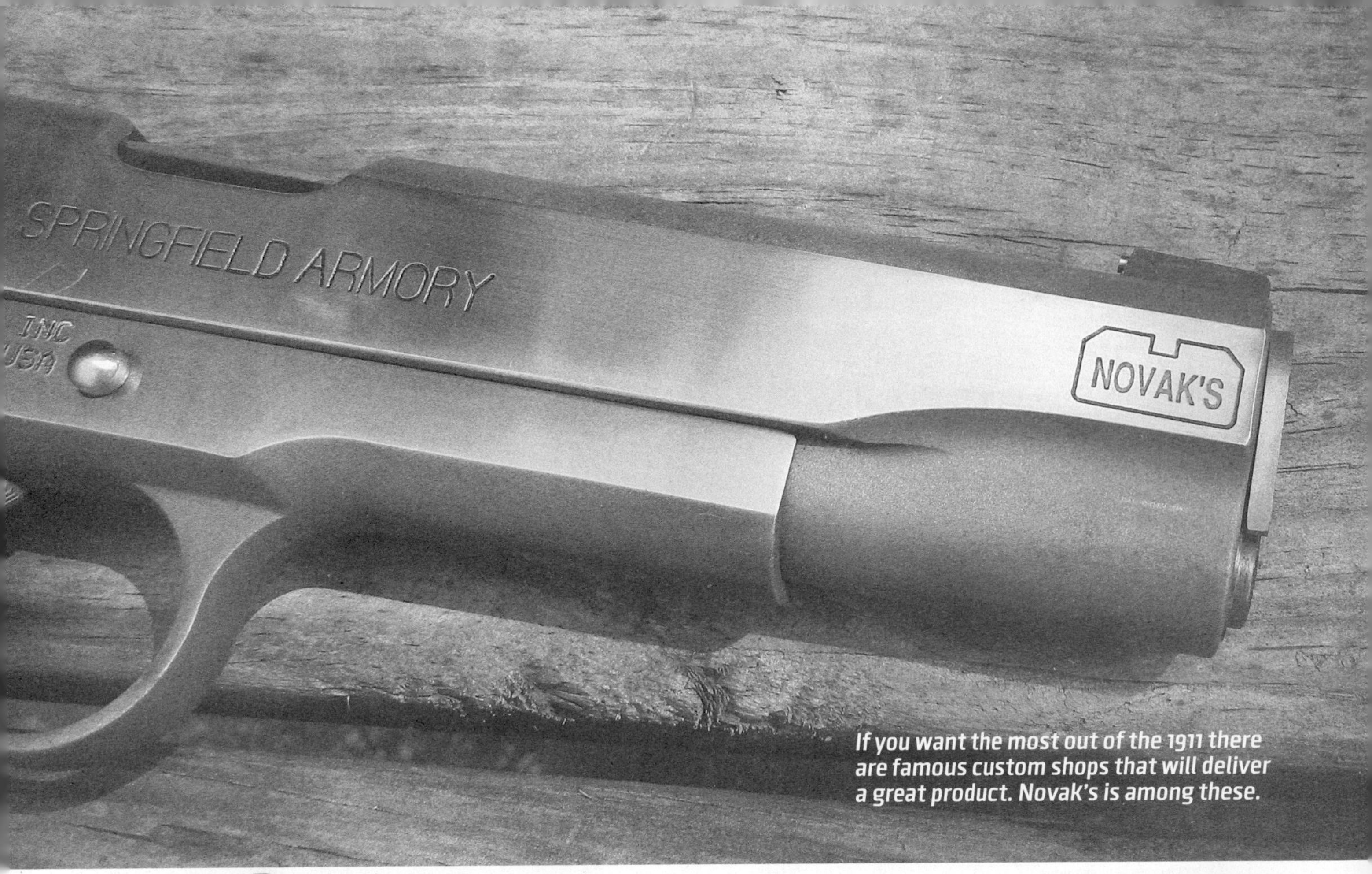

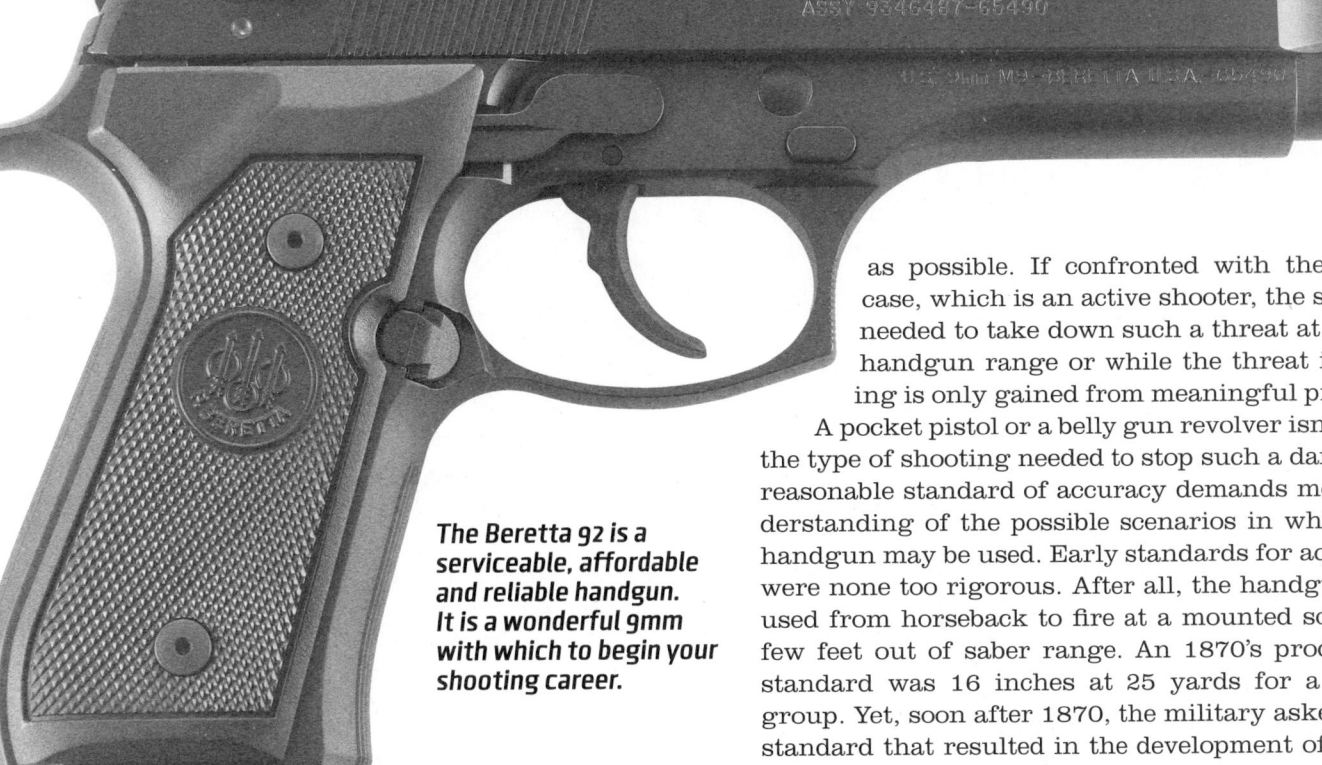

If you want the most out of the 1911 there are famous custom shops that will deliver a great product. Novak's is among these.

The Beretta 92 is a serviceable, affordable and reliable handgun. It is a wonderful 9mm with which to begin your shooting career.

as possible. If confronted with the worst case, which is an active shooter, the skill set needed to take down such a threat at longer handgun range or while the threat is moving is only gained from meaningful practice.

A pocket pistol or a belly gun revolver isn't up to the type of shooting needed to stop such a danger. A reasonable standard of accuracy demands more understanding of the possible scenarios in which the handgun may be used. Early standards for accuracy were none too rigorous. After all, the handgun was used from horseback to fire at a mounted soldier a few feet out of saber range. An 1870's production standard was 16 inches at 25 yards for a 5-inch group. Yet, soon after 1870, the military asked for a standard that resulted in the development of one of the most powerful and accurate military handguns of all time.

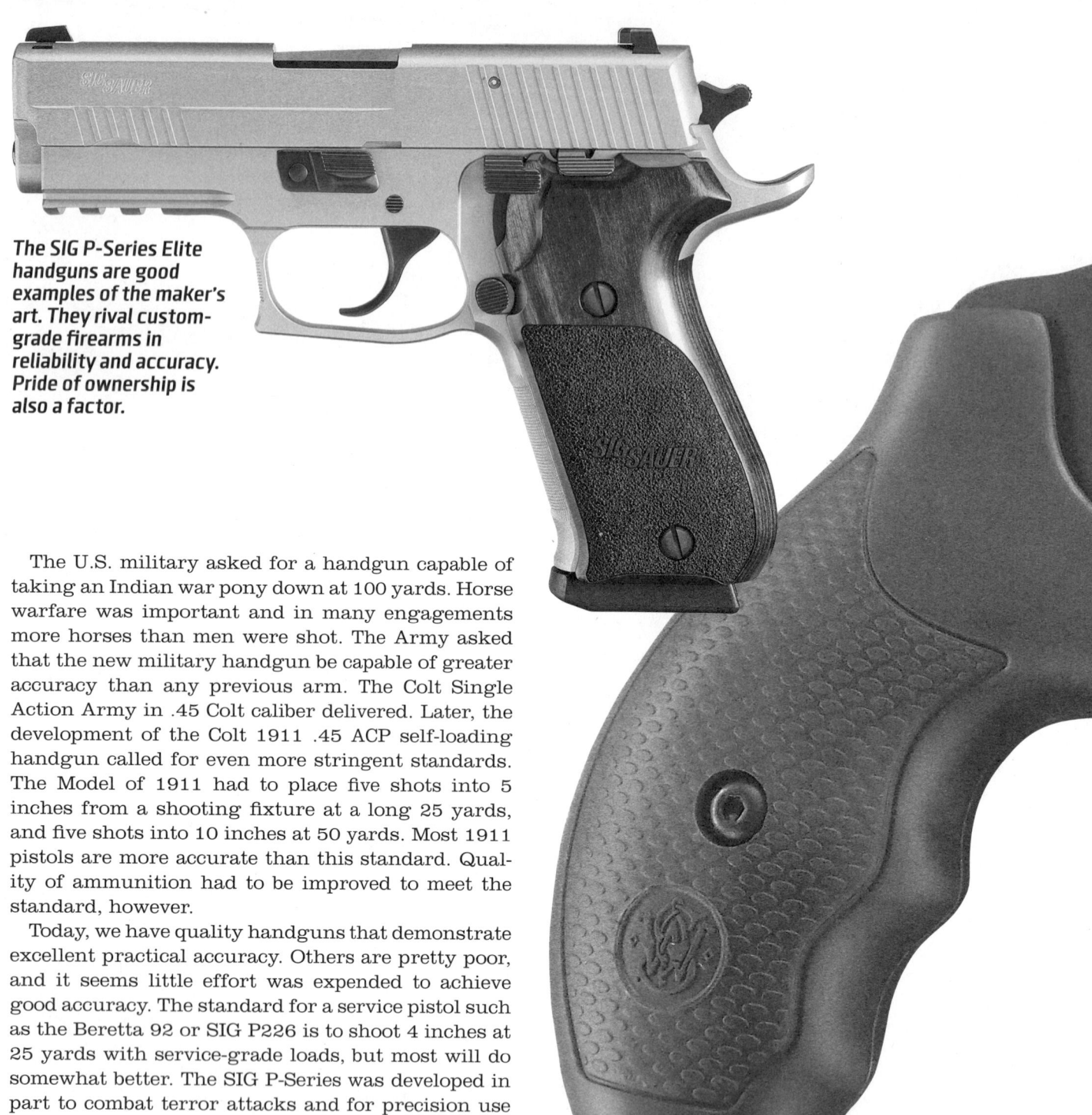

The SIG P-Series Elite handguns are good examples of the maker's art. They rival custom-grade firearms in reliability and accuracy. Pride of ownership is also a factor.

The U.S. military asked for a handgun capable of taking an Indian war pony down at 100 yards. Horse warfare was important and in many engagements more horses than men were shot. The Army asked that the new military handgun be capable of greater accuracy than any previous arm. The Colt Single Action Army in .45 Colt caliber delivered. Later, the development of the Colt 1911 .45 ACP self-loading handgun called for even more stringent standards. The Model of 1911 had to place five shots into 5 inches from a shooting fixture at a long 25 yards, and five shots into 10 inches at 50 yards. Most 1911 pistols are more accurate than this standard. Quality of ammunition had to be improved to meet the standard, however.

Today, we have quality handguns that demonstrate excellent practical accuracy. Others are pretty poor, and it seems little effort was expended to achieve good accuracy. The standard for a service pistol such as the Beretta 92 or SIG P226 is to shoot 4 inches at 25 yards with service-grade loads, but most will do somewhat better. The SIG P-Series was developed in part to combat terror attacks and for precision use during hostage rescue. They were the first service-grade handguns intended to be accurate enough for hostage rescue work. It isn't unusual for those in the P-Series — the P220, P226, P228 or P229 — to cluster five shots into 2-inch groups at 25 yards. The single most accurate factory service grade handgun I have ever fired was a SIG P220 .45 ACP. It delivered five rounds of Black Hills 230-grain JHP into 15/16-inch at 25 yards in a startlingly accurate demonstration. While this was a singular event, other P220s have demonstrated similar performance. And while the average groups with this handgun was 1.5 inches with certain loads it liked, the occasional 1-inch group was demonstrated. When testing handguns

for a police agency, I found the P226 would group five Federal 124-grain Hydra-Shok +P+ loads into 1.25 inches. Another exemplary showing was a CZ 75B that grouped five shots of Black Hills 124-grain JHP into 4 inches from a solid braced firing position at 50 yards.

The intrinsic accuracy of some of the lighter defensive handguns can be surprisingly good, depending upon the type of firearm. Efforts have been made

The Smith and Wesson Model 360 .38 Special revolver is short and light, yet its heavy barrel and large hand-filling grips make it a good shooter.

One of the great things about the 9mm is control. Note the author has two spent cartridges in the air over his shoulder, and another at his knees as the Honor Guard fires again.

to achieve good accuracy potential in the CZ2075 RAMI and the SIG P228, for example. As for handguns smaller than the RAMI, the problem is that it is difficult to fire the handgun up to its potential due to a short sight radius, small grips and heavier recoil. Most shooters retain a higher standard of accuracy when shooting offhand with the full-sized service pistol than with a lightweight or compact handgun. You retain the advantages of the service-size gun while the compacts are more likely to be off target. You may find a compact-size handgun hopeless past 10 yards, but this need not be true if you have practiced diligently with the carry gun.

The Smith and Wesson Model 360 double-action .38 Special revolver with 2-inch barrel is a quality piece with a smooth action and excellent barrel fitting. The chambers, barrel throat and cylinder are well-machined to tight tolerances. Firing carefully off of a benchrest will yield surprising results with the Smith and Wesson snubnose. Five-shot groups of 3 inches or less at 25 yards are possible. But firing carefully off of a benchrest is a different story than firing offhand during a critical incident. You

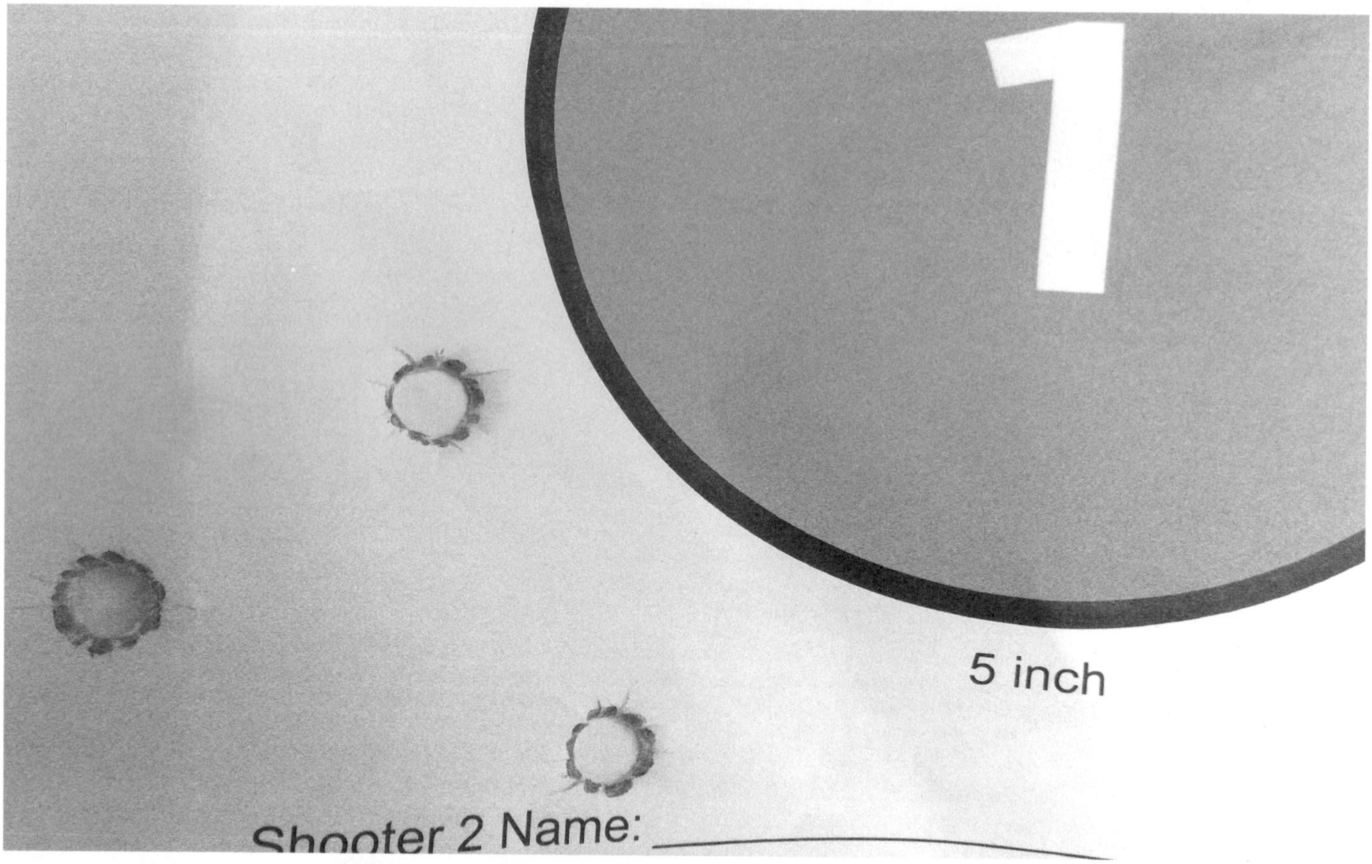

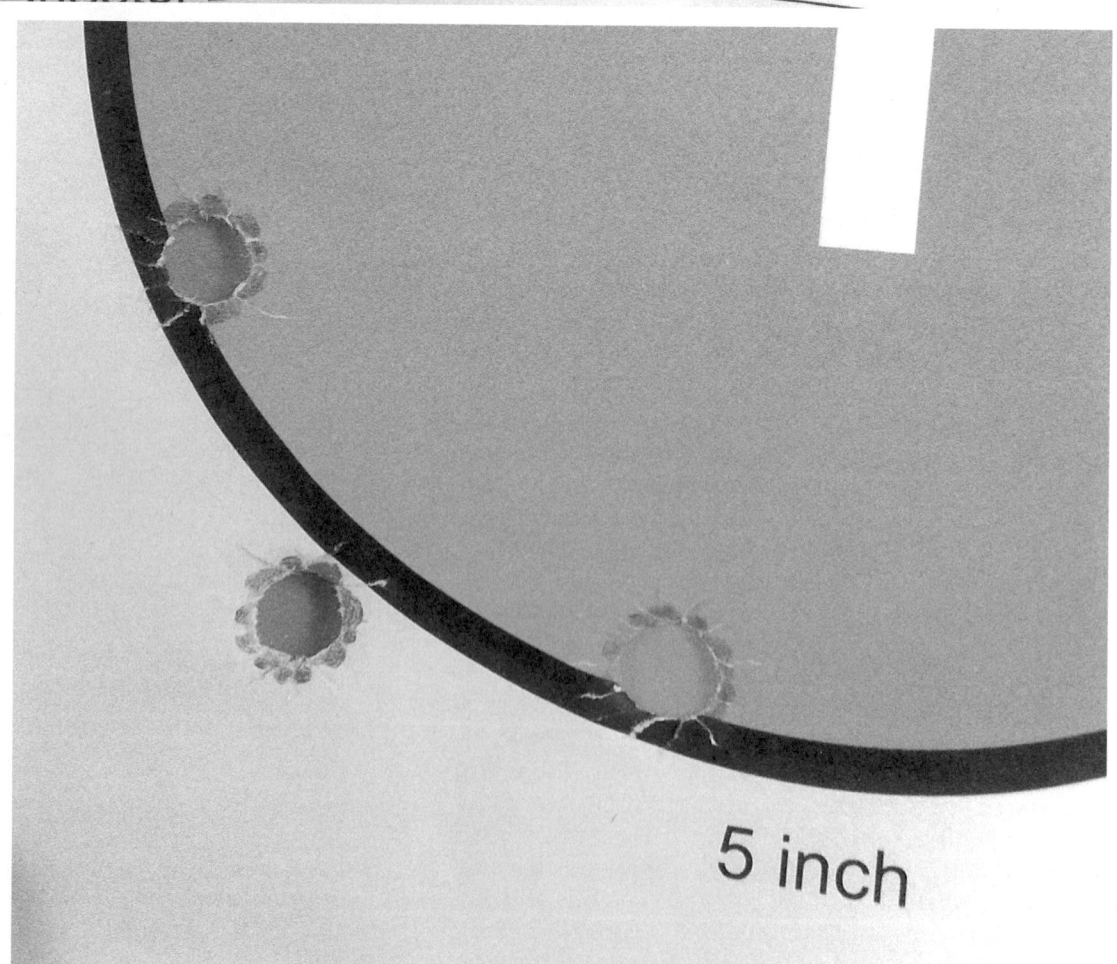

5 inch

Shooter 2 Name: _____

(above) This group, shot with a 1911 stocked with SIG Elite ammunition, is excellent at 25 yards.

(right) Firing at a larger bullseye makes for an easier aiming point. This is a good group at 25 yards.

5 inch

will retain a greater degree of accuracy with a service-grade pistol than with a sub-compact or a snubnose revolver. Just the same, if caught in a bad situation you will find that the snubbie is up to the task of making center hits past 15 yards if you are up to the task. A 2-inch barrel double-action only revolver with thin grips isn't going to be as easy to use well. After some experiments on the range and firing a few hundred handloads in the Model 360, I find it would not be out of the question to center punch a bad guy well past 25 yards — but this type of shooting falls more into the stunt category than true competence. Could a cool head pull it off at 50 yards? Maybe. But the odds are against this type of shooting.

Intrinsic vs. Practical Accuracy

The intrinsic and practical accuracy of a handgun are two very different things. In practical use, a compact 9mm or a snubnose .38 Special revolver should group five shots into 3 inches at 15 yards. We use 15 yards rather than 25 yards as a test in deference to the short sight radius and other short-comings of the compact handgun. With a solid benchrest firing position, you can confirm accuracy and also the pistol's proper sight regulation. A service pistol, such as the Glock 19 or a Commander .45, should do 3 inches at 25 yards all day long. Most institutional users specify 4 inches at 25 yards. This is a reasonable standard for modern production and today's ammunition, but many handguns will beat this standard considerably. Some, such as the Honor Defense Honor Guard in 9mm, shoot right up with lightweight service-grade handguns. The problem in practical use is that it takes an accomplished handgunner familiar with the firearm to shoot it to this standard. A CZ P01 will be much easier for the average to good shooter to wring the best accuracy from it. My personal standards for a go anywhere, do anything handgun is 2.5 inches at 25 yards. Quite a few of my .357- and .45-caliber revolvers and .45 ACP autoloaders will beat this standard.

Handgun Hunting Accuracy

The standard for a hunting handgun is dictated by the game. A squirrel's body is pretty small and the

(left) This is a decent group for any handgun shot at 25 yards, but it is too far to the right. The sights need adjustment.

(below) The Bullshooters pistol rest from Brownells is a great addition to any shooter's gear. The handgun is held rigidly as the test progresses.

The CZ variants are often very accurate. This is the Swiss AT 84 version of the 9mm CZ 75.

distance at which the pistol will group five shots into an inch is probably the best range, even shorter if you demand head shots. The size of the game and the distance is the determining factor for accuracy standards. If your squirrel community is skittish and allows a shooter no closer than 20 yards or so you have a challenge! Deer-sized game has a vital area of about 8 inches. So, 8 inches at 100 yards would be your accuracy standard. Quite a few Magnum revolvers and even a number of .44 Special and .45 Colt revolvers will meet this standard. The problem in the field is that you are not going to shoot this well. And 8 inches is generous, I like to figure closer to 6 inches and a

little less for a heart shot. Most deer-sized game are taken well within 50 yards.

The last two deer this writer has taken with handguns were at 15 and 30 yards, respectively, both downed with one shot from the .45-caliber 1911. For hunting, I would like to have better accuracy than a 4-inch group. Each of these handguns were go anywhere, do anything handguns, the first a Commander capable of 4 inches at 25 yards, the second, a Government Model capable of 2 inches at the same distance. With a 4-inch group, each shot should be within 2 inches of the point of aim given perfect conditions. Circumstances are seldom perfect and you should always take a broadside shot at game.

Magnum hunting revolvers are among the most accurate handguns ever made and may exhibit a 3-inch, 50-yard group with good ammunition. At 50 yards some of the better examples will group five shots into 2 inches, an excellent standard. Occasionally, a rather lucky combination comes your way that will perform beyond expectation. With this level of accuracy you can make hits past the sure killing range of the cartridge, another consideration. The primary concern is to master the handgun and load combination. I like to pack pistols such as the 4-inch .44 Magnum, the 4 ¾- or 4 5/8-inch .45 Colt, the 4-inch .357 Magnum or the 5-inch 1911 .45. These handguns will do everything I need to do at this point in my life and deliver excellent all-around performance. Competition-grade handguns are another matter.

In rapid fire the CZ 75 gives up nothing to any other 9mm handgun in control.

Accuracy of Common Defensive and Practical Carry Handguns

Table 8-1

Rock Island Armory .380 ACP Baby Rock 3.75-inch barrel. Groups fired at 25 yards.		
Winchester 95-gr. FMJ	980 fps	4.6 in.
Winchester 95-gr. JHP	960 fps	4.0 in.
Gorilla 95-gr. JHP	940 fps	4.3 in.
Black Hills 90-gr. JHP	910 fps	4.0 in.

Table 8-2

Rock Island Baby Rock 3-inch barrel. Groups fired at 25 yards.		
Black Hills 60-gr. Extreme Defense	1,201 fps	4.7 in.
Black Hills 90-gr. JHP	880 fps	3.5 in.
Gorilla 95-gr. JHP	900 fps	3.5 in.
Fiocchi 95-gr. FMJ	870 fps	3.4 in.

Table 8-3

Smith and Wesson 360 .38 Special 2-inch barrel. Groups fired at 25 yards.		
Magnus 124-gr. SWC/WW231	800 fps	4.0 in.
Hornady 110-gr. Critical Defense	930 fps	3.8 in.
Buffalo Bore 158-gr. SWCHP	980 fps	4.6 in.
Black Hills 148-gr. WC	690 fps	3.75 in.

Table 8-4

Smith and Wesson Model 19 .357 Magnum 2.5-inch barrel. Groups fired at 25 yards.		
SIG 125-gr. JHP	1,211 fps	2.0 in.
Hornady Critical Defense 125-gr.	1,260 fps	2.25 in.
Hornady 158-gr. XTP/Blue Dot	1,050 fps	1.9 in.

Table 8-5

Ruger SP101 .357 Magnum 2.5-inch barrel. Groups fired at 25 yards.		
Hornady Critical Defense 125-gr.	1,301 fps	3.0 in.
Hornady 125-gr. XTP	1,317 fps	3.1 in.
Federal 180-gr. JHP	960 fps	2.8 in.

Table 8-6

Smith and Wesson Model 19 .357 Magnum 4-inch barrel. Groups fired at 25 yards.		
Black Hills 125-gr. JHP	1,415 fps	1.6 in.
Winchester 145-gr. Silvertip	1,320 fps	1.5 in.
Hornady 180-gr. XTP/H110	1,060 fps	1.4 in.

Table 8-7

CZ RAMI 2075 compact 9mm 3.05-inch barrel. Groups fired at 25 yards.		
SIG 125-gr. V Crown	1,099 fps	2.0 in.
Hornady 147-gr. XTP	880 fps	1.9 in.
Federal 115-gr. JHP 9BP	1,110 fps	2.25 in.
Fiocchi 124-gr. Extrema	1,054 fps	2.25

Table 8-8

Glock 19 9mm 4.01-inch barrel. Groups fired at 25 yards.		
Federal 124-gr. HST	1,178 fps	3.2 in.
Federal 147-gr. HST +P	1,100 fps	3.4 in.
Winchester 115-gr. USA FMJ	1,124 fps	3.5 in.
Winchester 124-gr. PDX +P	1,177 fps	2.9 in.
Gorilla Ammunition 135-gr. JHP	940 fps	3.0 in.

Table 8-9

Smith and Wesson Shield .45 ACP 3.3-inch barrel. Groups fired at 25 yards.		
American Eagle 230-gr. FMJ	740 fps	3.6 in.
Speer 230-gr. Gold Dot JHP	760 fps	3.5 in.
Fiocchi 230-gr. Extrema	756 fps	3.8 in.
Magnus 200-gr. SWC/Titegroup	840 fps	4.0 in.
Hornady 200-gr. XTP/Titegroup	875 fps	3.9 in.

Table 8-10

Traditions SAA .45 Colt 4.75-inch barrel. Groups fired at 25 yards.		
Black Hills 250-gr. FP	750 fps	3.0 in.
Winchester 250-gr. FP	780 fps	2.5 in.
Winchester 225-gr. PDX	850 fps	2.25 in.
Magnus 250-gr. FP/WW231	880 fps	2.6 in.

Table 8-11

Springfield Mil-Spec 1911 .45 ACP 5-inch barrel. Groups fired at 25 yards.		
Black Hills 230-gr. JHP	855 fps	2.65 in.
Fiocchi 230-gr. JHP	860 fps	2.9 in.
Fiocchi 230-gr. Extrema JHP	800 fps	2.4 in.
Hornady 230-gr. XTP+P	933 fps	2.7 in.
Winchester W1911 230-gr. FMJ	866 fps	2.9 in.
Remington UMC 230-gr. FMJ	840 fps	3.7 in.

Hunting Handguns

Table 8-12

Smith and Wesson Model 686 .357 Magnum 6-inch barrel. Groups fired at 25 yards.		
Black Hills 125-gr. JHP	1,430 fps	1.8 in.
Winchester 158-gr. JHP	1,270 fps	1.5 in.
SIG Elite 125-gr. JHP	1,360 fps	2.0 in.
Hornady 125-gr. XTP/H110	1,412 fps	2.0 in.
Hornady 158-gr. XTP/H110	1,355 fps	1.5 in.

Table 8-13

Smith and Wesson Model 629 .44 Magnum 6-inch barrel. Groups fired at 25 yards.		
Winchester 250-gr. JHP	1,230 fps	1.2 in.
Black Hills 300-gr. JHP	1,100 fps	1.5 in.
Hornady 240-gr. XTP/WW296	1,319 fps	2.0 in.

Table 8-14

Ruger Blackhawk .45 Colt 4 5/8-inch barrel. Groups fired at 25 yards.		
Hornady 250-gr. XTP/W296	1,000 fps	1.8 in.
Magnus 250-gr. FP/WW231	990 fps	2.25 in.
Buffalo Bore 250-gr. HC/SWC	1,030 fps	2.6 in.

CHAPTER 9

HOW ACCURATE ARE FACTORY HANDGUNS?

The SIG P320 is easy to shoot well and is very reliable. It may not be the most accurate modern handgun, primarily due to the trigger action, but it is useful.

Although we have tested many handguns and loads in this book, the question of how accurate factory handguns truly can be may not have been completely answered. The question really is: how accurate is a specific handgun with a given load, and how accurate is the shooter — the human element and variable. In many cases, wrong conclusions about handgun accuracy are reached due simply to the use of the wrong type of ammunition and/or by poor shooting. On the other hand, accuracy is certainly relative to the mission.

As an example, I published a review recently in which I was able to secure a 2-inch 25-yard group with a quality handgun and ammunition. It was satisfying shooting, above the norm for the type of

This is interesting, but for most handgun shooters what really matters is combat shooting and control. A shooter that is able to place ten rounds into 4 inches offhand at 10 yards is capable. Benchrest accuracy is a means of testing both the handgun and the ammunition but not the best gauge of combat accuracy. Let's consider this. My 2-inch group means that the handgun will deliver every shot within 1 inch if I do my part. Moreover, a 4-inch group means that the handgun will deliver every shot within two inches of the point of aim. The pursuit of accuracy is worthwhile but must be taken into perspective. When testing factory handguns it is best to self-evaluate your shooting style and reappraise from time to time. Are you getting it right?

Lubricating the trigger action makes a performance difference in some handguns.

Dry-fire practice or training with CB caps (where safe and legal to do so) sharpens the marksman's skill.

handgun tested. A reader sent a correspondence and noted that they were able to fire only a 4-inch group at 15 yards from the benchrest with their personal handgun of the same type. What was wrong? There are many explanations. First, when shooting from a solid benchrest firing position over a sandbag, and with plenty of time to fire, I was able to demonstrate a group of five shots into less than 3 inches at a long 25 yards using a number of different handguns. A trained shooter or competitor may produce this level of accuracy under similar conditions. I have been at this a long time. (A very few competitors may shoot about as well offhand — they are true athletes!) A shooter that is beginning/proficient, where most young and trained shooters fall, may print a group of 4 inches off the benchrest at 15 yards. Some will shoot as well as the old hands after just a few years practice; after all, a handgun is only so accurate.

Among the most interesting new introductions is the Rex Zero 9mm handgun. This is a pistol well worth its price, and it is accurate enough to solve most problems.

Handgun Fit

Accuracy is simply shooting without missing. And there are many variables that cause misses. One critical relationship of handgun geometry is how it fits your hand. You need to explore this in your selection of a handgun. But a truly telling measure-   ment that you cannot overlook is the relationship between trigger pull weight and the handgun itself. Some handguns have a very heavy trigger, particularly the double-action first-shot pistols. Some are so heavy they are not useful for personal defense. I think that a number of foreign-made double actions loosely based on the Browning Hi Power were the worst I have seen. Yet, the FEG Hi Power clone is often a decent handgun. I once tested

the AMT backup .45 and found that the double-action-only, or DAO trigger was right at 20 pounds! The Beretta, CZ and SIG are much better. The Glock DAO breaks at 5.5 pounds or 85 ounces against a 30-ounce gun. A rough double-action, or DA trigger as found on bargain-grade handguns may run 15 pounds! On such a beast it is difficult to pull the trigger against the handgun's weight and keep the pistol steady at the same time. Even relatively compact handguns are difficult to manage if the trigger is heavy.

(left) The sight picture must be perfect to make hits at longer range. The Ruger GP100 .44 Special features a fiber optic front sight that many will find works well for them.

(right) With the proper sight focus, the front sight is sharp and clear. The Ruger fiber optic front sight is ideal for this application.

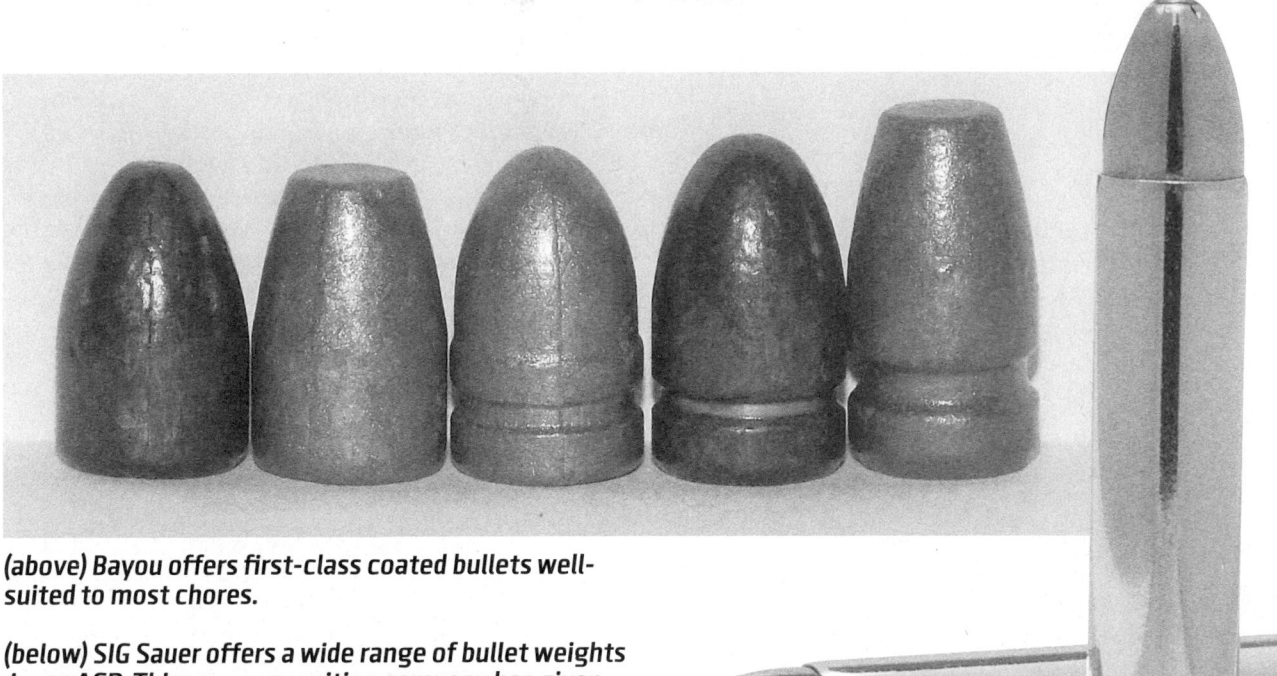

(above) Bayou offers first-class coated bullets well-suited to most chores.

(below) SIG Sauer offers a wide range of bullet weights in .45 ACP. This new ammunition company has given the author excellent all-around results.

The .22 Magnum can be an accurate cartridge in the right handgun and it hits harder than the .22 LR.

al defense, and you wish to use a handgun that offers a sure steady shot when your nerves are frayed, the heavy trigger action of the DA first-shot and the DAO pistols are a viable choice. When learning marksmanship, or if you have a desire to be an accurate shooter capable of placing hits at long handgun range, you need a smooth trigger and a reasonable ratio of trigger weight to pistol weight. A middle of the road handgun with a good trigger will often perform better than a well-made one with a heavy trigger action. Trigger reach — or trigger span — also means a lot. If your trigger finger has good leverage you will be able to control the heavy trigger better. If your trigger reach is such that your trigger finger is continually stressed to simply press the trigger (much less control the trigger) then you have yourself a difficult little problem. I have actually tested double-action handguns that stressed the tendon in my trigger finger after just a few shots. No wonder so many shooters practice cocking the hammer of a DA pistol rather than controlling it. I have seen my sons control the Beretta double-action and make hits in DA fire all of the way out to 25 yards. It can be done with a smooth trigger pull that isn't intolerably heavy, but an action requiring over 12 pounds of pull isn't very manageable.

A heavy trigger action prevents control of the trigger, which leads to missing the shot and the bullet landing where it was not intended to go. You must

This aspect of handgun geometry and leverage must be understood. The answer is to grasp the handgun tightly and manage the trigger. The DA first-shot pistols have a single-action option and the Glock can be controlled pretty well with the proper technique. Just the same, some handguns are difficult to manage. When the goal is close-range person-

learn to control the trigger and hit the target every time. You must engage in constant dry fire practice. Lubricate the trigger action and chances are it will become smoother. Triple check the firearm to be certain it isn't loaded and dry fire against an object that would stop a bullet if you make a God awful mistake. Do not aim for a large object. Aim for a small object of no more than an inch in diameter. Dry fire against this object and observe the sights as the trigger falls. There should be minimal to no disturbance of the sights as the hammer drops.

(above) Federal Match ammunition is legendary for accuracy and reliability.

(right) Standard defense loads can provide you with excellent accuracy. Federal has earned a well-deserved reputation for cartridge integrity.

(below) The Browning Hi Power offers first-class reliability and will often prove quite accurate.

Laser Sights

A great aid to marksmanship training and dry fire practice is the laser light. These are available for as little or as much as you would like to pay. My favorite is the TruGlo Tru-Lite. This robust and affordable unit performs well for use in everything ranging from everyday practice to a personal defense situation. Its combination laser and light can be used simultaneously, or each separately. The laser dot is a great training aid. Turn the laser on and attempt to keep the dot on the target as you press the trigger. You will find that the dot jumps around the target. (This isn't a red dot sight, the laser fires a red dot.) No matter how well-practiced you are, there will always be some wobble. The beginner will look ridiculous until having trained considerably! Dry fire practice with a laser pays off. And if you are going to use the laser for personal defense you might as well practice with it in dry fire. The final goal is to press the trigger with no movement and to hit the target every time. The more you practice, the more this goal seems obtainable. Dry fire practice teaches trigger control and sight alignment without distracting flash and ear-splitting report. Of course, always follow the safety rules. Treat all guns as if they are loaded, triple check to be certain the firearm isn't loaded, keep your finger off of the trigger until you actually fire, and be certain of your target. Since you are practicing dry fire, do not be lulled into complacency. Be certain the point of aim and the backstop would stop a bullet if need be.

With this type of dry fire practice you will be better armed to test firearms for accuracy. Hitting the target involves having the handgun properly sighted in. In addition, there are several holds to master, including the six o' clock and dead-on hold. Most fixed-sight revolvers are sighted for the six o' clock hold. The same goes for fixed-sight self-loaders. Occasion-

(left) Brittany Caton achieved what few do, she is a certified NRA instructor.

(below) The proper grip is vital to any pistol shooter. Strive for perfection in all of your practice.

The Kimber fully adjustable sight is among the best in the business.

ally, a handgun will be found that is badly off-center. Heavy bullets strike higher than light bullets. This is because the heavy bullet recoils more, is slower, and dwell time in the barrel longer. A lighter bullet is going faster and will exit the barrel lower in the recoil arc. As a rule, fixed-sight 9mm handguns are sighted for 124-grain loads; 40-caliber pistols for 180-grain loads; and .45 ACP pistols for 230-grain bullets. A service pistol such as the Colt 1911 Government Model will be sighted to fire high at close range. This gives you a fighting chance at 50 yards. It is possible to bump the rear sight in the dovetail to account for windage. The front sight can be filed a bit to allow the point of impact to be moved up. Good quality adjustable sights are ideal for use with an all-purpose handgun, but they are not found on most personal defense sidearms. As for out-of-the-box accuracy in factory handguns, the answer is very accurate indeed. Many of the more popular autoloaders are capable of putting five rounds within 1 ½ inches of the point of aim for every shot — that is, a 3-inch group — at 25 yards. But to see that level of precision, you must do your part behind the trigger.

The Beretta 92 9mm has many good attributes. One of these is limited muzzle flip and modest recoil.

The author tries his hand with the fixed-sight Traditions .45 Colt revolver.

Accuracy Results

Table 9-1

Handgun	Load	25-Yd. Group
Kel-Tec PMR 30 .22 Magnum	Hornady 45-gr. Critical Defense	4.0 in.
	CCI 40-gr. JHP	3.8 in.
Ruger SP101 .357 Magnum	SIG 125-gr. JHP	3.65 in.
Springfield Mil Spec 1911	SIG 200-gr. JHP	3.0 in.
	SIG 230-gr. JHP	2.8 in.
Glock 41 .45	Federal 230-gr. Match	2.25 in.
	Federal 230-gr. American Eagle	3.4 in.
Glock 35 .40	Hornady 155-gr. XTP	2.65 in.
	Federal 165-gr. Hydra-Shok	3.2 in.
Arex Rex Zero 9mm Compact	Aguila 115-gr. FMJ	4.6 in.
	Black Hills 124-gr. JHP	3.6 in.
	Federal 115-gr. American Eagle	3.5 in.
	Federal 124-gr. HST	3.0 in.
CZ 75D Compact	Black Hills 124-gr. JHP	2.5 in.
	Hornady 124-gr. XTP +P	2.6 in.
	Gorilla 135-gr. JHP	2.8 in.

ACCURACY TEST PROCEDURES

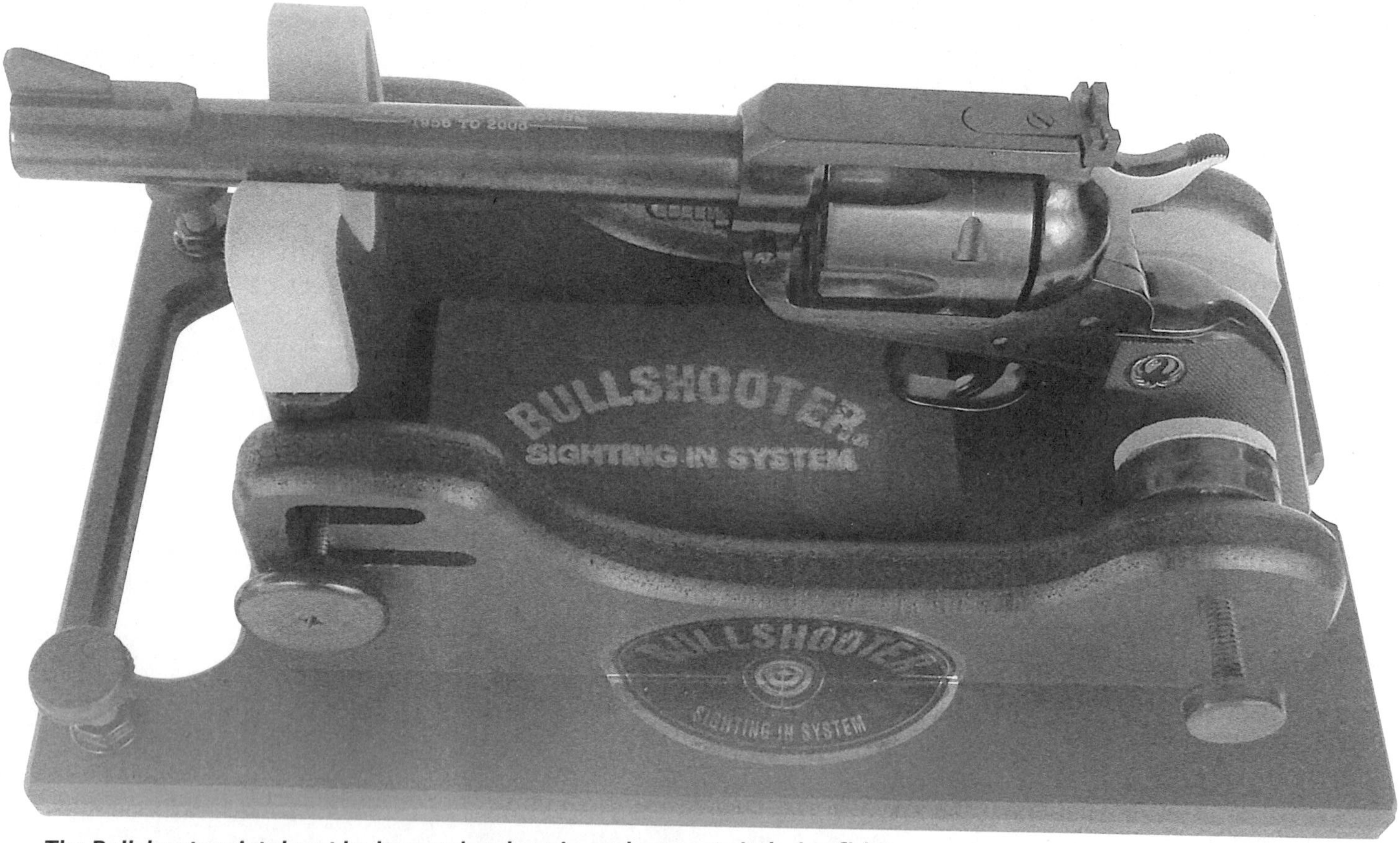

The Bullshooter pistol rest locks your handgun in, and supports it during firing.

You need to have a procedure established to test handguns. Only then can you fire a handgun and deem it accurate or inaccurate. The process much be repeatable and verifiable. Comparing inconsistent results — that is, those that are apples to oranges — will not mean anything. There will be no validity. It may take shooting a top-quality handgun with different loads to verify its true accuracy potential, and there are handguns that are not going to rise above mediocre with any load. You have to learn how to test these handguns and how to judge accuracy. Consistency is everything. The grip and the tension with which the handgun is held must be as consistent as humanly possible. The sight picture and sight alignment must be as nearly perfect as possible, and most of all consistent. Trigger control must be exact and painstakingly executed. Fire from a solid benchrest to gain every advantage for accuracy. (The handgun will not be fired from a bench in the field, although you may find a tree, large rock or a natural setting to get a solid firing position. The bench rest position is for pure accuracy testing.)

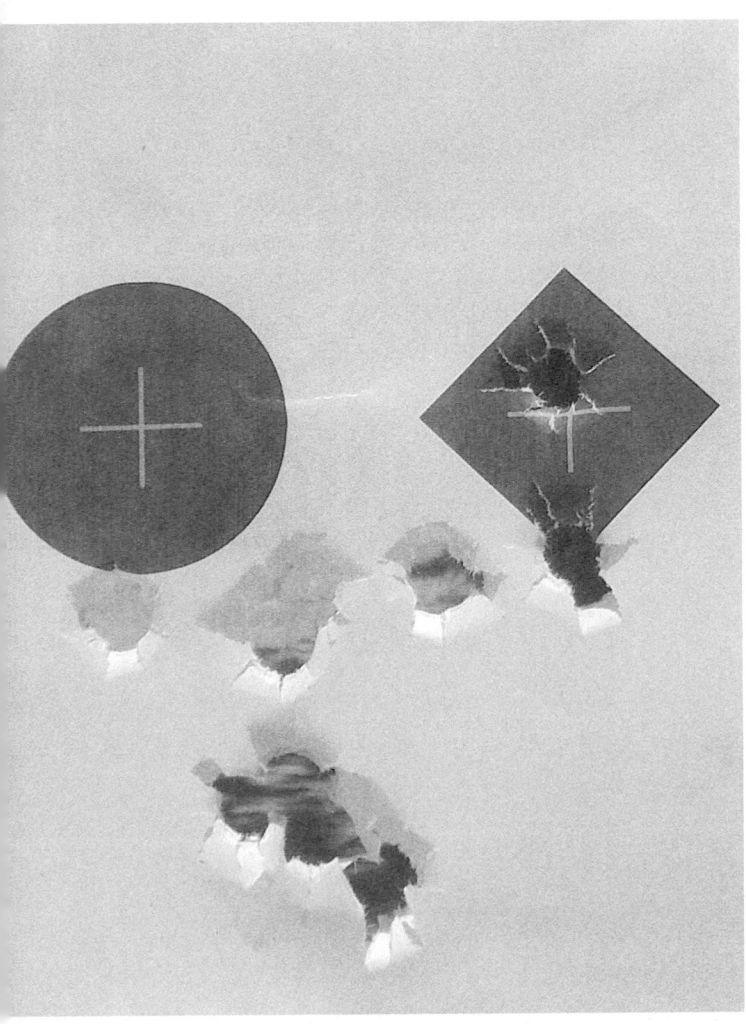

An excellent group fired at 25 yards from the Bullshooter rest.

While small groups are one goal, having the bullet strike exactly where you want it is another, and a vital component to accuracy. When shooting from a bench, use a purpose-designed sandbag or cushion to use as a rest. I have used variations over the years and, for informal work, particularly at 15 yards, I often simply use a range bag. It works for me, but I have been at this a long time. A properly designed sandbag rest is for the best when firing for maximum accuracy. When shooting from the sandbag your body should be relaxed. Both feet should be planted on the ground. This isn't like shooting offhand or being ready for tactical movement, you are not going anywhere. Use a second set of sandbags for resting your elbows. Take the handgun in hand firmly and place it on the sandbag. Keep the same force in the grip as when you are firing offhand and your handgun will shoot to the same point of aim whether on the bench or while standing. It doesn't always work that way, but with care and attention to the grip you will be dead-on target no matter your position.

Careful handloading is one means of maintaining control over accuracy potential.

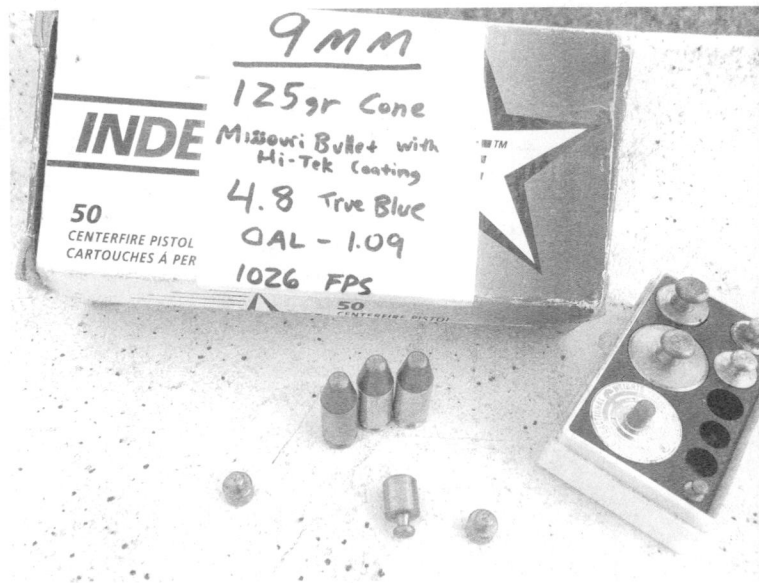

When resting the handgun on sandbags or a heavy shooting bag, the gun's frame should be resting on the support. The revolver barrel will tend to recoil away from a rest and accuracy will be terrible if you use the barrel to rest the revolver. Keep the frame stabilized. Your hands should not be butted against a hard surface or you will abrade or sting them when the gun fires, which leads to poor accuracy. Always keep movement of the firearm and the shooter as limited as possible. By following these rules and applying the proper trigger press, sight picture and sight alignment consistently for each shot you will be able to fire accurate groups that will be a true test of the handgun's accuracy potential. The primary goal is consistent accuracy. When you sight the handgun in from the benchrest, do so for the maximum number of scenarios. Keep your head upright — if you scrunch down, your eyes will become tired and blood flow will be affected causing your vision to blur.

Ruger's high-visibility sights are superior to most fixed sights in the author's opinion.

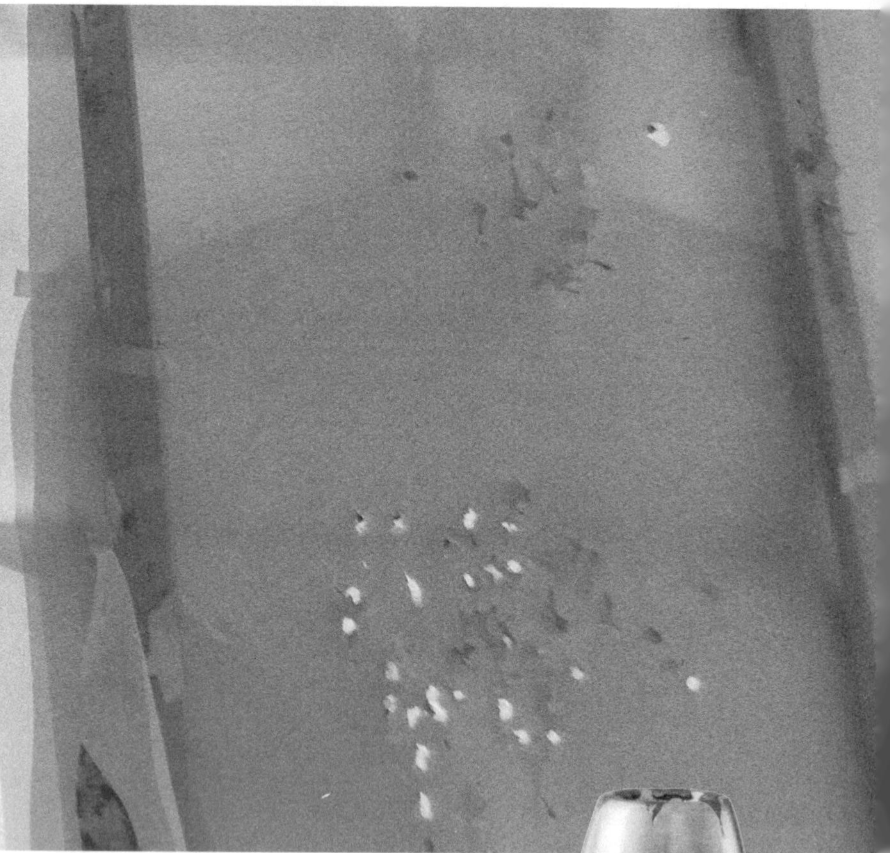

When benchrest testing my personal handgun I use only good quality ammunition. Inexpensive burner loads are fine for offhand practice, but when you wish to be all you can be, top quality is dictated. Use the same load you will in the field for the zeroing process. When striving for top accuracy, I use handloads that I have personally loaded, or ones put together by my son, Alan. He is the best and most accurate loader I know and has been at the game for over 20 years. If the handgun doesn't shoot well and I am doing my part, it isn't the ammunition, so it must be the handgun. Be aware of various handgun cartridge trajectories. You should sight the hand-

(above) Accurate, rapid fire depends on you, but the gear must also be up to the chore.

(right) Some ammunition is more accurate than others. The Speer Gold Dot, as an example, usually gives excellent results.

This is life-saving accuracy that few shooters or handguns can duplicate.

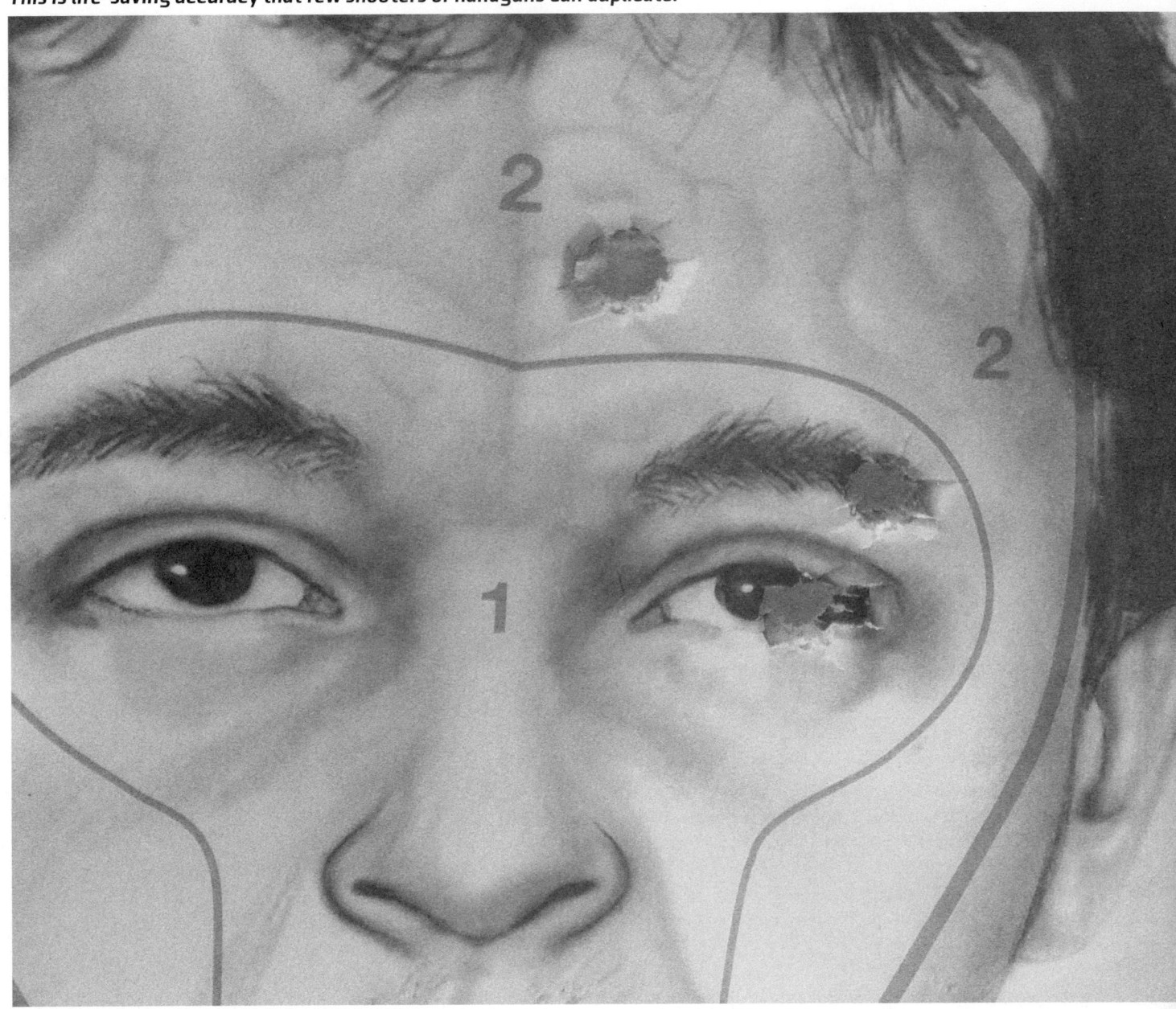

gun in for the range at which it will be used. This means 15 yards for small game for most of us. For predators, you can engage coyote at short range or up to 100 yards, so a zero that places the bullet a bit high at 50 yards is good for this application unless you are certain you will encounter varmints at even longer distances.

One of my friends has consistently taken coyote at rather long range with his 7.62 Tokarev, a flat-shooting and accurate combination, so success doesn't necessarily demand an expensive handgun, but an accurate shooter. Handguns simply do not fire as flat as rifles; their trajectory drop should be understood. The .357 and .44 Magnum revolvers are more accurate than anything, but only the best shooters can hold and are useful well past 100 yards, having practiced and sighted their handguns

properly. Handguns will shoot off-center due to the manner in which they are held, and how grip pressure is applied. The handgun is in recoil before the bullet leaves the barrel. You must keep the grip consistent from shot to shot, maintaining a steady grip as you manage the trigger and keep the sights properly aligned. Once you have the pistol sighted in at the bench, be sure to shoot it from the standing and braced firing position (such as leaning against a tree to confirm the field zero).

It is just as important to sight a personal defense handgun as one for competition or hunting. At close range, you must know exactly where the bullet is going. If you have only a few inches of the adversary exposed from behind cover, you must be able to hit that area. Once the bullet leaves the barrel, you can't call it back — keeping innocent bystand-

ers safe makes close-range accuracy even more critical. When learning to sight the pistol in, it is fine to start at very close range. When you have a little practice under your belt, begin sighting the pistol in at 10 yards. This seems a ridiculously close range, but it is a standard beginning distance for handgun shooting. If you have engaged in firing offhand in a less organized manner, you may need to relearn good habits to properly sight the handgun in a repeatable and efficient manner. Begin at 7 yards and progress to 10 and 15 yards. Actually, 15 yards is a standard for properly sighting personal defense and

small game handguns. You should work up to firing small groups at 15 yards while confirming your accuracy procedure.

As you progress, you will find that you are able to hold groups that are right up to the potential of the handgun. This comes with practice, attention to detail, and ignoring distractions. When you have the procedure mastered, only then will you wish to get into the mechanics of properly sighting the handgun for hunting and competition. As an example, if you are going to use a long-barrel .44 Magnum for hunting purposes, you may take a 100-yard shot.

Black Hills load. That load's momentum, superior weight and added penetration are excellent for game from hogs to the largest deer.

Also, some loads, including 250- and 270-grain .44 Magnum may not be on the ballistic charts. You will have to shoot the handgun to confirm zero and that is the only means of being certain.

Defining Handgun Accuracy

A few years ago, I was at a public range and a young shooter was directed to me by a range master who knew I was a certified instructor. The young man was shooting a third-rate revolver at 15 yards. His .357 Magnum featured a 4-inch barrel, fully adjustable sights, and a five-shot cylinder. Its best feature was hand-fitted wood grips. He'd splattered 15 shots all over the target — some high, some low — with the group an estimated 15 inches. He asked if he needed to adjust his sights! I groaned. After recommending he begin with .38 Special loads from a rest, I think I set the young man on the right track. I have seen others engage soda cans at 25 yards and never seem to miss, yet do not shoot paper targets.

When testing your handgun for accuracy, you need a standard against which you can draw valid comparison. What is good accuracy and what is satisfactory for the average shooter? Consider accuracy by class of firearms. For example, 6-inch barrel magnum revolvers are one class, 9mm service pistols another and 1911 .45s a third. Accuracy isn't necessarily the measure of a single group, but how closely the handgun places each shot together on the target over multiple groups. How small will the grouping be time after time when the shooter is capable of shooting the handgun for accuracy? The term used a century ago was mean dispersion, a term that has much validity. If your handgun is accurate enough for the chores to be done in the role it performs, and is consistent in its accuracy with more than one load, then it is an accurate handgun.

If the handgun has a high level of dispersion then it isn't accurate. As mentioned earlier in this book and it bears repeating, there are two levels of accuracy. First, accuracy that is a result of the design and manufacture of the firearm and its intrinsic tolerances. This is intrinsic accuracy. Good barrel fitting and proper slide to barrel fit, as well as tight machining and proper steel result in good intrinsic accuracy. Practical accuracy is how easily the handgun produces good accuracy in the hands of a proficient shooter. Practical accuracy is affected by the sights, trigger, and even such things as a sharp

This isn't unreasonable considering the accuracy of the big revolver from a braced position and the generous 8-inch kill zone of deer-sized game. The handgun should be sighted to hit high at 50 yards. This is easily corrected for during a 50-yard shooting session — sight it in to hit 3 inches high at this yardage. With my personal 240-grain JHP hunting load, a 3-inch high 50-yard sight-in will place the bullet dead on the bull at 100 yards. My .44 Magnum is presently zeroed for the standard 240-grain JHP. I am seriously considering changing the sight setting on my Blackhawk for the exceptional 300-grain

SIG has recently introduced its Legend series. These are excellent handguns and, while not inexpensive, are well worth their price.

edge (or lack thereof) on the grip tang. Mechanical accuracy is easily tested. Simply bolt the handgun into a machine rest. It doesn't matter if the pistol has sights or not. I do not use a machine rest, but I admit that it is the best means of testing a handgun's performance in a mechanical sense. Then you need only attempt to learn to shoot up to the handgun's mechanical limitations.

Practical accuracy is more difficult to quantify. Nothing fits my hand like the 1911. When I grip the 1911, something says friend. When something has saved your life more than once, you may feel that way, too. In common with the Single Action Army, military service has ensured a long afterlife with ol' slab sides. While I enjoy the 1911 immensely, the marvelously modern Beretta Neos is among the best-shaped and ergonomically practical handles I have ever felt. It is as close to perfect as possible for my personal needs. Yet, I avoided the piece for several years due to its wild look. That is to my detriment. The Smith and Wesson Victory .22 is another beautifully shaped handgun. Others like the feel of the Glock, CZ or the SIG. To be fair, I recognize the SIG series as among the most accurate handguns in the world. I find the CZ 75 pistol suits me better overall, though, and I take the gun on its own merits. In practical terms, I am able to use one as well as the other in offhand fire. I never point shoot; but some handguns do have a better natural point of aim, an aid in getting the handgun lined up with the eyes quickly. Heft and balance are important attributes to consider when shooting offhand. The terms natural point and comfortable grip mean a lot in accuracy testing. No individual shooter is correct in his recommendations on hand fit as this comfort level varies from one shooter to the next. But intrinsic accuracy is a constant. A handgun is only so accurate. A good shot may shoot right up to the capability of a pistol, but he cannot make it do more than it was able to do from the factory. If the trigger is heavy and the sights poor, you will not be able to shoot up to the handgun's capability whatever that may be.

The shooter is much the same. We all have different capabilities and hand sizes as well as differences in vision. Personally, I simply cannot grasp my hands around the Glock 21 and use it well. Yet, I can shoot it well enough to know that it is a soft-kicking .45 and quite accurate. Much the same goes for the Glock Model 20 10mm, which I feel is the most accurate production Glock. You have to decide how much accuracy is adequate for your tasks. For competitors, the bar is raised higher and higher. However,

THERE ARE TWO LEVELS OF ACCURACY. FIRST, ACCURACY THAT IS A RESULT OF THE DESIGN AND MANUFACTURE OF THE FIREARM AND ITS INTRINSIC TOLERANCES. THIS IS INTRINSIC ACCURACY. GOOD BARREL FITTING AND PROPER SLIDE TO BARREL FIT, AS WELL AS TIGHT MACHINING AND PROPER STEEL RESULT IN GOOD INTRINSIC ACCURACY. PRACTICAL ACCURACY IS HOW EASILY THE HANDGUN PRODUCES GOOD ACCURACY IN THE HANDS OF A PROFICIENT SHOOTER.

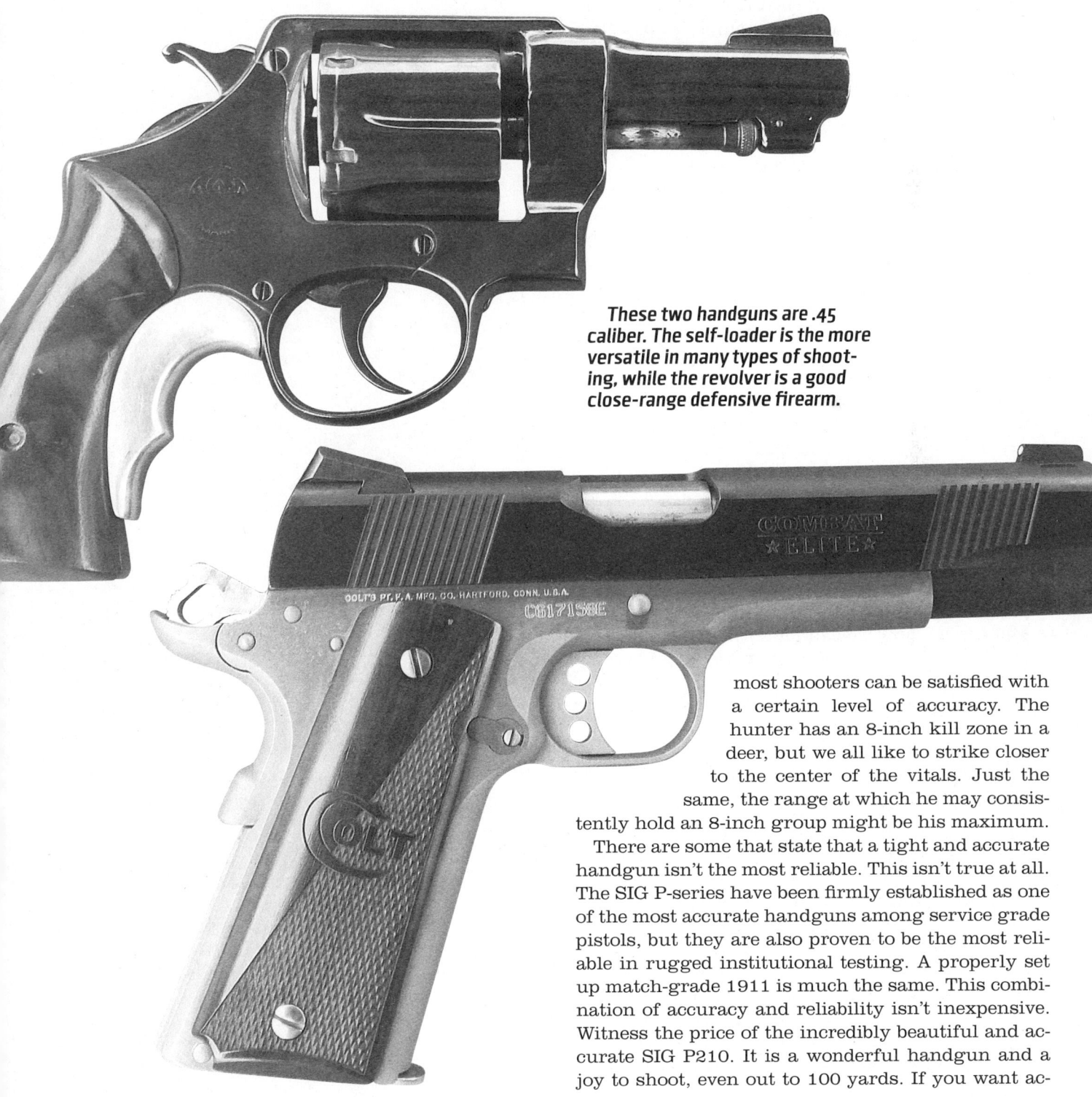

These two handguns are .45 caliber. The self-loader is the more versatile in many types of shooting, while the revolver is a good close-range defensive firearm.

most shooters can be satisfied with a certain level of accuracy. The hunter has an 8-inch kill zone in a deer, but we all like to strike closer to the center of the vitals. Just the same, the range at which he may consistently hold an 8-inch group might be his maximum.

There are some that state that a tight and accurate handgun isn't the most reliable. This isn't true at all. The SIG P-series have been firmly established as one of the most accurate handguns among service grade pistols, but they are also proven to be the most reliable in rugged institutional testing. A properly set up match-grade 1911 is much the same. This combination of accuracy and reliability isn't inexpensive. Witness the price of the incredibly beautiful and accurate SIG P210. It is a wonderful handgun and a joy to shoot, even out to 100 yards. If you want accuracy, however, a Browning Hi Power with a Bar-Sto Precision barrel will run right at the heels of the SIG and perhaps equal its accuracy in a much less expensive package.

When the pucker factor is high and your life is on the line, service grade accuracy is more than enough. This is generally stated to be 4 inches for five shots at 25 yards. I have tested most of the service grade handguns. While the practical accuracy of the Glock 19 9mm, as an example, isn't on a par with the tighter and more ergonomic pistols at longer range when firing offhand or from a solid benchrest, the Glock is more than accurate. But, you have to fire the pistol properly to test and evaluate this accuracy. Frankly, too many shooters simply do not shoot well enough to notice any practical accuracy among such handguns. A Glock, SIG, or Beretta is all the same and the simpler the better. And yet I have to admit this isn't necessarily a bad thing. While it is great to have personal preferences, if I were issued the SIG P226, Beretta 92, CZ 75 or Glock 17 I would not wax poetic over the considerable differences in handling, sights and trigger action but would instead master the piece to the best of my ability. The bottom line is that there is little that can be done, tactically, with one that cannot be done with any of the others. Sure, perhaps I would prefer the Rex Zero 9mm over them all, but then I could easily pass a qualification course with any of these handguns. If you are after the bottom line in accuracy you need to learn to shoot first. Only then do the differences between models become glaringly apparent. With the service grade 4-inch group, all shots should be within 2 inches of the point of aim given a perfect trigger press and sight alignment. I have higher standards than that, but do not wish to give house room to a handgun that groups into more than 3 inches at 25 yards. But then, I am able to test and evaluate the handguns and tell the difference.

Match Accuracy

When testing a handgun for competition, the term "match accurate" is often used. There are semi-custom factory handguns such as the Ed Brown 1911 that are guaranteed to group three shots of quality ammunition such as the Federal 230-grain Match into 3 inches at 50 yards. Few shooters will be able to shoot a 3-inch group at 25 yards. Professionals and interested students find the match standards thrilling and enjoy firing these handguns.

When you are ready to move up to this type of accuracy, it will be because the run-of-the-mill handgun has disappointed. You have reached the point

that you know you can shoot better. I have seen more than one shooter do incredible work with factory handguns — usually a SIG or 1911. Testing the handgun for accuracy is critical. Not only should you know just how accurate the handgun and shooter combination are, you should know where the gun shoots at all practical ranges.

Firing quickly offhand the author has utilized the standing barricade brace to enhance accuracy.

CUSTOM BARRELS

The Bar-Sto barrel, right, is more finely machined than the factory Glock barrel, left, and also offers superior case head support.

I am sometimes surprised by the accuracy potential of modern factory handguns. Quality pistols such as the SIG P220 and Springfield Range Officer are very accurate, well-made, and offer impressive reliability. But there is room for improvement and among the upgrades that can be had is the fitting of a match target barrel. A properly fitted barrel will offer considerable accuracy improvement. A barrel of match quality will be tightly fit-

ted, which means less slop and eccentric wear. That translates into greater accuracy and longevity in the long run. Eccentric wear is a result of slop in the mechanism, a condition that rears its ugly head in some handguns that have loose tolerances in order to enhance reliability. Yet, a properly fitted barrel of tighter specifications does not affect reliability, but will increase accuracy potential.

Again, it is important that the aftermarket bar-

The Wilson Combat Glock barrel is a viable option.

The Wilson Combat barrel not only allows the use of lead bullets in the Glock, but makes for greater accuracy.

muzzle has an 11-degree match crown, versus the rounded profile of standard factory barrels. The precision cut lands and grooves afford you much greater precision and accuracy potential.

Not Just 1911s

While most of my barrel work revolved around 1911 handguns, a change came with the introduction of the Glock pistol. Glock shooters realized that polygonal rifling of the factory barrels wasn't compatible with lead bullets. It didn't take long for aftermarket barrels to be offered that were suitable for use with lead bullets. These conventionally rifled barrels offer good accuracy. While there are several makes available for the Glock, if you are going to fit a barrel that offers good economy and compatibility with lead bullets then you might as well go ahead and fit a Bar-Sto match-grade or semi-fit barrel. Accuracy has been considered improved in the

rel is fitted properly. After installation you may notice an accuracy increase, but the barrel may not have been fitted to its greatest potential. The secret is painstaking care in fitting, working slowly to achieve the best results. When working with aftermarket barrels, unless the customer has a preference, I recommend Bar-Sto Precision (Barsto.com). Bar-Sto has been producing excellent quality barrels since 1967 and remains a family business. While fitting is important, Bar-Sto barrels sport features that make them superior to factory production parts. The

Note excellent machine work with the Wilson Combat barrel.

examples I have fitted and tested. Among the first was a Glock 22 .40-caliber. When the .357 SIG was introduced, I wished to test that cartridge without obtaining another firearm. (The .357 SIG is far from a favorite cartridge after much experience. I have yet to see a truly professional-grade shooter with one, and the cartridge is hard on the gun.)

I ordered a semi-fit Bar-Sto barrel for the G22, only in .357 SIG. At the time, the average Glock 22 was capable of perhaps 4-inch groups at 25 yards with the limited choices in ammunition. Truth be told, many would turn in 6-inch groups — even with Winchester 180-grain JHP loads, probably the most accurate load of the era. I added a set of Novak sights that helped immensely with practical accuracy. Intrinsic accuracy was still poor. However, with the Bar-Sto .357 SIG barrel installed, several loads — including the CorBon 115-grain JHP — averaged less than 3 inches, a great improvement over the factory barrel. It is true that the caliber was changed with the barrel swap, but the results were encouraging. I have also used a Glock Model 36 with a .45 ACP Bar-Sto barrel. That drop-in barrel was ordered primarily for economy and use with lead bullets. It was originally ordered in ported form and lowered recoil somewhat. Accuracy was excellent. At a later date, the owner elected to have the barrel shortened by cutting the ported section. Accuracy remained good to excellent.

There are two types of barrels offered by Bar-Sto: match target and semi-fit. Critical dimensions are oversized in the match barrel. Semi-fit barrels usually drop right in the SIG and Glock without fitting. With the 1911 version, some fitting is often needed as 1911s are as individualistic as shooters themselves. Not too many years ago, a semi-fit pair of barrels for a 1911 — one in 9mm, the other in .38 Super — each dropped right in and ran from the start in a Colt Government Model. The match target barrels for the European pistols tend to be oversized in dimension in the barrel hood and the lower lugs. The big difference between Bar-Sto barrels and factory ones is in the precision of machine work. I have read and heard some pretty ridiculous notions regarding chambers and tighter bores that simply are not true. The fit of the barrel to the slide and the precision of the rifling are what make a match-grade barrel. SIG and Glock pistols butt the barrel hood into the ejection port for lock up. The barrel hood of a match target tube is oversized. This barrel hood must be filed in order to achieve a good fit. The process isn't complicated, but you must take your time. If you simply remove metal until the barrel fits and the handgun functions you have fitted the barrel and there will be an accuracy improvement by virtue of the part's inherent precision.

The barrel hood is marked with a red or blue Sharp-

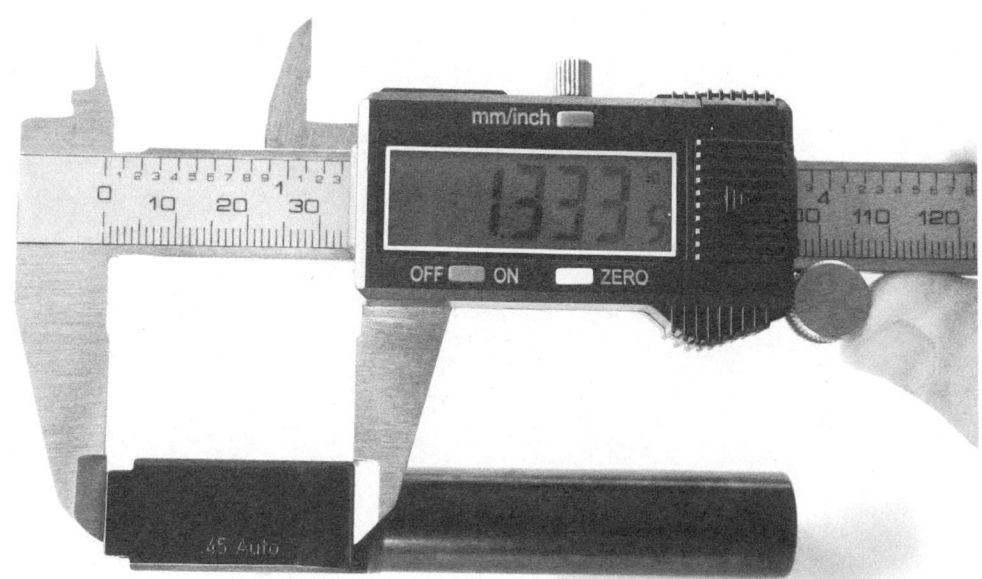

Measuring the original Glock barrel with a digital caliper.

(below) The Bar-Sto barrel is slightly oversized compared to the factory part. Once fitted, it will exhibit excellent accuracy.

ie for reference. Compare the match barrel to the factory one. You will have an idea of how much metal will need to be removed. It isn't much! Drop the new barrel into the slide and attempt to lock it into the slide. When the barrel is removed, the marking will be smudged where the oversized barrel hood is preventing the barrel from locking up. The barrel hood is carefully filed and fit into the ejection port, a little at a time, until the barrel fits snugly but may be removed with just slight finger pressure. The locking or camming surfaces on the lower barrel are marked and the barrel fitted into the frame in the same manner. Take your time, using single strokes of the file. Don't remove metal until the barrel locks up, or you'll remove too much, too soon. Take your time on this project and understand the difference. It is rather easy to file the barrel to fit, but more difficult to achieve a gunsmith fit. The goal is to gradually file the barrel until optimal fit is achieved. If the barrel easily drops into another handgun then perhaps the fitting wasn't ideal — the fit must be tight to the individual handgun. I have fitted the barrel until the slide has the slightest hesitation in locking. Then

A Kart 1911 barrel after fitting.

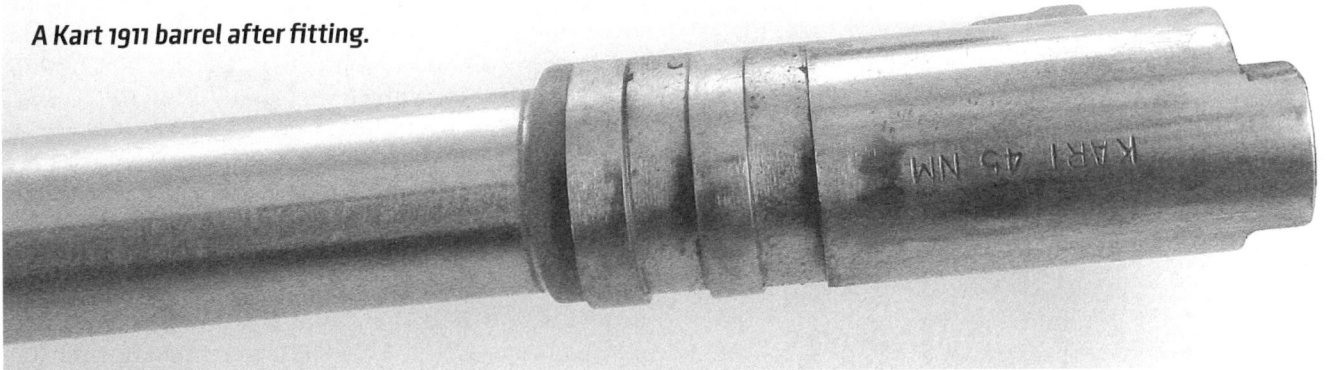

A match-grade 1911 9mm barrel from Kart.

I have heavily lubricated the handgun and fired a magazine to seat the fitting. It works for me, some will debate this procedure. It is similar to the break-in period of a tightly fitted match grade handgun.

For the semi-fit barrel, the first step is to drop the new barrel into the slide and examine the fit. Most often with SIG and Glock-type handguns the result is a good fit without any type of fitting. The improvement in accuracy potential is there for those who are capable of shooting a handgun accurately. As for the improvement in accuracy, it is incremental in some handguns and surprising in others. I am

beating a dead horse concerning accuracy problems with the first .40-caliber Glocks, but they were not as accurate as the more modern Glock 22s. The Bar-Sto barrels installed by shooters to allow safe use of handloads and lead bullets often cut 25-yard group sizes in half, when accompanied with Novak or Warren sights. As one shooter said, the Glock became a 50-yard gun instead of a 25-yard one. A good SIG 9mm may see improvement from a 2.5-inch group down to a 1.5 to 2.0-inch standard with quality ammunition. I stress the importance of using quality ammunition. While I use fairly ordinary ball am-

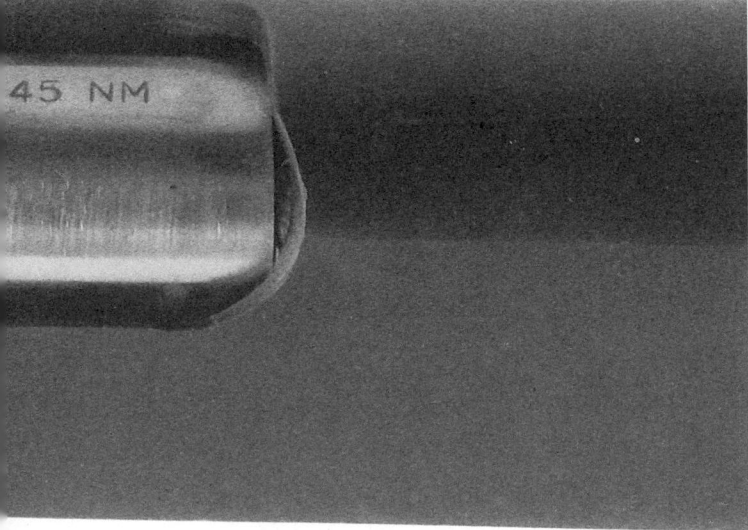

The Kart barrel gives excellent results after proper fitting.

munition to test handguns for function and general accuracy, Federal Match stands alone for testing Bar-Sto barrels. A standard handload of the Magnus 200-grain SWC over TiteGroup for 900 fps gives similar results in the .45 ACP, while Fiocchi 124-grain Extrema works extremely well in the 9mm. There are few truly accurate factory .38 Super loads but the SIG 125-grain FMJ load gives acceptable results. In the 1911, drop-in barrels often provide a good improvement. The difference will be a group size of an inch smaller on average. If you fit a Bar-Sto tube to a Rock Island 1911, the difference is more profound, on the order or 2 inches compared to the factory barrel of this handgun.

The 9mm/.38 Super

In factory handguns, the .38 ACP Super has a well-deserved reputation for accuracy that is inferior to a similar 1911 in .45 ACP. On average, though, the new 9mm variants seem as accurate as the average .45 ACP. The situation is different when the Bar-Sto Match Target barrel is fitted. A handgun so customized will be as accurate as the .45 ACP with Bar-Sto barrel. The .38 Super has enjoyed a small but loyal fan base for many years and the Bar-Sto replacement makes the .38 Super accurate. Later, Bar-Sto began properly chambering the barrel to allow the cartridge case to correctly headspace on the case mouth

The barrel bushing must be properly fitted to the Kart barrel.

rather than the cartridge case rim as the factory Colt did. The Colt was a throwback to the 1900 .38 ACP and its semi-rim. The result was greatly improved accuracy. The Colt .38 Super went from a 4- to 6-inch group gun at 25 yards to a 2-inch tack driver with the fitting of this barrel. That is significant.

Aftermarket Barrel Fitting Process

Recently, I had a good experience with the new Ruger SR1911 9mm. The Ruger is quite accurate for a 9mm, features a lightweight frame, and overall this Commander-style 1911 has much to recommend. Ruger even improved the 1911 by changing the plunger tube to a permanently affixed rather than staked-on style. After some thought, the inspiration came to convert the pistol to a .38 ACP Super. In this case, the work was actually done by Bar-Sto, but the step-by-step procedure is worth discussion. I have fitted several Match Target 1911 barrels with excellent results, and also filed a few of the drop-in ones that were not quite … drop-in.

Barrel fitting is pretty simple as long as the same program is followed with each barrel fitting. The barrel hood should fit into the slot in the breech face, but the slide should not make contact. You just need a few thousandths of an inch clearance on each side. The width of this slot is .442 inches. The average match barrel hood is .451 inch, so some fitting is needed. File the barrel hood until the fit is tight and the barrel drops into the slide and contacts the breech face. That is width. Barrel hood length

is fitted next. The barrel will not usually travel far enough to the rear for the locking lugs to lock into the slide. The hood length of the barrel may be 1.33 inches, as an example, and the recess in the 1911 slide may be 1.314 inches — this is close work and must be exact. That means .016 inches of material is what you have to work with. These measurements may differ on various 1911s and calibers but let this example be a guide. The barrel hood will lock properly and just touch the breech frame without binding. It must fit evenly. The final touch involves lapping compound and tapping the barrel in and out for the final fit. But you are not done yet!

The lower locking lugs must also be fitted in the match barrel. When the pistol is in battery, the barrel is wedged between the slide stop at the bottom and the locking lugs of the slide with no movement. There is a definite stop as the barrel locks. While the inexpensive 1911s just don't have it, Colt, Kimber, Springfield, and Ruger do — at least to a certain extent. A match-grade barrel feels better and performs

Note excellent fit of the Wilson Combat bull barrel for the Beretta 92.

BARREL FITTING IS PRETTY SIMPLE AS LONG AS THE SAME PROGRAM IS FOLLOWED WITH EACH BARREL FITTING. THE BARREL HOOD SHOULD FIT INTO THE SLOT IN THE BREECH FACE, BUT THE SLIDE SHOULD NOT MAKE CONTACT.

better. Slide stop pins are available in oversize configuration but, for the most part, the factory slide stop works fine. Both lower lugs must be fitted in order to put pressure on the slide stop evenly as they bear on it while in battery. If you mark the slide stop pin with heavy markings you will be able to see just how the lower lugs bear on the slide stop as the gun goes into battery. Often, one lug will show more contact than the other. You must file the lug with greater wear until both bear evenly on the slide stop pin. Cut the locking lugs until the slide locks up tight, and for a super-accurate match target fit, the slide will require the slightest nudge to fully close when slowly returned to battery. I like this type of fit for superb accuracy, but unless you are very familiar with the process you may not achieve both good accuracy and excellent reliability.

In addition to parts for the 1911, Wilson Combat offers match-grade barrels for the Beretta 92. The locking wedge is rigid, making a great upgrade option for America's current service pistol. Bill Wilson started his business making first-class parts and then built his famous competition-level handguns. The Wilson Combat Beretta is a first-class 9mm no equals. Wilson Combat also offers Glock barrels and 1911 handgun parts.

The Kart match barrel is an excellent aftermarket part that will improve handgun accuracy.

CLEANING THE HANDGUN

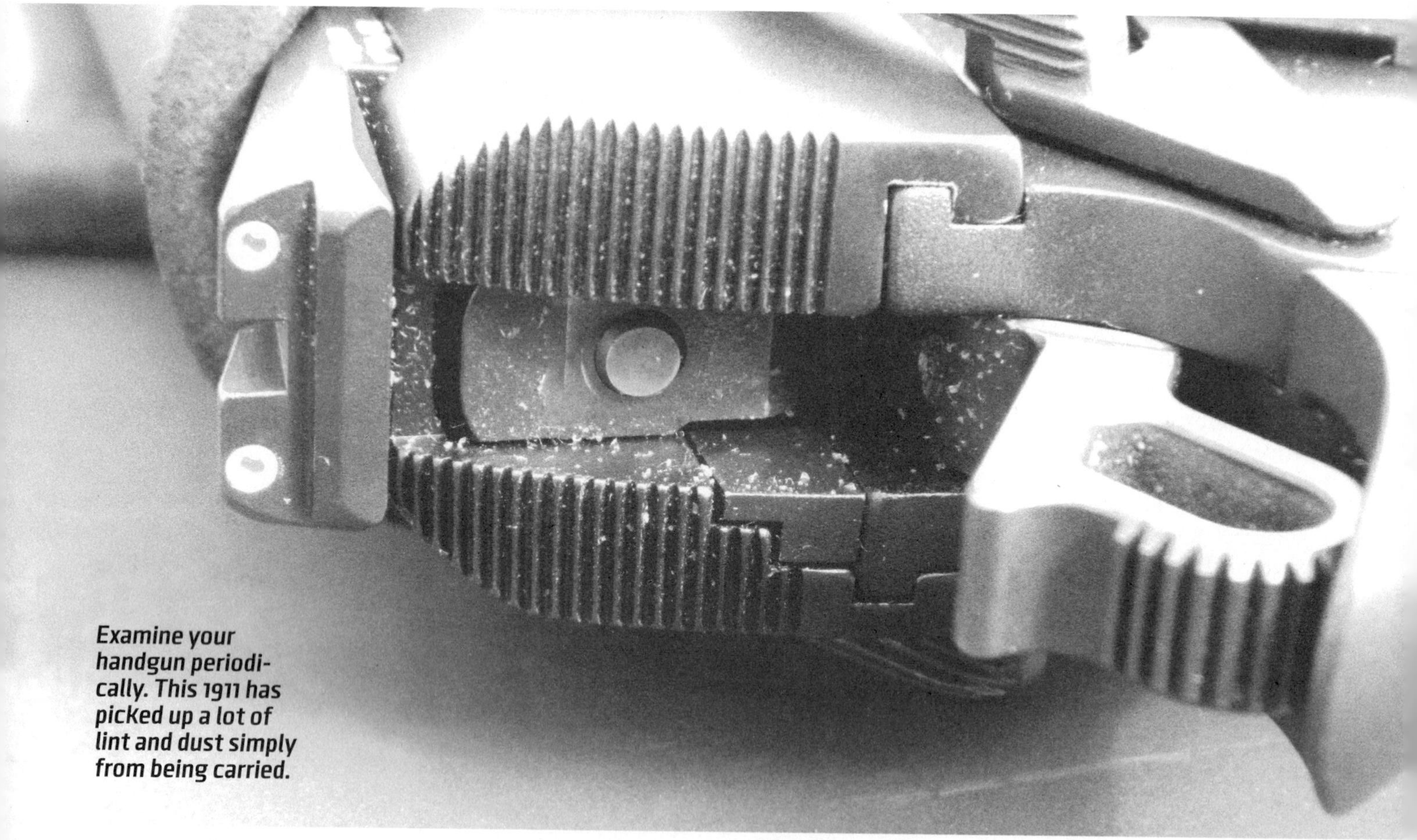

Examine your handgun periodically. This 1911 has picked up a lot of lint and dust simply from being carried.

The more I test and use handguns, the more respect I have for the operating reliability of these machines. Modern firearms are as reliable as any other well-designed machine. The tolerances held by Kimber, Colt, Springfield, Ruger, Smith and Wesson, SIG and CZ are excellent. When you use a firearm — either on the range or in some dark alley for self-defense — you should have every confidence that it will fire time after time without any type of problem. Thankfully, today's machining tolerances ensure that handguns are reliable. After all, many are indeed based on service pistols that were designed to function in horrific situations. The Colt 1911 is famous for operating when soaked in mud or snow. The SIG P226 has come out on top of the field in a rigorous test in which 228,000 cartridges were fired in a grueling test program.

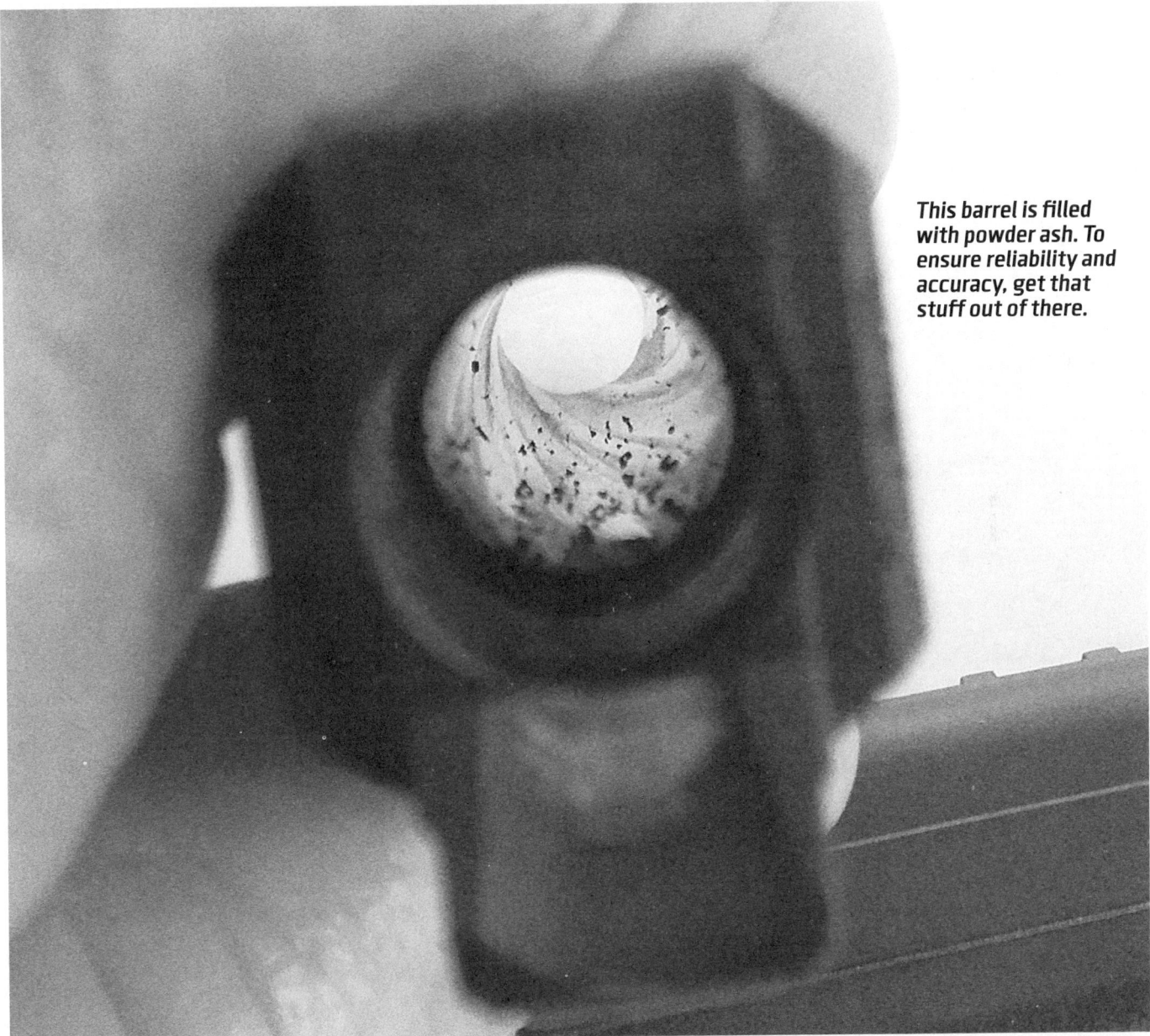

Clearing the Crud

Just the same, these handguns need maintenance — regular cleaning and lubrication. As for service handguns such as the Colt 1911, Springfield Operator, SIG P220 and the CZ 75, they will run dirty but they will not run dry. If a handgun isn't cleaned properly, eccentric wear will impede function. Normal wear is simply even wear. The finish is worn and the pistol becomes worn as it is used. The springs eventually wear and need to be replaced. The bore becomes worn. Eccentric wear is different. Either the finish or the handgun's parts can be gouged by foreign material. Dirt, grit and unburned powder make for eccentric wear. The handgun must be cleaned to maintain optimal performance. If the tolerances are such that good accuracy is guaranteed, the pistol simply will not be as accurate if the operating mechanism is filled with powder ash from firing. Lead buildup is even worse.

How often should you clean your handgun? The answer really depends upon the firearm. For instance, .22-caliber rimfires should be cleaned most often. The powder used in this caliber makes it the dirtiest cartridge in common use. Few .22 handguns will go more than three hundred rounds without a malfunction if they are not cleaned. Accuracy will be degraded. A modern 9mm self-loader firing good, quality factory jacketed bullet loads may go several thousand rounds before function becomes sluggish due to the buildup of unburned powder, but don't test that out by abusing your firearm. Even handguns that will perform well without cleaning throughout a high round count still demand lubrication.

The handgun, like your vehicle, needs periodic

Note powder build-up in this HK barrel. It's time for a cleaning.

going since World War II without changing the springs, but don't count on these for optimal performance. True, you purchased a high-end pistol so that you would not have to worry about reliability, but maintenance is part of every firearm.

Firearms that are seldom used are seldom cleaned. I have handguns that are used for testing a specific caliber that I keep on hand for reference and for training students. As an example, the .40 Smith and Wesson isn't my favorite cartridge, but there are plenty of new developments in the caliber, so I keep one handgun so

After cleaning, the barrel is slick and clean. Now comes peace of mind that it will be as accurate and reliable as possible.

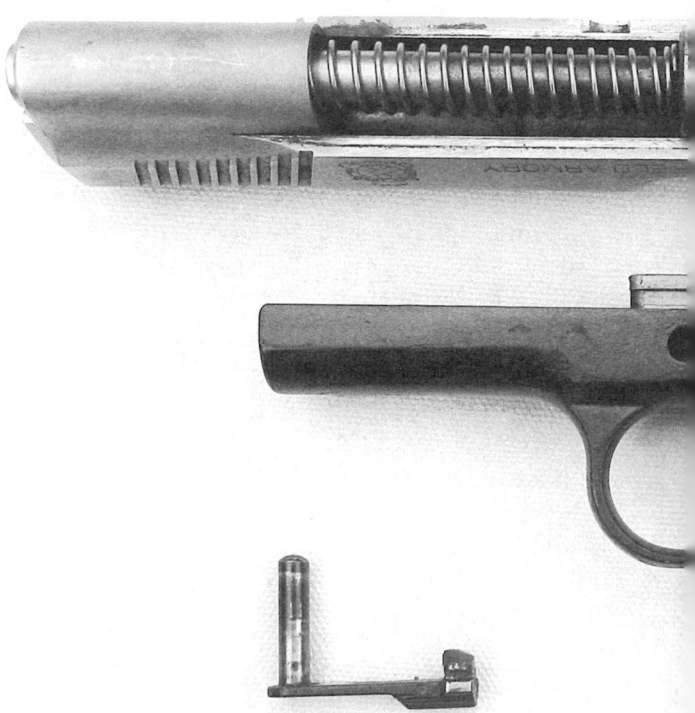

This Springfield has been properly maintained and has fired well over 20,000 cartridges without fail.

maintenance including changing the springs at regular intervals. Revolver springs seem never to go out of whack as they are not compressed when in storage. Self-loading pistols should have their recoil spring changed every 3,000-5,000 rounds in the case of the 1911 .45 and, at a similar timeframe with the Glock, SIG, Beretta and other quality autoloaders. We all know of handguns that have been

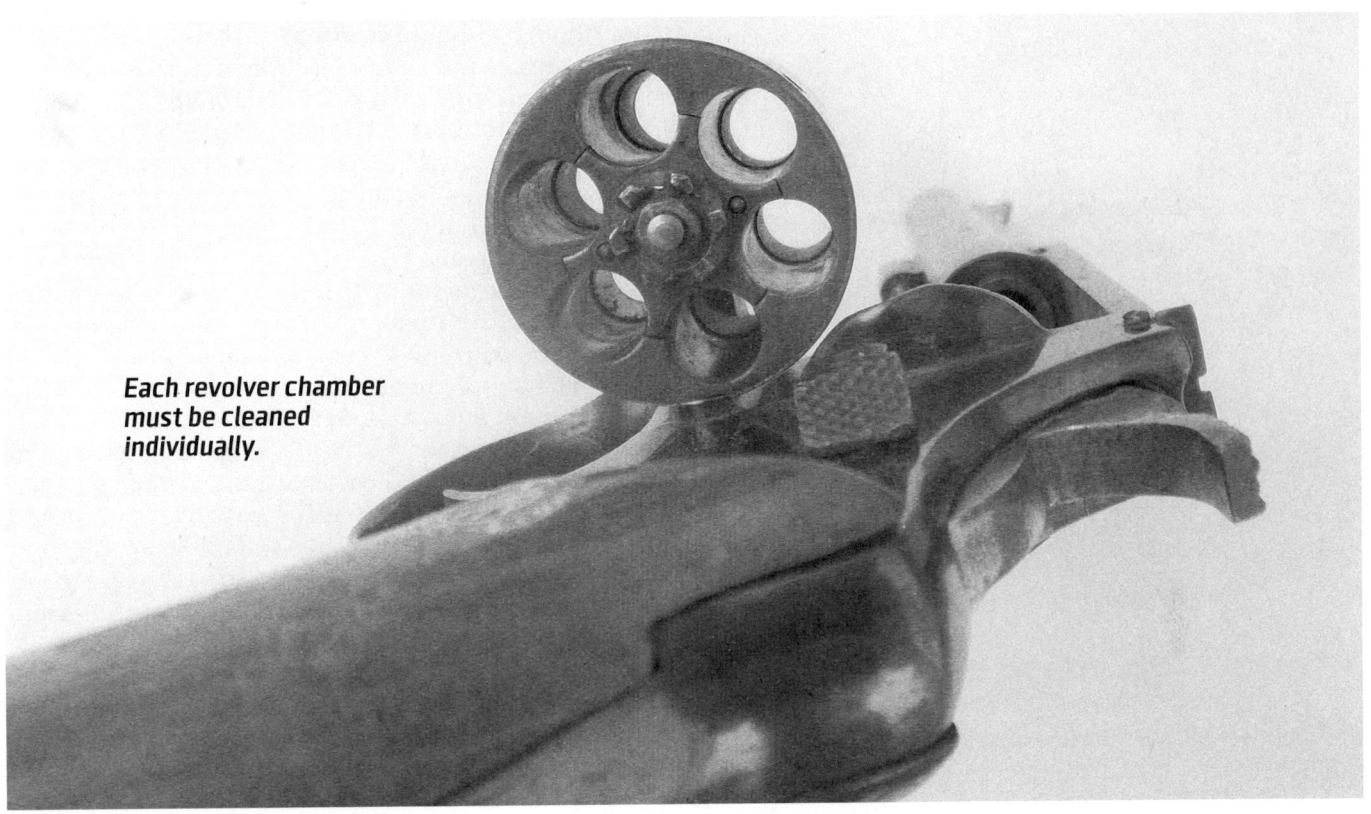

Each revolver chamber must be cleaned individually.

chambered. I don't keep up with rounds fired, it isn't used for critical missions, and I clean it once a year. The handguns that I use on a regular basis include my Ruger .22 MKIII and the Colt 1911. The Ruger .22s are recreational firearms and are cleaned as needed. When the chamber begins to look cruddy and the bolt seems greasy with lubricant and powder ash I clean the MKIII. After the pistol is clean, lubricant is judiciously applied for function. When powder ash is present there is a muddy soup. I really like a clean gun and keep my carry guns sparkling and well-lubricated. When you go to the range, plan on lubricating your handgun more frequently if you fire hundreds of rounds of ammunition. A carry gun is best served with a thin application of lube. Fieldstrip, wipe down and lubricate the carry gun after every practice session. Give it a thorough field strip and inspection every five-hundred rounds or so. When you are faced with a critical incident, there are many factors beyond your control. One thing you can control is that your handgun will be clean, ready, and well-lubricated so it's in top firing condition.

Field Stripping

Owner's manuals usually have good information on field stripping the handgun. Field stripping simply means removing the slide from the frame of the self-loading handgun and then separating the barrel, spring, and recoil guide from the slide. Revolvers usually do not need to be field stripped at all, al-

One chamber shows greater powder accumulation after firing.

(below) Get the bore clean or there goes your accuracy!

though you will need to learn to remove the cylinder from a single-action revolver for proper cleaning. A professional will learn detail stripping in order to properly maintain the trigger action, but a hobbyist has no need to do so. Most agencies have an armorer to maintain issued firearms. If you seek to modify an agency issued handgun, let's hope you and the Chief are on a first name basis. It is quite easy to damage the ejector, extractor or firing pin by attempting disassembly of the firearm without knowledge of the correct procedure. It is easy to field strip a Series 70 1911. The firing pin simply slips out after removing the firing pin stop. A modern Series 80 with a firing pin block is another matter. Some pistols have blind holes and other variances that really make a difference. There is only one correct way to do things and that means study. Something as simple as allowing a spring to launch across a room may not be serious (if found) but small parts can take flight and disappear forever.

As a rule of thumb, the better quality firearms are simpler. Smith and Wesson revolvers follow a template that hasn't been changed in many years, save for an upgrade to a transfer bar ignition. Less expensive clones of the Smith and Wesson have small parts that are easily lost, such as springs in blind

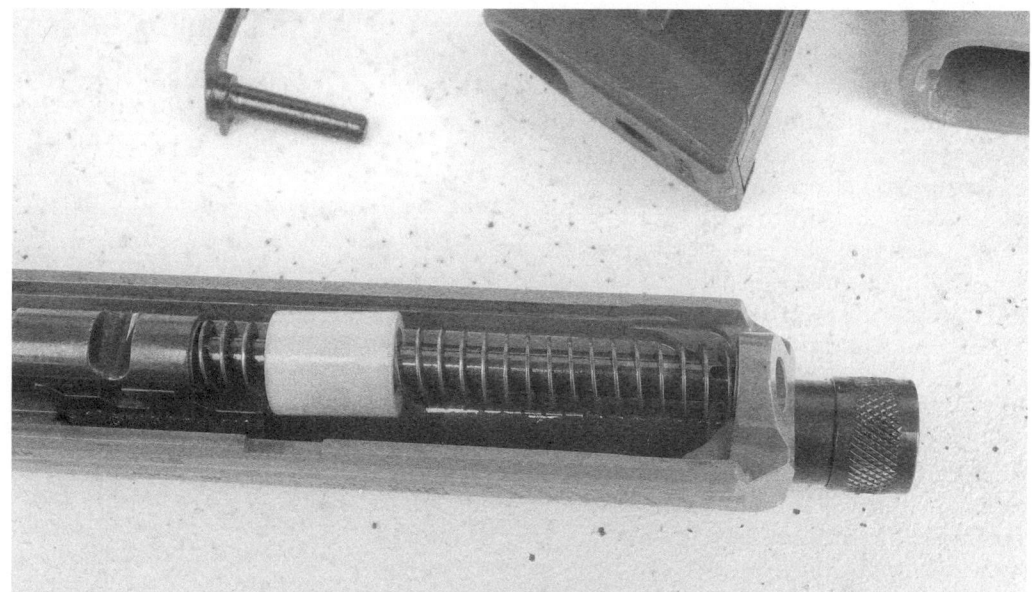

Check the recoil spring from time to time and keep the handgun well-lubricated.

(below) Perform maintenance with only the proper tools, so that you do not mar the pistol when field stripping.

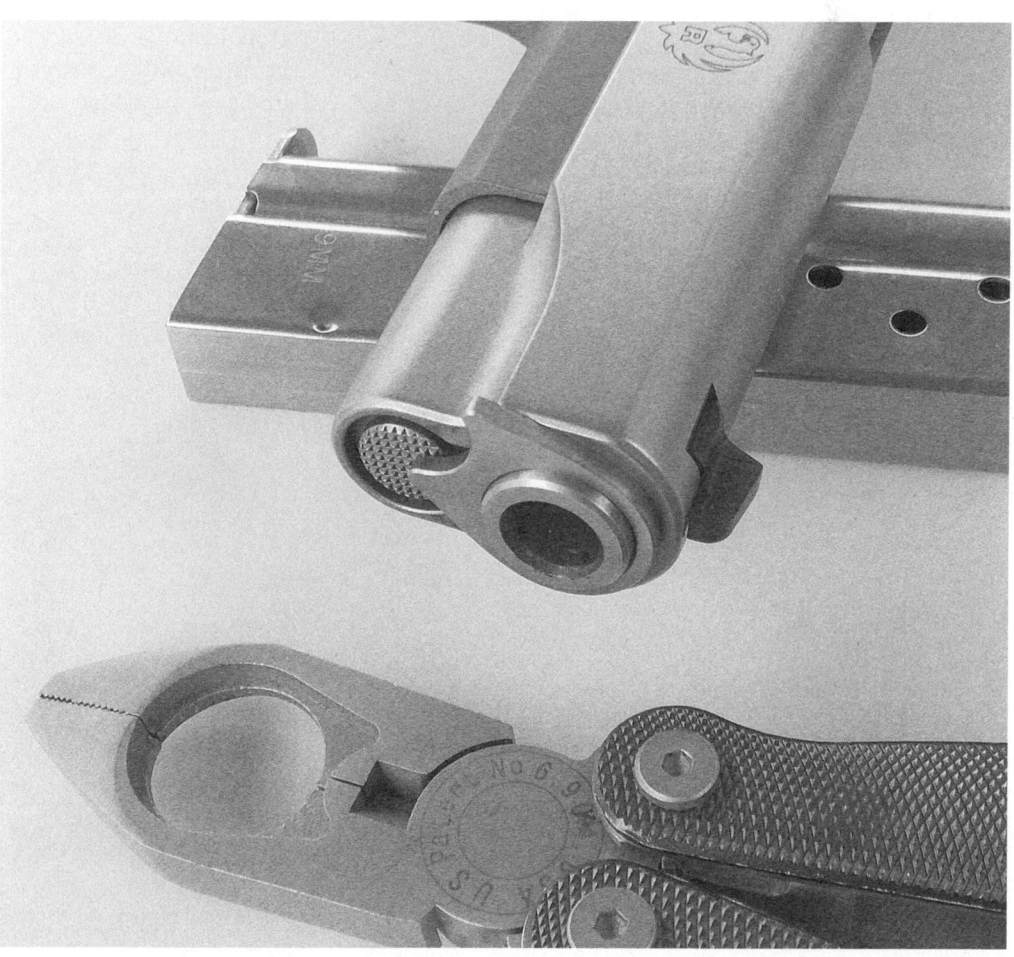

holes on the side plate that complicate disassembly. On the other hand, Ruger has made the revolver simpler and more durable and has taken the SR1911 automatic and permanently attached the plunger tube, resulting in one less item of concern in this venerable design. Take each handgun as a problem unto itself and be completely familiar with the design and takedown. Depending upon make and model, disassembly spans the gamut from simple to difficult. Possibly the simplest to take down and clean are the Beretta 92, SIG P226, and Walther P1-type selfloaders. Simply press a takedown lever and move the slide forward to perform routine maintenance. The CZ 75 is a little more complicated and the 1911 even more so, although not difficult. The smaller the handgun, the more difficult in some cases, as downsizing parts results in design compromise. Difficulty in field stripping can be a deciding factor in choosing your handgun.

Work Area

Get in the habit of setting aside a designated work area. The cleaning materials you use can be dangerous, although the primary concern is the strong smell. This odor is more pronounced in a small work area. A well-ventilated area is important. You are dealing with chemicals that have certain properties intended to cut through lead and powder deposits. A heavy plastic covering over a table is good. A waste basket will serve to handle your cleaning patches when you are done with the chore. Cleaning is necessary and should be done safely.

Before you clean any handgun be double certain it is unloaded. Make sure ammunition isn't in the same room. Many of the chemicals used in cleaning can kill the ammunition's priming compounds so keep such material well separated from ammo. Double check the handgun's chamber after unloading. Be certain the magazines are unloaded, they will need attention as well. Always wear eye protection. There will be droplets of solvent thrown in the air as you vigorously clean the barrel. Do not clean over an expensive tablecloth! Field strip the pistol into its basic components. If cleaning a revolver, simply swing the cylinder open. Carefully remove the stocks or grip panels before cleaning if you are going a bit deeper than field stripping.

The 1911 isn't terribly complicated to field strip, but demands attention to detail for proper maintenance.

The Cleaning Process

The bore of the handgun is where most of the cleaning is needed. Powder and lead deposits are found in the grooves of the barrel. It takes a bit of effort to clean the bore even if you have used only full metal jacketed bullets and do not use lead. There is nothing wrong with lead bullets, they are both accurate and economical, but they do leave more deposits in the barrel. Take the bore brush and screw it into the cleaning rod. Run the brush into the solvent bottle to make it sopping wet. Push the brush through the barrel several times, loosening the deposits in the bore. After doing this several times a mixture of solvent and powder residue will run from the barrel. Switch to cotton patches next, running them through the barrel. Some of the first patches will be black with powder ash. Keep going until the patches come out clean. If the deposits are very heavy you can move back to the bore brush. Soak the cotton patch in solvent and run it through again as well. The final patch should be solvent-free, with only a light coating of gun oil. This helps preserve the bore from rust.

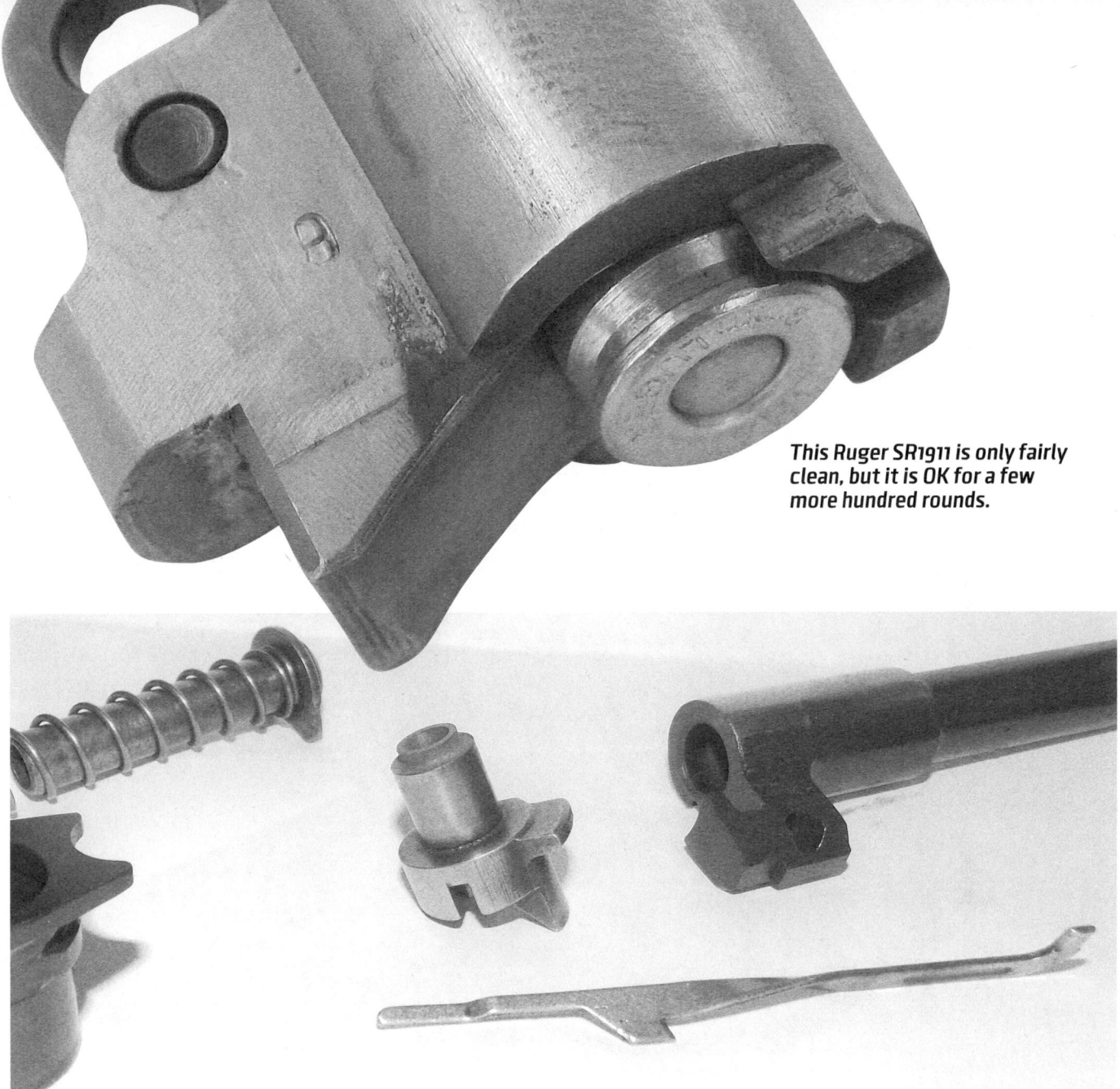

This Ruger SR1911 is only fairly clean, but it is OK for a few more hundred rounds.

This is the floating chamber of a Colt .22-caliber conversion unit. This chamber must be clean and well-lubricated for good function.

The procedure is modified with the revolver. While the barrel is cleaned in the same way as an autoloader, each individual chamber of the revolver cylinder needs cleaning. The area at the chamber step often collects powder and lead residue and should get particular attention.

Next move to the receiver of the self-loader. Wipe the slide rails and long bearing surfaces. The feed ramp and the outside of the barrel should be clean. Check the cocking block and the locking lugs. Look for collected grit, powder ash and lead. The firing pin channel collects powder ash and even brass particles so clean it occasionally. On pistols, the breech face gets dirty and must be addressed. The recoil plate of the revolver gets cruddy, which can impede function. This area should be cleaned often. You do not have to bathe the handgun in solvent, but be certain that you use an adequate amount in cleaning.

Once you have cleaned the handgun it should be lubricated.

The self-loading pistol should be lubricated on the long bearing surfaces where metal contacts metal. Some handguns — the 1911 in particular — need to be well-lubricated; the Glock needs but a single drop. Heavy lubrication is needed when shooting a match or during long practice sessions. Lighter lubrication is needed for carry. After cleaning and lubrication, reassemble the handgun and wipe the slide and frame off with a clean rag. And that's it. Get this process down pat and repeat as necessary. If you do, you'll enjoy long, reliable service from your handgun.

STOCKS AND GRIPS

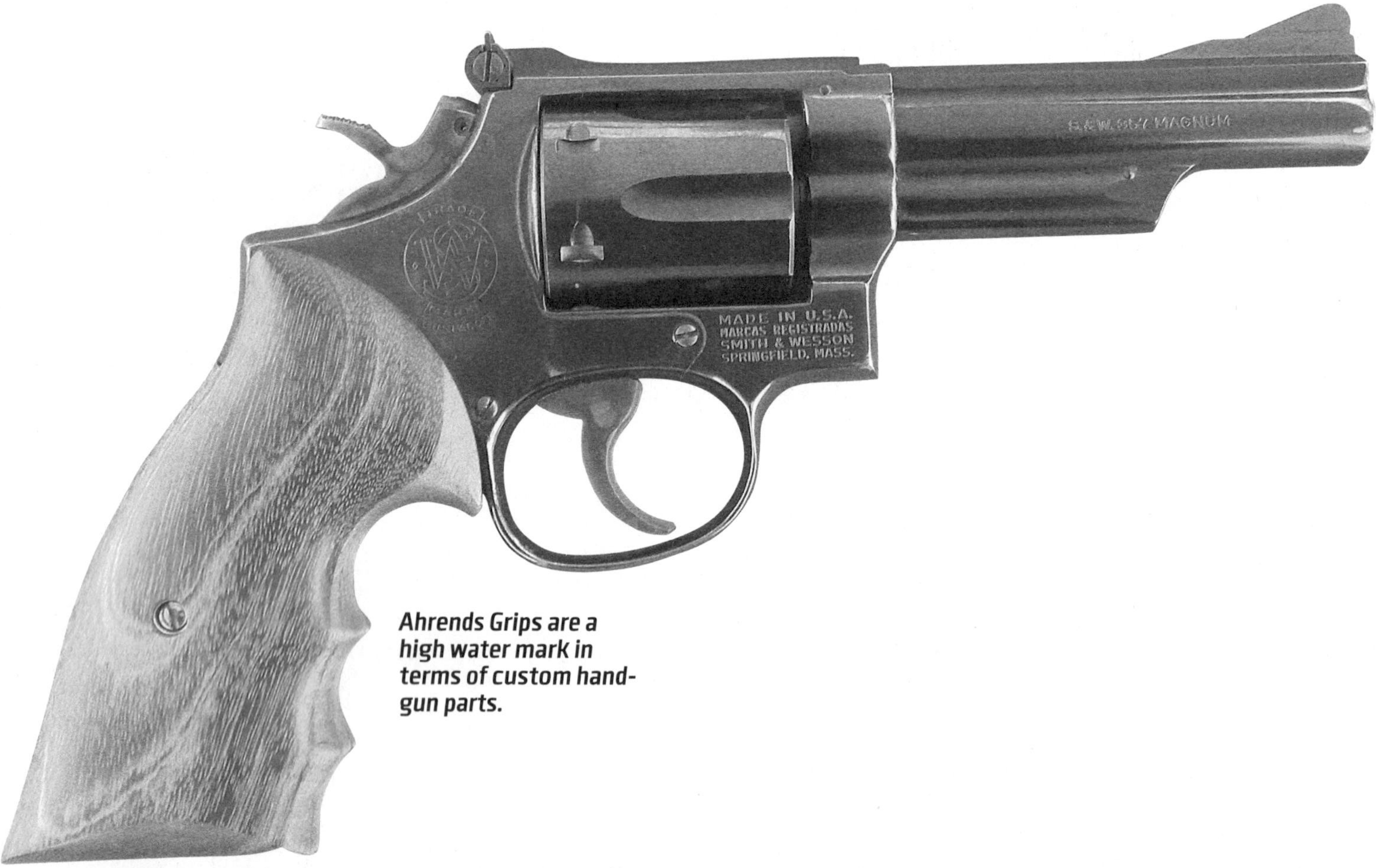

Ahrends Grips are a high water mark in terms of custom handgun parts.

The grip, or stock of the handgun, is more important than many shooters realize. Some handguns do not have removable grips. Those include the Glock, Smith and Wesson M&P (Military and Police), and Springfield XD. These handgun grips can be modified, however, and to a large extent the basic geometry of a self-loading handgun grip isn't subject to change. Revolver grips offer much more opportunity for change. All handgun parts are important, but the grip frame is the foundation. The frame sits in the hand and allows you to manipulate the trigger and controls and to properly align your sights. The grip frame must allow comfortable use of the handgun and not overly stretch the average hand size. A frame that does not fit your hand correctly can be managed well enough from the bench. But from offhand fire, especially in dynamic movement, an oversized frame will be a serious liability.

(top) This Glock grip has been considerably improved with custom reshaping.

(above) It isn't terribly complex but, done correctly, grip reshaping alters the fit and feel of the Glock considerably.

There are several reasons for modifying or changing handgun grip panels. The first is for a proper fit. The second is for pure vanity — to increase the eye appeal of the handgun. There is considerable latitude between those extremes when it comes to choosing grips and adapting the grip frame. In this section, I examine the grips available and divide them

by handgun type. When you are dealing with the Glock or SIG, considerable effort is needed to accomplish a better fit. Just the same, there is always some procedure to follow.

Grips for Polymer-Frame Automatic Pistols

If the Glock, Heckler and Koch or Springfield XD does not fit your hand, you are practically helpless without the aid of a good gunsmith. But there are some do-it-yourself (DIY) avenues to be pursued. The primary attraction of such modifications is to reduce the grip frame circumference and to produce a distinct 'beavertail' that aids in more comfortable shooting. The Glock 21, for example, is a reliable and powerful handgun but one that stretches the average hand size for comfort. This may result in a lack of control in rapid fire or even short cycles as a result of a weak grip. Do not get the grinder out! Study first. Automatic pistol geometry must be understood. The frame is a foundation. The handgun must recoil against a solid foundation in order to function correctly. This is the one measure of modification that should be left to a professional.

Robar Industries offers a credible modification for polymer autoloaders that offers both comfort and controllability. I fired several on the pistol range and the fit and feel is excellent. The original Model 21 grip truly challenges my average size hand. However, the Robar grip frame is a different proposition. Comfort and controllability are part of the package. The change is subtle, but good. There are other companies doing such modifications but at present Robar seems to be ahead of the game by a considerable margin.

These factory Colt grips are much too thick and offer no adhesion during firing.

Grips for 1911 Pistols

Those who use the 1911 handgun usually change the grip for vanity. They wish to add a personal touch or simply mount a pretty set of grips. That is fine as far as it goes. In fact, you can even mount a smooth-sided set of 1911 grips and get by in most instances. But getting by and being all you can be aren't the same thing. Occasionally, you'll find a set of grips (typically pearlite) that are too large for good control.

Cherokee Hills grips are first class all of the way, with excellent fit and finish and a great personal touch. They also offer a superior gripping surface.

Ahrend's classic skip-checkered grips are ideal for 1911 handguns.

Sometimes you need a rougher grip for best control in extreme drills such as competition or in maximum effort accuracy exercises. I have used a custom set of grips from Cherokee Hills with excellent results. These are dark wood with a deeply engraved emblem. The Celtic knot and crossed swords design keeps the hand stable and makes for excellent control. The grips are also attractive and make a personal statement. In fact, a classic set of double diamond skip-checkered grips rides on my Commander .45. These grips are from Ahrends grips. I have used more Ahrends grips than any other over the years and they provide excellent function and superb quality. A new maker is Crystal Powell, of Texas. She has taken a classic talent for wood engraving and turned to the 1911 pistol. Her grips have a personal motif and offer good stabilization while making the handgun a personal extension of the hand. One set was commissioned for my son when he returned from a tour of duty in the Middle East. Captain Campbell was well-pleased with the grips illustrated.

In factory grip panels, Hogue grips offers many options. The Hogue rubber grip is ideal for most handguns, available for the CZ 75, Hi Power, and others and makes for a good base for accurate fire and good hand fit. My personal CZ 75 has been fitted with European-quality Krinksy grips. These grips are expertly engraved and offer a well-designed thumbswell for positive aiming. They are better suited for target use than fast-paced combat firing and offer excellent utility. If I had to pick a single pair of handgun grips that are both versatile and effective, it would be the Tactical Grips offered by Kim Ahrends. These grips are half checkered and half smooth. The theory is that the smooth component offers in-

Crystal Powell's 1911 grips offer plenty of adhesion with a personal touch.

The author's .38 Super wears Crystal Powell's grips.

Challis grips are first-class, one-of-a-kind additions to the 1911.

stant adjustment while the checkered section affords you good purchase. In practice, the grips work exactly as designed.

There are those who prefer the fit and feel of rubber grips. There are several different compositions of rubber in use, from hard to soft to pebble grain and tacky. The classic handgun grip remains the Pachmayr. Pachmayr grips feature a hand-filling grip that not only allows good purchase in every climatic condition but also absorbs recoil. The Pachmayr is especially well-suited to big bore handguns such as the Ruger Super Blackhawk. The Pachmayr has a great advantage for enthusiastic 1911 handloaders. In certain variations there is a steel insert. This insert may have originally been added to give rigidity, but it also offers excellent safety in the case of a ruptured cartridge. Perhaps the finest set of grips I own are a set of stag grips from MDGrips.com.

Hogue grips are not expensive, but offer an excellent option for comfortable shooting.

Krinsky grips are first-class, European-styled for the CZ 75.

This Krinksy pattern is a good choice for the CZ 75.

The stag grip, I admit, is something of a vanity, but that isn't the full story. It's roughened and the natural bark allows excellent purchase. The grip is sturdier in the hand than a smooth or lightly checkered grip. Only the checkered tactical grips are superior.

Revolver Grips

For single-action revolvers, the durable urethane grips from Gripmaker are ideal. They are durable — I have confirmed that — and they also age well, turning a nice antiqued yellow with age. These grips are delivered oversized in order to ensure perfect fit for the common 1873 single-action grip frame. There is

An inexpensive ATI .22 wears attractive target-style grips.

a wider variation among grips for these revolvers that most realize, as they have been manufactured by Colt, Great Western, Pietta, Uberti, JP Sauer, and Ruger, among others. As such, it is best that they are delivered oversized in order to allow the owner to cut and file them for a perfect fit. The one piece grip set comes with a spacer between the grip halves. They are excellent for most shooting needs, attractive, and the ribbing in the molded grip allows a better handle and control than standard smooth single-action grips.

These stag grips from MDgrips.com are first-class additions to the classic 1911.

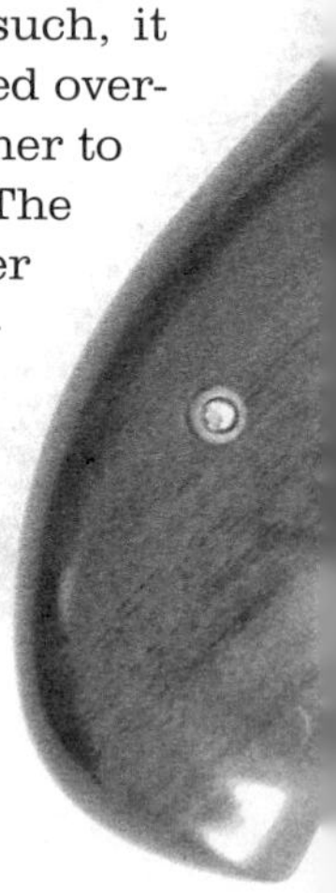

Culina makes excellent high-quality grips for Smith and Wesson revolvers as well as the Colt Python.

Note Culina hand-filling grips, left, and the factory Charter Bulldog, right. The oversize Culinas help with .44 Special recoil.

My personal Model 21 .44 Special is fitted with the Culina grips. These grips were fitted because the factory ones were the worst I have seen on any factory revolver! They were quite small and, while the Model 21 is a retro-type revolver, far from period authentic. The Culina grips are perfectly fitted to my hand and offer good control by geometry rather than checkering. Culina also offers fine-checkered grips, but the finger groove smooth grips I have used are ideal for carry and packing handguns.

Why does hand fit matter? On a firing range, with no stress and a target that doesn't shoot back, a large grip is manageable. Or a grip that is too small can be managed as well. When shooting in dynamic competition or attempting to connect at long range, the situation is different. The handgun has to fit your hand correctly. The geometry of the grip is such that the handgun is centered in the hand and the eyes lead naturally to the sights, given the proper grip design. Even when the handgun is taken firmly in a two-hand grip, at some point the handgun will come out of line. The handgun grip that is ideal is one

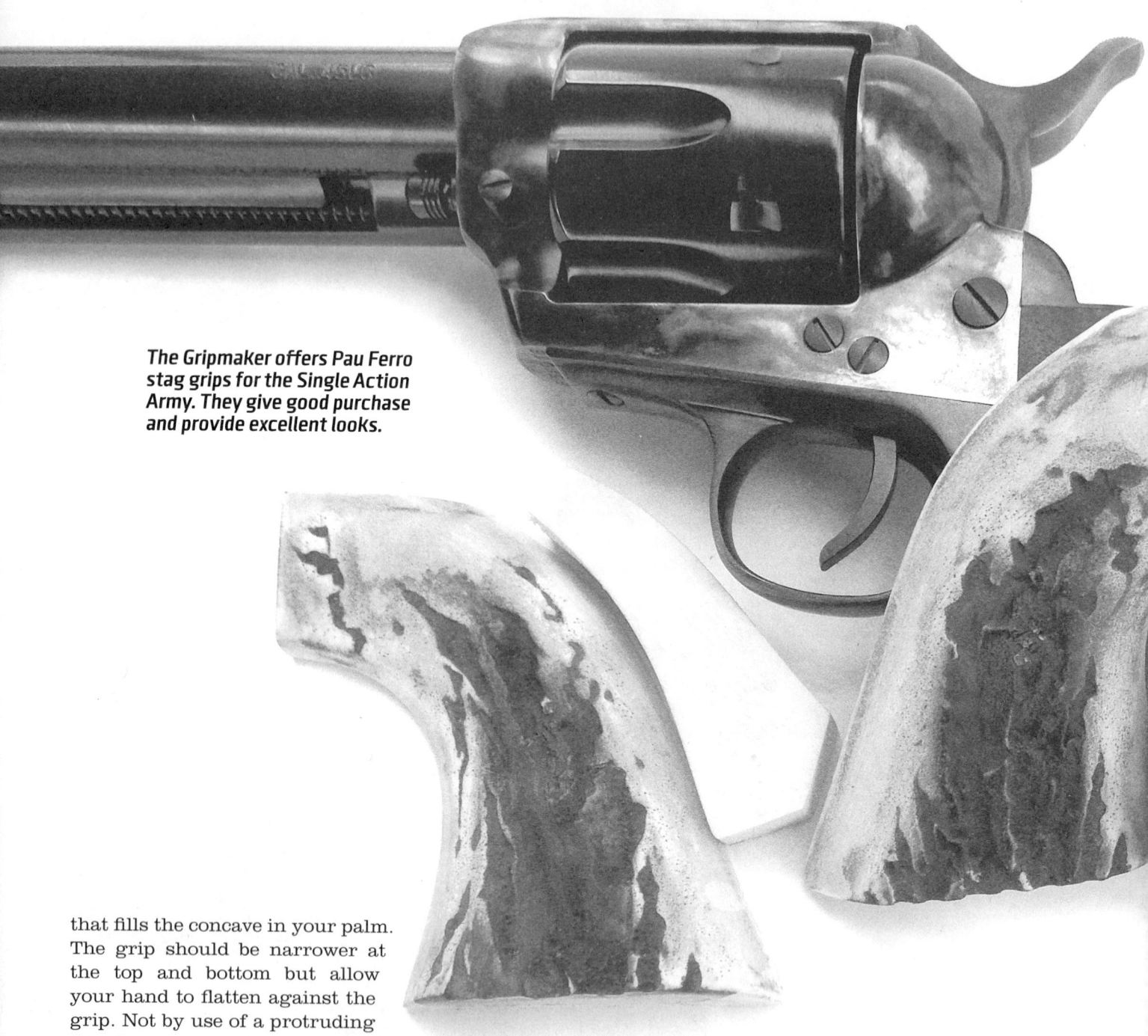

The Gripmaker offers Pau Ferro stag grips for the Single Action Army. They give good purchase and provide excellent looks.

that fills the concave in your palm. The grip should be narrower at the top and bottom but allow your hand to flatten against the grip. Not by use of a protruding thumb swell, but by the slightest natural swell in the flat grip of a self-loader or revolver. Revolver grips are often badly shaped from the factory, with a pronounced swell in the bottom of the grip, exactly the wrong place. When a grip is too large, you will shift the gun away from yourself to find a way for your finger to reach the trigger. When you do this with a hard-kicking revolver, the chances are you will get hit hard on the firing thumb and this is never pleasant. You must control recoil. A proper firing grip is needed to do so. When the grip is stretched, your trigger finger doesn't properly move independently of the hand. A poorly shaped grip is bad news all the way around.

Some handgun grips work because the frame is so functional. The Ruger MKIII .22-caliber autoloader uses thin slabs in most models. Due to the grip angle of the pistol they work just fine. Most 1911 grips, even the smooth ones, work well. But there is plenty of room for improvement! The bottom line is that when the handgun is held in a normal firing grip you must be able to reach the trigger without straining or placing the finger against the frame, and with the proper leverage against the trigger face. If you are not properly controlling the trigger, the pistol will be pressed to the right or left, the shot will be off, and accuracy will suffer.

When choosing a handgun, consider the grip before you purchase. Sure, a shorter grip frame makes for easier concealment, but then a lot depends upon a proper holster. The gun may be easier to conceal, but it will be more difficult to control — and to fire accurately. If you cannot get a full firing grip on the handgun grip, then accuracy potential will be adversely affected. If you have to cock the gun to one side or the other to operate the magazine release or the slide lock, then the handgun is too large for your hand. It may be better to choose a low-capacity handgun that you can shoot well than a high-capacity one that doesn't fit your hand.

REVOLVER GRIPS ARE OFTEN BADLY SHAPED FROM THE FACTORY, WITH A PRONOUNCED SWELL IN THE BOTTOM OF THE GRIP, EXACTLY THE WRONG PLACE. WHEN A GRIP IS TOO LARGE, YOU WILL SHIFT THE GUN AWAY FROM YOURSELF TO FIND A WAY FOR YOUR FINGER TO REACH THE TRIGGER. WHEN YOU DO THIS WITH A HARD-KICKING REVOLVER, THE CHANCES ARE YOU WILL GET HIT HARD ON THE FIRING THUMB AND THIS IS NEVER PLEASANT. YOU MUST CONTROL RECOIL.

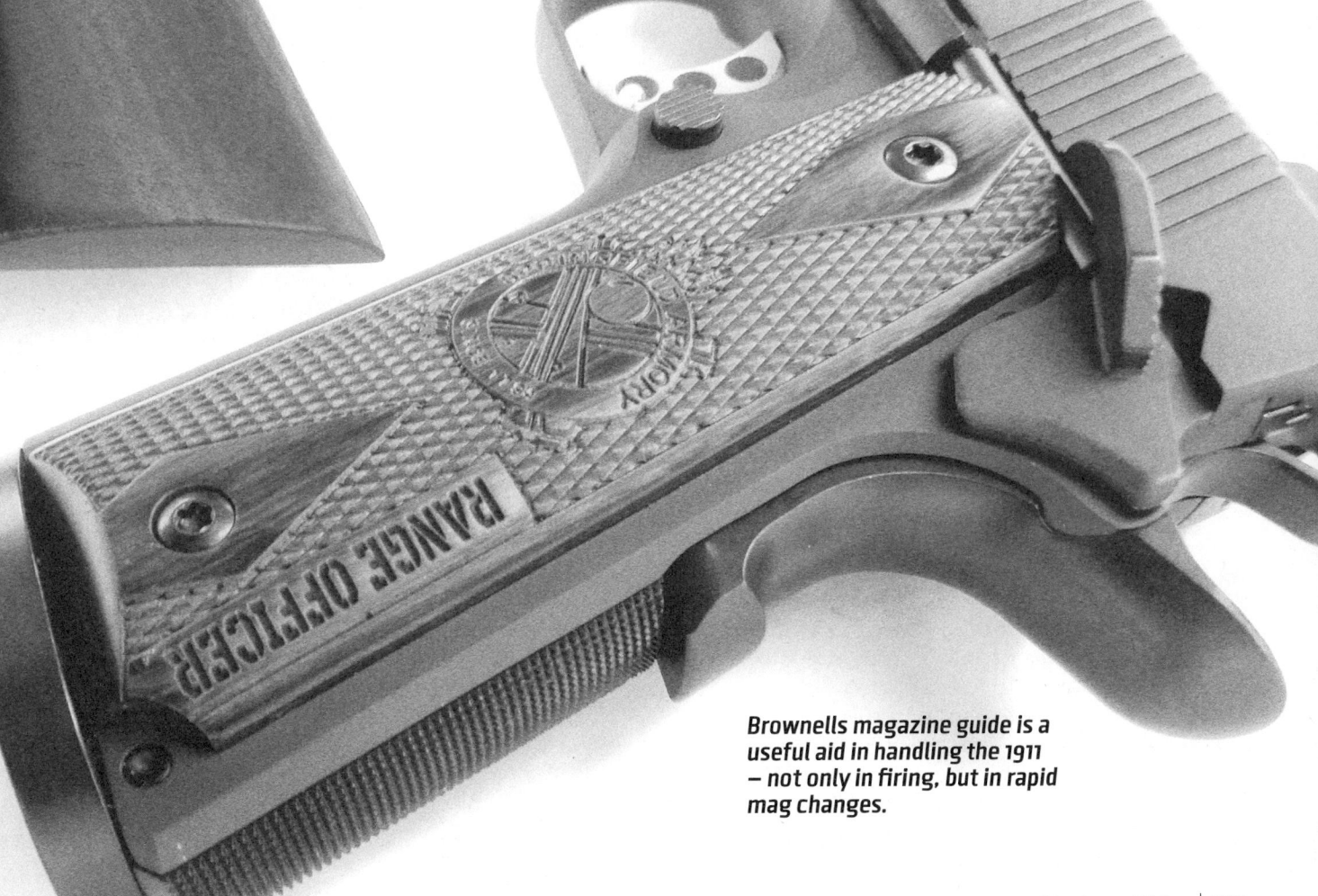

Brownells magazine guide is a useful aid in handling the 1911 – not only in firing, but in rapid mag changes.

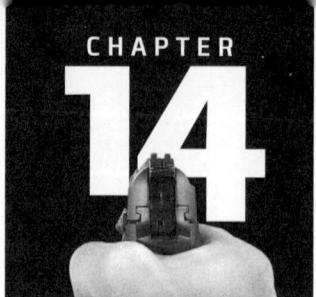

THE GLOCK

The Glock is a tactical service handgun that is reliable above all else.

I have often stated that the Glock is a baseline for choosing a handgun. When personal defense is the primary mission, the Glock is a good choice. Handguns less expensive than the Glock often cannot be trusted for reliability. If you spend more money on a handgun than the cost of the average Glock, it should have significant features that make its purchase desirable compared to the Glock. The Glock isn't perfect, far from it, especially for those desiring the greatest accuracy. But it is a good baseline for reliability.

Glock Sights

The Glock's primary shortcoming is, in my opinion, its factory sights. They have ample room for improvement. Glock has missed their chance, through several generations of new releases, to improve the sights. They've improved the grip-frame fit by supplying various inserts for their next generation handguns. But there has been no significant improvement in sighting equipment. But that doesn't mean there aren't options. In fact, the factory Glock night sight option is one well worth exploring. The steel night sights offer considerable improvement in sight picture. The Glock is rugged, reliable, and combat worthy. About the only modification that is critical is the addition of a set of aftermarket sights. The factory Glock features a rear sight with a .150-inch wide rear notch coupled with a .140-inch front — leaving very little light between the front post and the rear sight notch. When fitting a quality aftermarket front sight, the thinner .115- to .125-inch front post offers better precision. When choosing a set of sights to improve the sight picture it pays to invest in Tritium sights. Night sights add a greater dimension to the utility of the firearm.

Another reason to discard factory Glock sights is fragility. They do sometimes get knocked out of alignment or are sent flying off of the gun; after all, they are plastic. Glock changed the front sight's anchoring system a few years ago, but steel sights are still better. Most night sights consist of steel parts with a Tritium insert in a sleeve.

You must install aftermarket Glock sights properly. It isn't unusual for a Tritium ampoule to burst during installation if you use a brass punch and hammer. The MGW sight pusher was used during my testing. This tool provides a degree of precision to the process and is indispensable in changing Glock sights. The first step is to choose the proper sights, which we will cover shortly. Next, either

Many female shooters find the Glock 19 9mm to be their all-around ideal pistol.

take the pistol to a gunsmith or invest in a sight tool. I cannot imagine doing this type of modification with only a hammer and punch! Before you remove the factory sights, mark their exact position. This will allow centering the replacements and, if

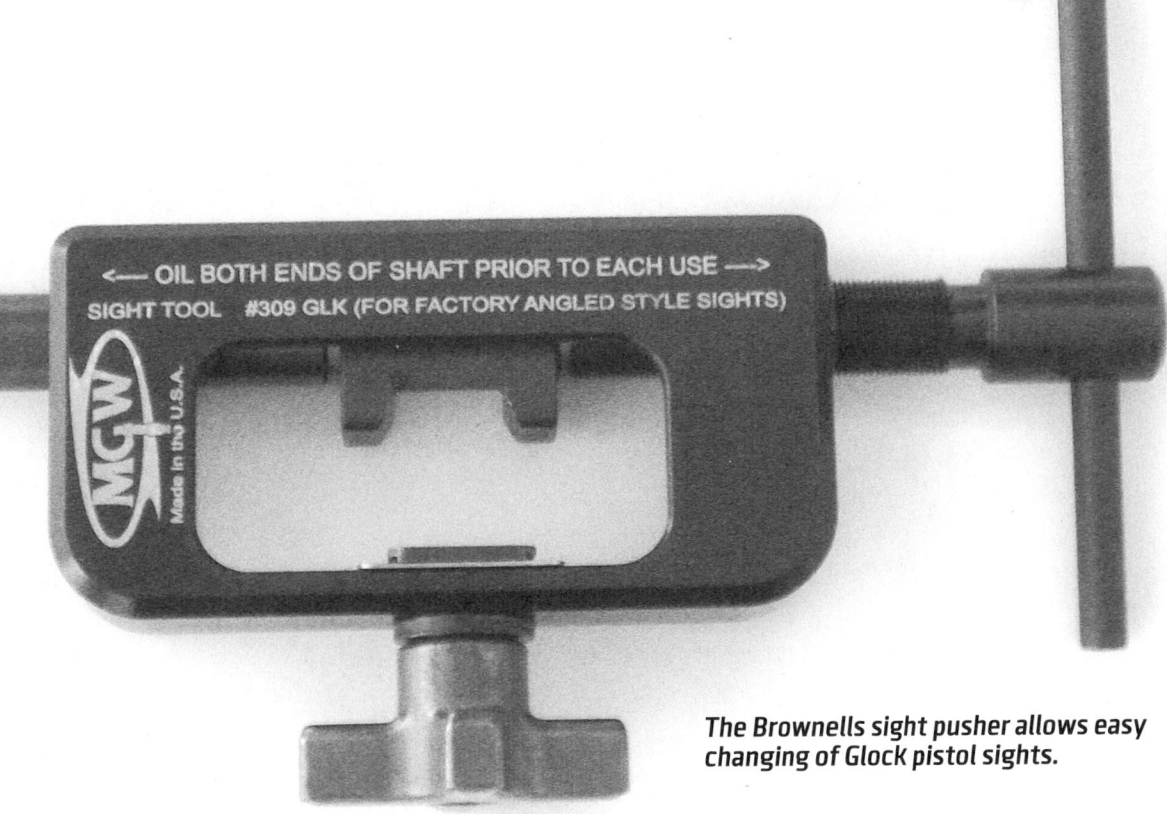

The Brownells sight pusher allows easy changing of Glock pistol sights.

done properly, only minor adjustment will be needed after they are mounted. Mark the center of the replacement sights — this will be aligned with the mark on the slide.

Use the sight pusher to remove the rear sight. The slide is locked solidly into the sight pusher on either side of the rear sights. The screw handle is turned to move the sights from the frame. The front sights were once simply pulled out, but (finally) Glock began using a screw attachment starting with the Generation 4 guns. Clean

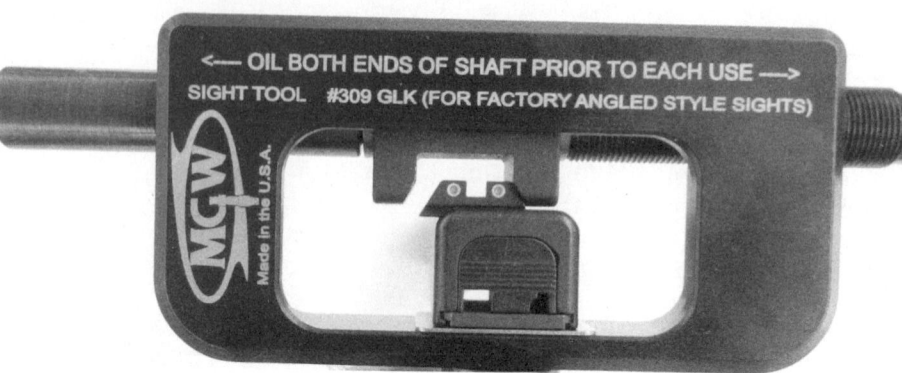

This sight tool, available from Brownells, is essential for changing Glock sights.

Be certain to mark the front sight before replacement.

The Battlehook rear sight is perhaps the best all-around combat sight yet designed for the Glock, in the author's opinion.

the rear dovetail of the slide. Begin to press the rear sight in the dovetail, right to left, by turning the sight tool handle. Remember to consult the registering marks to be certain that the sights are properly aligned.

XS Sight Systems Big Dot

I have used most of the aftermarket sights at one time or another. I am going to cover the most interesting. The sight system known as the 'Big Dot' or 'Express' system is offered by XS Sight Systems. Patterned after the old-style Express sights found on dangerous game rifles, the big dot is highly visible in dim light conditions. The front dot is held with a retaining screw after the factory front sight post is removed and the XS part pressed into the slide. The rear sight slides into the Glock dovetail easily. Tighten it up with the supplied tool and two set screws in the body of the XS rear sight. The front Big Dot is visible, but the Tritium dot itself is fairly small; it is centered in a white outline post. The result: In daylight conditions, fast hits at 7 yards. The Big Dot covers a portion of the target and recovery is rapid during firing strings. The problem is accuracy. At 25 yards it can be difficult to shoot a good group with the Big Dot sight. Consider this option carefully depending upon the goal for the handgun.

TruGlo Glock Sights

Another option I have used on several Glocks is the TruGlo night sight. TruGlo sights use a combination of Tritium and fiber optic tubes. This is a contrast to the standard-type night sights installed in an ampoule and mounted in an aluminum sleeve in a steel sight. These glow the brightest of any tested in a dark room I use for evaluating night sights. During firing tests in the daylight, the TruGlo sights gave excellent, accurate results. Shooting in dim light conditions they also yielded impressive results. The combination of good accuracy in all conditions, excellent luminosity and general good quality gives this combination a great deal of utility.

Battlehook Glock Sights

I have also tested the Battlehook sight system. Battlehook sights are a tight fit in the dovetail. Set screws in the rear sight provide rigidity. The rear sight is designed to give operators a surface for snagging the rear sight in order to rack the slide or clear a malfunction when only one hand is available. With a wounded arm or a hand busy with other gear the Battlehook works as designed. This extra option certainly is worth consideration. The front sight is bright and offers a good aiming point in darkness. The single dot provides a fast sighting option. When testing the single dot in dim light, if misaligned, the broad rear sight posts cover the front sight. Carefully realign the sights and you have a dot. This isn't the night sight for the average person, but for a very specific shooter. And, I feel, a well-trained shooter. I found this design gave the best sight picture for absolute accuracy and also the most tactically efficient for personal defense. The Battlehook sight actually increases the sight radius slightly due to the overhang on the rear of the slide. I liked the serrated rear side. Accuracy was excellent in daylight conditions. If you are headed to the sandbox, get this one. Machine work is excellent.

There are a variety of sights available for the Glock pistol. Self-luminous iron sights are well-suited to personal defense while larger target sights work good in competition. You must decide if the pistol is primarily defensive or sporting in nature. The Wilson Combat sight is the best all-around replacement sight I have used with the Glock. This sight gives a good sight picture and excellent utility. And the Warren competition sight is a good bet, too, proven in contests.

Glock Mods

The Glock pistol receives its fair share of modifications from shooters. Glock perfection is perhaps overstated, just as 1911 perfection or revolver perfection would be a misnomer. There is always room for improvement. The Glock benefits from improvements that stress and complement its good traits.

These include reliability and easy shooting. There have been terrible modifications, including triggers that are way too light and barrel and slide porting that have ruined good guns. The trigger can be fixed if chopped up but porting the barrel and slide cannot. Gun butchers have ruined their fair share of 1911 handguns, and the Glock has also had its day on the operating table. Some, it seems, were in for a fast buck while others were interested in craftsmanship and actually improving the Glock handgun.

Another area for upgrade is hand fit. The Glock features a polymer frame that actually can be modified to suit your hand. The best bet is to invest in the grip reduction from Robar industries. This is particularly well-suited to the Glock 20 and 21 large frame handguns. The Robar grip modification will leave the Glock with a lowered bore axis and a grip frame that fits the hand better. The roughened surface also results in better control in shooting. The ability to use different grip inserts no longer exists after this modification, but in the end you will have a superior fit that aids in getting the pistol on target quickly, improved control, and laying down accurate fire.

The Glock trigger must be learned to be properly managed. The trigger has about 1/2 inch of travel from beginning trigger compression to breaking the sear. The Glock action is very consistent and can be learned and managed well enough to deliver

The Glock is in wide use with American police.

TO MY PERCEPTION, THE GLOCK ACTS LIKE A SINGLE-ACTION PISTOL WITH A HEAVY TRIGGER SPRING. A STRAIGHT-THROUGH PRESS WORKS WONDERS. WHILE I PREFER THE CRISP SINGLE-ACTION TRIGGER OF THE 1911, I ALSO VERY MUCH LIKE THE SINGLE-ACTION TRIGGER OF PISTOLS SUCH AS THE CZ 75 OR REX ZERO, BUT ONLY AFTER YOU HAVE GOTTEN PAST THE INITIAL DOUBLE-ACTION PRESS OF THESE GUNS.

good accuracy. The factory Glock trigger demands a 5.5-lb. compression. Trigger reset is fast and allows excellent rapidity of fire, and accurate firing. The Glock trigger is different from the 1911, as one example, but superior in combat shooting terms to the double-action pistol. In the double-action types, your trigger finger must lay on a shelf above the trigger and come down to touch the trigger and press it to the rear. To my perception, the Glock acts like a single-action pistol with a heavy trigger spring. A straight-through press works wonders. While I prefer the crisp single-action trigger of the 1911, I also very much like the single-action trigger of pistols such as the CZ 75 or Rex Zero, but only after you have gotten past the initial double-action press of these guns. Some that fire the double-action first-shot pistol never address the double-action trigger. That's fine for a target gun but not for a combat pistol.

The proper cadence with the Glock trigger press and reset makes for remarkably accurate shooting, same as the 1911. There are skilled craftsmen who polish the Glock and produce a smoother — but not necessarily lighter — trigger.

Glock Trigger Idiosyncrasies

In terms of Glock trigger action, think of the connector as a drawbar in double-action first-shot terms. I have shot the Glock 17L with the 3 ½-lb. connector. It is easy to use well. I have also fired a law enforcement Glock Model 22 with the 8-lb. trigger, which I did not care for. There is a point concerning Glock trigger

actions that is often overlooked: No matter the trigger weight, the amount of travel is the same — a half inch. The weight of the trigger compression can be adjusted, but the length of travel remains the same. Trigger discipline, rather than weight of the press, is the answer. You may have seen disturbing videos and heard of Glock accidental discharges. I am quite certain most were with the standard trigger action, and equally certain that an 8- or 12-lb. trigger would have made little difference. Some occurred while preparing to field strip the pistol and others while holstering. Trigger pull weight would have made no difference in my opinion. Only keeping the finger off the trigger until you intend to fire, and by using trigger discipline and common sense, will you prevent accidental discharges.

So, the Glock trigger is OK as issued but can be improved for competition shooting. Use caution. I own a couple of 1911s with 3.5-lb. triggers but all of my Glocks have the factory 5.5-lb. action.

Glock Slide Releases

Another non-issue is the Glock slide release. This item has been produced in aftermarket versions with an enlarged area. Predictably, there were problems. The only Glock I have used that suffered a slide lock open during firing was a Glock 26. A slight indent in the grip frame made the slide stop protrude farther than with the Glock 19, and I locked the slide when my thumb rode into the part during a firing string. An extended Glock slide lock will do the same. The Model 37 features a slightly redesigned slide lock that I find a bit faster and easier to handle than previous pistols, but it remains unobtrusive. As is the case with the 1911, Glock slide stops should be left stock.

THERE ARE TWO TYPES OF GLOCK BARRELS –
DROP-IN AND FITTED. GLOCK BARRELS FROM
BAR-STO ARE TYPICALLY OF THE DROP-IN
VARIETY, IF SPECIFIED. FOR THE BEST RESULTS
WITH A FITTED BARREL, THOUGH, LET BAR-STO
FIT IT FOR YOU. THE GLOCK IS NOT A
DIFFICULT PISTOL TO FIT PROPERLY, BUT IT IS
CONSIDERABLY DIFFERENT FROM THE 1911.

*The Battlehook sight
is well-secured.*

A few simple tools are all that is needed to change the Glock front sight.

Glock Barrels

A few years ago, it was common to see monstrosities with four to eight ports in the barrel and slide. These pistols produced ear-splitting blast and serious function issues. They simply could not be fired with anything other than full extension of the hand. If fired at closer quarters, in retention position, or below eye level, hot gas and jacket material would be blown into your face and eyes. The lightened slide sometimes did not function well with original strength recoil springs. The big bore Glock does not need ports. In my experience, the Glock 21 .45 ACP is among the softest-kicking of all factory .45-caliber pistols. However, as Gary Paul Johnston has pointed out, the pistol is not at its best with +P loads. One writer pointed out that the Glock 21 was a hard kicker with CorBon +P, so he tried the porting system. The result was a Glock ported nearly to the chamber with six ports! After the modification, why, the pistol kicked a lot less. However, he also noted that the load was reduced from 1,140 fps to 980 fps. Now, the CorBon load gives those of us wishing for a little more thump an option. But if we thought the pistol kicked too much why not simply load the Winchester Silvertip at 980 fps? I do not recall ported barrels being competitive. These pieces did not last long as those who actually fired the pistol soon discovered their faults. If you own one, a new barrel will cure the problem but you will still have a lightened slide.

There are three reasons for replacing a Glock barrel. (A worn out barrel is not a reason. I have never seen a worn out Glock barrel.) The first is the need to fire lead bullets; the second, to increase accuracy; and third, to change the caliber. The Glock factory barrel features polygonal rifling. This type of rifling is fine for general use. In fact, the polygonal barrel will often prove quite accurate. It may produce more velocity than a conventionally rifled barrel of the same length. But polygonal rifling is quite different from standard rifling. Such rifling features shallow grooves that do not deeply engrave the bullet, but which give the jacketed projectile adequate spin. The combination results in good accuracy, high velocity and low wear. However, the standard Glock barrel does not support the case head as well as some designs. This is a product of a design that above all else is intended to feed every bullet style every time — and the Glock is feed reliable. Regarding lead bullets in the factory barrel, there is nowhere for the lead to go. Without the traditional grooves, the lead smears in the barrel and simply increases pressure. For economy, a conventionally rifled barrel is demanded. If, like myself, you are a believer in hardcast bullets, then an aftermarket conventionally rifled Glock barrel is a good step. I suppose Glock doesn't understand, as lead bullets for automatics are practically unknown in Europe. I have used Bar-Sto barrels in the Glock that turn in excellent results. I have also used a .357 SIG Bar-Sto in the Glock 22, originally a .40-caliber pistol, with stellar results.

There are two types of Glock barrels — drop-in and fitted. Glock barrels from Bar-Sto are typically of the drop-in variety, if specified. For the best re-

While the Glock isn't always recommended for hand-loaded ammunition, excellent results can be had if you are careful with load practice.

sults with a fitted barrel, though, let Bar-Sto fit it for you. The Glock is not a difficult pistol to fit properly, but it is considerably different from the 1911. A fitted Bar-Sto barrel coupled with good sights will convince you of the Glock's accuracy potential. In no case should you allow a new barrel to affect the reliable function of your pistol. My friend Lee uses the standard Glock barrel in his carry pistol but fires the Jarvis barrel with lead bullets for practice, and this works for him.

The Glock Consensus

Anyone who has worked extensively with the 1911 will be able to avoid pitfalls and approach the Glock with a mature understanding of how to customize the pistol. A generation ago, we reached a consensus on the 1911 and what it needed to be a first-class handgun: A set of sights, a speed safety, and a trigger job was the consensus. Some added barrel throating to feed hollowpoint bullets. The Glock consensus includes good sights and a proper hand fit. Today, we have the option of different frame sizes for the Glock, with the Model 23, 37 and 21 all having different grip circumference, while the 1911 is always the same except for length. True, the G22/G23 is a .40 S&W, but it seems good enough for per-

sonal defense. After quite a few years of back and forth, and love and hate with the Glock, I think I may just hang on to the few Glocks I now own. I find it a worthwhile pistol that responds well to carefully considered modifications.

Shooting Polymer Framed Handguns

There are other handguns to be considered. When approaching any quality firearm keep an open mind. If the pistol is manufactured to high standards, and is of good material, it should be serviceable even if it isn't what you would describe as your dream gun. But, you can give the piece a fair shake and perhaps you will find it to be a practical solution. When looking over the popular European handguns — such as the SIG P220, CZ 75 and others — and the American Smith and Wesson M&P, ask yourself why the pistol is a success. Why would you buy one? What are the positive attributes of the handgun and how do they pertain to your needs? I have shot factory handguns that gave me quite a surprise. They were more accurate than I would have thought. I have also tested handguns from respected names that were less useful than I expected. Some of the results were dictated by personal preference; others by actual performance. Indeed, polymer-frame handguns have become very popular and, while I continue to prefer steel frame ones, the polymer choices have their place as service pistols and for defensive use. These handguns are proving they are not subject to excess

A .40-caliber Glock is back on target and a spent case in the air.

wear from hard use. They are immune to exposure to the elements and seem very durable and reliable.

When approaching any handgun, there is a certain basis for procedure that must be followed. When following this program, I find that many handguns I do not personally prefer are still good performers, they simply must be handled with respect to their unique trigger action or firing characteristics. There is much to be said for the tough and reliable modern handgun. And while I have found the grip frames of some of these too square for my hand and actually uncomfortable to handle and fire, grip frame modification changes that picture considerably.

When you consider grip frame modification, you are really talking about grip frame reduction. While I recommend Robar Industries for this work, it is possible to do the mod yourself. But do it correctly. I have seen the hollow in the backstrap filled and the backstrap ground and the pistol sprayed, but this doesn't always make for a nice fit, it just makes a smaller handle. Also, remember that while the backstrap reduction is a desirable feature for some folks,

The author found the G35 to be one of the best-balanced Glock pistols.

the resale value of such a modified handgun is very low. Be certain you love the gun and the modification before pursuing this avenue.

The hollow backstrap should not be filled just because it is trendy to do so. After all, the hollow actually 'gives' a little on firing and cushions recoil. But if you must, you can do the work yourself with care, a steady hand and a Dremel tool. The usual process is to heat the backstrap incrementally until malleable. A large candle or even a lighter will work on a small area. To reduce the area, the rear strap is pressed against a hard surface. Take it easy using the cut-and-dry method, which is to say you should work the grip a little and then consider if more needs to be done. I've done this mod myself, employing the gun safe as a hard surface upon which to press the backstrap. You can also beat and peen the grip surface to produce a good grip and superior adhesion over the factory pistol. Any tool used to burn wood will work. One tip is to practice on a piece of plastic scrap first, to get a feel for the "stippling." With this work done, the Glock fits most hands well.

It isn't a bad idea to replace Glock sights with Wilson Combat sights. They are among the best.

The Glock Model 21 is a soft-kicking and very accurate .45.

Some modifications should be avoided. Since most Glock pistols are carried for personal defense, the trigger action should never be modified. If the pistol is used in competition, then an aftermarket trigger with shorter travel and rapid reset is useful. However, for the carry gun, do not risk giving a prosecutor something to hang you with.

Mastering the Glock

As a peace officer, I was issued and carried the Glock professionally. It always worked and made for a great service handgun. It is outstanding for general issue to trained officers. The shooter with no prior experience tends to settle comfortably into the Glock sooner than someone who has extensive experience with other types of handguns. But all of us will find the Glock useful if we give it an honest try. The same is true of the Smith and Wesson M&P, a very similar handgun with superior ergonomics as far as hand fit goes. The Springfield XD is a quite different animal. It features a single action rather than a double-action only trigger. The XD is capable of being mastered by trained shooters. Good accuracy can be demonstrated by a shooter who strives to master the piece.

When the polymer frame handguns were designed, one of the criteria was acceptable performance but not match-grade accuracy. This is acceptable for most shooters because the Glock, Smith & Wesson M&P, and Springfield XD are personal defense handguns. They need not be as accurate as a match-grade handgun. Once instructors and interested shooters found their way around the Glock, they had serious reservations concerning its accuracy. The first .40-caliber handguns were particularly disappointing, but were improved in due course. Most of the Glock service pistols are capable of delivering groups better than the 'service grade' standard at 25 yards. A 4-inch 25-yard group is considered service grade, as revealed earlier in this book. You can do better with the Glock, but concentration is needed. Even without custom modifications the Glock can deliver 3-inch groups on demand with quality ammunition. Yet, a problem with it and other handguns is that the shooter simply doesn't invest the time in familiarization that he should. Dry fire is ignored and the pistol, not respected for its accuracy potential, isn't mastered in the way it should be. The typical law enforcement officer may feel he is too busy to master the handgun and reaches a level of competence he feels is adequate, and no more. The conception that the handgun isn't very accurate adds to this shortcoming. Practice and repetition take time and require investment in ammunition, but the results are always worthwhile. A key point in learning to shoot polymer frame handguns is to secure the proper hand fit as mentioned already. Modern Glocks are supplied with grip inserts that change the grip profile considerably. Use these grip inserts, change them out, and make a genuine effort to get the pistol fitting your hand. Chances are you will find a grip insert that makes for the perfect fit and trigger reach. If the grip is uncomfortable, accuracy will suffer every time.

Anyone who carries a handgun for personal defense should shoot it extensively before carrying. Yet, I see handguns deployed without more than a single magazine fired before the handgun is loaded and holstered! I will be the first to agree that the Glock is probably a handgun that will always fire when the trigger is pressed, but this level of familiarity with the handgun just isn't enough. Your life, or the lives of others, may depend upon the handgun's performance — and the shooter's performance is the true bottom line in any defensive situation. A minimum of three-hundred rounds should be expended in proofing the handgun and in familiarization of the shooter to the pistol. The National Institute of Justice states that handgun reliability is gauged by a standard of three hundred trouble free rounds between cleaning. This is an acceptable level, but one that is very conservative. A quality service pistol is capable of thousands of rounds fired between cleaning. This break-in period aids in ascertaining whether the handgun works as it should and in making certain that the shooter is reasonably familiar with it. With the 1911 and certain other handguns, the break-in serves to seat the locking lugs and remove burrs that may exist from manufacturing.

You should fire for accuracy offhand, testing the handgun — and yourself! — for control during rapid fire. This firing experience will pay big dividends as you get acquainted with the grip, sight picture and trigger action. This is simply essential in order to build accuracy potential. When training Glock shooters and practicing myself I have found steel reaction plates to be a great resource. The reason is simple: steel plates give instant feedback. If you hit to one side, the plate spins in the direction of the hit — right, left, or too high shows instant feedback. If you center punch the hanging plate properly then you get a straight to the rear action. Since

The Glock 35 in .40 S&W is a good all-around service and personal defense gun with a great deal of sporting potential.

most Glock shooters are defense-oriented, the rapid-paced shooting builds important skills quickly. The best means you have of training with the handgun (for an experienced shooter) is to begin at moderate range, 7 yards or so, and fire in a mix of fast and slow drills at a reaction target. Shoot and learn the handling characteristics of the firearm — how it recoils, how control is maintained, and how the trigger feels. Concentrate on trigger control, align the sights properly, and get good hits. Then move to 10, 15, and finally 20 yards. By mastering the handgun in this manner you will find that the Glock is a formidable choice for those who practice.

After you are familiar with offhand shooting and feel confident in your ability to shoot the Glock, move to the benchrest and shoot for accuracy. The first shots should be fired at 15 yards to gauge accuracy potential. There is a big difference between firing at 15 and 25 yards and even after many years of testing I often shoot the first test rounds at 15 yards in order to gauge sight regulation and get a feel for any new handgun. Use a sandbag or some type of rest that offers a solid platform. Take your time and use every skill you have learned. Exercise patience between shots and get the sight picture and trigger press correct. Use your skill to control the trigger press. The Glock demands coordination in firing, while the 1911 or Browning Hi Power demand concentration. The longer press is different from single-action .22-caliber target guns and must be mastered. The break is slower than with the single action; there is no changing that, but with practice you may find the Glock quite an accurate handgun.

While a factory Glock may never fire a 1-inch 25-yard group, the standard of 3 inches or less is easily met. I have shot a Glock 17 pistol capable of 2.5-inch, 25-yard accuracy. The Glock 21 .45 is perhaps the easiest of the Austrian line to master from the benchrest and is comfortable to shoot. Again, while hand fit is an issue with many shooters, those with larger hands will find the Glock 21 a great all-around .45 ACP handgun.

Best Glock Loads

A good number of shooters do not take the time to test their Glock with different types of ammunition, believing that the gun isn't accurate enough to test one load against another. This isn't true. Truth be told, the Glock has definite ammunition preferences that will show over time. Some ammunition for personal defense is well-designed and high quality. Other types are far less useful. Too much pressure, too light a bullet, or an odd bullet shape make for poor accuracy. There are many different types of ammunition and many different makers. Black Hills, Federal, Fiocchi USA, Gorilla, Hornady, Speer,

and Winchester offer first-class ammo for personal defense and target use. In my experience, the Glock performs best with what is regarded as standard bullet weights. These include the 124-grain 9mm, 180-grain .40 S&W, and the 230-grain .45 ACP. While it is possible and even probable that 115-grain 9mm and 200-grain .45 ACP bullets will give acceptable results, in my experience the Glock simply performs best with the standard or traditional bullet weights.

Testing ammunition can get expensive. Having a handgun that is reliable with the chosen loading is much more important than a small increment in accuracy. Even so, ammunition testing with the Glock is worthwhile once you have mastered the handgun's handling and trigger press. There are a number of loads that have an excellent reputation for accuracy potential. Federal's 124-grain 9mm HST is among these. If your Glock 19 9mm isn't accurate with this load I would seriously consider skill as the culprit. Most 180-grain .40 loads are good performers. A standout for competition use is the Fiocchi 170-grain .40 load, intended to make Major rating in IPSC with minimum recoil and maximum accuracy. The 230-grain loads shine in the Glock 21 .45. The Hornady 200-grain XTP will give excellent results in most handguns, but in the Glock the heavier 230-grain XTP is a better choice. I enjoy testing different loads, but if the Glock proves accurate with a certain loading it is wise to stick with that load, as experimentation is costly and may not produce material results in this handgun.

A trick with the Glock is to shoot three-shot groups instead of five-shot. Fewer shots means the concentration is such that you are more likely to produce the pistol's true accuracy potential. Find a load that is completely reliable, proof it for function, and determine its reliability. Once you have mastered your Glock through application of the basics of sight picture, sight alignment and trigger press, you may find the accuracy of the handgun is limiting your own potential. The application of aftermarket sights is the most basic and perhaps the best modification with the greatest accuracy potential. Another possible modification is the grip frame reduction addressed previously. A move I do not recommend is installing an aftermarket trigger system to lower the trigger pull weight. This is a terrible idea in a service or personal defense pistol. The standard 5.5-lb. trigger release of the Glock is ideal for most uses and may be mastered sufficiently for most chores.

A handgun intended for pure competition without any application in personal defense can be modified with a trigger disconnect that is as low as 3.5 pounds. The 3.5-lb. connector has been fitted to many Glocks. Those using it find that accuracy potential is enhanced in competition, but it won't make up for poor marksmanship. Rather, the only persons using this modified trigger should be those that have mastered the Glock and find the factory trigger limiting them. This is the rare bird indeed, and he or she knows who they are. The rest of us need to maintain and use the factory Glock trigger action.

Accurate Handloads for the Glock

Officers and competitors began to understand the virtues of the Glock. There were a number of spectacular blow ups. Without dissecting each individual failure — and there were quite a few with the .40 and fewer with the 9mm — I am certain that many were attempting to shoot loads that were +P or even 9mm Major pressure levels. But even more were trying to use lead bullets, which the Glock was not designed to shoot. Lead bullets are not the same as hardcast bullets. Lead bullets are soft and cheap. Hardcast bullets are alloyed with tin and antimony and take rifling well; they do not lead badly if used with quality lubricant. Many commercial bullets were too soft. As a result of these problems, Glock issued a prohibition on the use of lead bullets in their pistols. While many companies prohibit handload use for their products (and such use will typically void the warranty) this was the first straight across the board prohibition of lead bullet use of which I am aware.

Rifling Differences

Rifling is the grooves cut into a barrel. The grooves are separated by lands. The type of rifling varies by the maker. The standard form of rifling used in most handguns is easily recognizable with a cog-like appearance. However, polygonal rifling, as used in the Glock, Heckler and Koch, and a few other handguns, is smoother in appearance. There are only slight rises in the rifling. In such rifling there is a tighter gas seal and the bullet grips the barrel more tightly. Less bullet deformation, higher average velocity, and a bore that is easier to clean are among the advantages of polygonal rifling. As a rule, polygonal rifling exhibits no tool marks, which are common with traditional rifling. The bore sees less wear and the barrel will last longer. The only drawback for shooters — especially high-volume sport shooters — is that polygonal rifling isn't lead friendly.

When the bullet travels through the bore it is slightly oversized in order to take the rifling properly and secure a good gas seal; it becomes compressed as pressure heaves it through. Lead bullets lose some of their lead in the barrel. This is known as 'leading the barrel.' As an example, firing a soft lead bullet at high velocity in the .357 Magnum will quickly cause a badly leaded barrel — the lead fills in the grooves. With a polygonal barrel there is nowhere for lead to build up. It simply coats the barrel. This can result in a buildup of pressure after a relatively modest amount of ammunition is fired. Each successive bullet must overcome greater resistance to exit the barrel. The Europeans use jacketed bullets almost exclusively in their handguns. There, factory ammunition in the self-loading calibers is limited to jacketed bullets with few exceptions. For this and many other reasons Glock issued a warning not to use lead bullets in their pistols. When Glock issued this warning they created a market for aftermarket barrels. Bar-Sto Precision Machine offers first-quality aftermarket barrels for the Glock. These barrels are precision made and uniformly accurate. They are conventionally rifled and allow reloaders to use lead bullets.

I do not use soft swaged bullets or standard lead bullets in any of my handguns, instead opting for quality hardcast lead bullets only. By using hardcast bullets and loading my own ammunition I can fire three to four times as much ammunition on the same budget. This means more enjoyment and greater proficiency. I have owned Glock pistols with Bar-Sto barrels and the performance has been excellent. A combination of the Bar-Sto barrel and Novak Lo Mount sight when fitted to my first Glock 22 resulted in changing a 25-yard gun to a 50-yard shooter.

Accuracy Tests

Table 14-1

Conducted with Bayou Bullets coated in 9mm. Glock 17L long slide.			
115-gr. RNL	5.7 gr. Unique Powder	1,195 fps	2.5-in. 25-yard group
115-gr. RNL	4.2 gr. Red Dot Powder	1,120 fps	1.9-in. 25-yard group
125-gr. Bullet	5.8 gr. Unique Powder	1,280 fps	2.75-in. 25-yard group
125-gr. Bullet	4.5 WW WSF powder	1,088 fps	1.7-in. 25-yard group
124-gr. TCG	6.0 Unique	1,199 fps	1.9-in. 25-yard group
125-gr. bullet	4.4 WW 231 Powder	1,101 fps	2.4-in. 25-yard group

OTHER PISTOLS

The Wilson Combat Beretta is a first-class and very accurate 9mm.

When it comes to the other pistols — that is, those other than the 1911 and the Glock — you may be tempted to lump all of them into one group. This must be avoided. The fact is, these "other" handguns are individuals. There are Glock-like ones including the Smith and Wesson M&P. Then there are the double-action first-shot handguns including the SIG, Beretta and CZ. Few of these have any special programs for accurizing. Your best bet is to apply good techniques in order to achieve optimum accuracy with them. An exception is the Beretta 92. Army Marksmanship Units have developed accurizing procedures for it. The procedure has been taken even further by Wilson Combat.

The Walther P1, right, remains a service pistol with plenty of integrity. The author's favorite compact 9mm is the CZ P01, below.

The Beretta 92 was among the finest 9mm service pistols ever produced. The Wilson Combat enhanced version will supply the needs of any Beretta fan and serious shooter. The handguns are accurate, barrels excellent, and the trigger action properly tuned. But if you can't spring for a Wilson Combat Brigadier, you can add a D-type hammer spring to enhance the trigger action on a factory 92. Military gunsmiths add a special barrel bushing that is hand fit one by one. If you are capable of holding 2-inch groups at 50 yards in stringent national competition, then Wilson Combat offers improvements over the standard Wilson Combat Beretta. The Beretta is a proven pistol and the Wilson Combat modifications are a great addition to a fine handgun.

Browning Hi Power

The modern Hi Power 9mm is pretty much ready to go as it is issued. The modern trigger action breaks from 4.5 to 5.5 pounds, much better than some of the handguns I wrestled with back in the 1980s. The best addition to the gun is a Bar-Sto barrel. The drop-in version almost always works as-is without filing or fitting in any generation of Browning Hi Power. I once dropped in a Bar-Sto barrel into a WWII 1943 FN High Power [post-1950s Browning guns are called "Hi Power," original FNs "High Power" — Editor]. The gunsmith helping me with this handgun noticed it had soft steel, but since it was what I had, and the barrel did not need fitting, we proceeded. That High Power was a wonderfully accurate handgun when we were done. Now, a classic Hi Power will often print a 2.5-3.5 inch group off the benchrest with quality ammunition. Some, well used and abused, will not meet that standard. A Bar-Sto barrel will add much to a Hi Power.

I installed one such barrel in the most accurate Hi Power I have owned. The result was stellar accuracy, including a single 1.1-inch group at 25 yards with a personal handload using the Hornady XTP bullet. For a Hi Power with a truly heavy trigger, the C and S-Trigger Pull Reduction Kit from Brownells is the best means of gaining a superior trigger action. Be certain the action cracks the primers of the duty load after this modification.

WILSON COMBAT BERETTA 92 ELITE SPECIFICATIONS

With a few judicious upgrades and excellent sights – not to mention barrel fitting – the Beretta 92 becomes a top-performing tactical 9mm.

Wilson Combat handguns offer the option of tactical illumination.

The Beretta Brigadier tactical is an enhanced handgun with great appeal to fans of the Beretta.

- M9A1 frame with 92A1 round trigger guard profile and improved checkering
- Dehorned 92G Brigadier slide
- Enhanced slide-to-frame fit
- Trijicon tritium dovetail front sight
- Stainless barrel with recessed crown, 4.7-inch Elite II length, black finish
- Oversize steel magazine release
- Steel de-cocking levers
- Skeletonized Elite II hammer
- D hammer spring
- Lanyard loop pin
- Lanyard loop, aluminum
- Steel trigger
- Wilson Combat rear u-notch battle sight
- Wilson Combat fluted steel guide rod
- G10 Dirty Olive grips with Wilson Combat logo medallion
- Wilson Combat logo on slide
- 3 15-rd. M9A1 Beretta sand resistant magazines
- 9mm caliber only

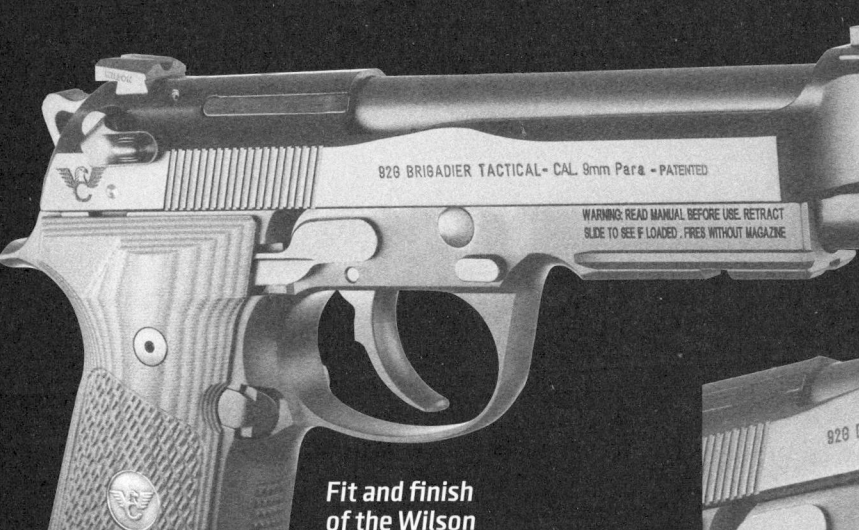

Note the tight, exacting fit of the barrel to slide in Wilson Combat Beretta 92.

Fit and finish of the Wilson Combat handgun is excellent.

More Options

- G configuration ambidextrous decocker only
- All steel components (decocker, trigger, magazine release, guide rod)
- Checkered frontstrap and backstrap
- Beveled magazine well
- Rail for mounting light or laser
- Special serial number range with WC prefix
- IDPA Stock Service Pistol approved
- USPSA Production Division approved
- Not CA Compliant (Unless LEO purchase) Only Two Custom Upgrades at This Time
- Action tune
- Mag guide

A great advantage of the Wilson Combat Beretta is the proprietary sight system.

Note the extended magazine release and excellent-quality grip panels of the Wilson Combat Beretta Brigadier.

The author shooting a Browning Hi Power in a combat drill.

Tactical Sport is a heavier pistol at 44 ounces loaded. This makes for a very stable handgun that handles the hottest 9mm loads easily. The balance is ideal and accuracy is there for those who master it. Much of the extra weight of the pistol is in a monolithic dust cover that adds recoil-dampening weight to the muzzle end. There is aggressive checkering on the frame straps and the trigger guard as well. And one detail that may help when running a combat course is that the magazines hold twenty rounds of 9mm Luger ammunition. At 5.4 inches, the barrel is longer than the standard CZ 75B and gets the most from the hottest 9mm ammo. The sight radius is a long 7 3/8 inches. This sight radius really makes for superior shooting.

CZ 75

Every pistol should have a well-defined purpose, whether for concealed carry, hunting or recreational use. The Czech CZ 75 is a war dog that has served in the Middle East and other hot spots worldwide, not to mention special operations by Russian units. I have been gravitating toward the CZ and away from the Hi Power for some time, and this is partly because of the variations available for the CZ. The full-size CZ 75 is a capable 9mm. The Tactical Sport variant is a credible performer for IPSC and USPSA divisions. For pride of ownership and accuracy work, the pistol is an alternative to the expensive SIG P210. The trend is toward reduced weight in carry guns, but the

This original CZ 75 has been fired a great deal and remains a reliable and effective handgun.

*Firing offhand the CZ 75
in .40 S&W is accurate
and hits hard.*

Heckler and Koch

If you are using an HK USP 9mm, then you have one of the finest handguns made. I like the P30 and recently moved to the VP9. Its finesse and construction is simply first quality. The trigger action of the VP9 required considerable acclimation. While usable, it isn't quite as sharp as the P30's single-action press. But overall, for combat shooting and ease of training, the VP9 is a great all-around handgun. There isn't much to be done with HK save keep it clean. The trigger action is the primary concern and the HK shooter (like the Glock shooter) is advised to keep the pistol

All CZ 75 handguns feature rails that are machined the entire length of the receiver. These rails ride inside the frame. The slide rides lower than most pistols and this lowers the bore axis. This slide design helps the pistol maintain its good accuracy — a trait that crosses over into the Tactical Sport model. That model is a competition pistol designed to win matches and nothing else. It is supplied with a crisp single-action trigger that breaks between 2.5 and 2.75 pounds, in the models I've tested. It takes a marksman to master a trigger pull that light, but when you do, the CZ 75 Tactical Sport is very accurate. My example was tested thanks to a shooter and CZ fan that stood over my shoulder as I fired his expensive handguns! In firing 50 rounds of Federal American Eagle FMJ loads and 50 rounds of Federal 124-grain HST hollow points, results were excellent. The front sight simply hung on the target. Shooting from a solid barricade rest, standing, I put ten rounds of the HST load into 3 inches at 25 yards. This dog will run and should be significantly more accurate than the shooter.

For home defense the CZ 75 with mounted combat light is a formidable tool.

(left) As the author fires the HK VP9, a cartridge case rides his line of sight.

(below) The HK VP9 is a credible performer and quite accurate for a polymer frame pistol.

clean and lubricated and practice with it to the exclusion of all others. The HK features a polygonal rifled bore. Like the Glock the barrel isn't lead friendly but often gives good accuracy and higher velocity than similar length barrels with conventional rifling.

HK VP9 Test Results

I conducted an accuracy test of the VP9 at 15 yards to answer some of my own questions concerning accuracy. While the test was strenuous (in mastering the trigger) the results were excellent. Recorded were three-shot groups.

Two great HKs: the VP9 and the HK P7M8.

There is no handgun with a greater range of hand adjustment than the VP9.

Table 15-1

HK VP9 — 15 yards	
Black Hills 115-gr. FMJ remanufactured	.8 in.
Black Hills 115-gr. +P JHP	1.25 in.
Black Hills 124-gr. JHP	.75 in.
Federal 124-gr. HST	.9 in.
SIG Sauer 115-gr. FMJ	1.5 in.
SIG Sauer 124-gr. V Crown JHP	1.0 in.
Winchester USA 115-gr. JHP	1.75 in.
Winchester 124-gr. PDX +P	1.4 in.
Speer Gold Dot 124-gr.	1.3 in.
Handloads	
Hornady 124-gr. XTP/WW231 powder/1,120 fps	.75 in.
Bayou Bullets 135-gr. plated/ww231/980 fps	1.5 in.

A few years ago, Heckler and Koch introduced a new handgun designed with the hope of achieving a military contract. It became the HK45, and is a viable pistol for use by the Special Operation Command (SOCOM) or any military entity. The HK45 builds upon HK's slide-to-frame design that features more contact between parts than most polymer-frame pistols — resulting in greater rigidity and accuracy potential. The single greatest advantage of the HK45 over the HK USP is the slimmed grip. For many of

After firing the HK45T, a case flies while the pistol is back on target.

The 10-round magazine of the HK45 allows a smaller frame than the company's USP model, but is still a large pistol.

The HK45T proved accurate with every load tested. Right out of the box it's an easy shooting and accurate handgun.

us, the USP's grip, particularly in .45 caliber, is too large. The HK .45 grip is more similar to those of the VP 9 and P30, although sized up for the .45 ACP cartridge. Since the grip is thinner, magazine capacity is limited. The HK45 magazine holds ten rounds of ammunition. The pistol reviewed here is the HK45T, the tactical model of the HK45. This variant features a threaded barrel and night sights as well as the popular dark earth finish.

The HK's slide and frame manage to eliminate some of the slide-heavy feel plaguing many of the polymer-frame handguns. Its frame is nicely stippled for good adhesion. Make no mistake: This is a big gun. But it feels lively in the hand, more so than a Glock 21, and the grip frame is more ergonomic. The pistol features Meprolight Tru-Dot night sights. The front of the slide features cocking serrations. This is a must-have for tactical handguns. The ejection port is generous for administrative handling. The pistol features the Browning locked breech design. Practically every modern self-loader — save the Beretta, with its oscillating wedge — uses this lockup.

That is, the barrel and slide remain locked together in recoil and separate when the bullet exits the barrel. The pistol features the requisite frame rail for mounting combat lights. I used several lights during the evaluation, notably the LaserMax Spartan.

The HK45T barrel features an O-ring to enhance lockup. It is intended to increase accuracy potential by tight slide-to-barrel fit. The difference is probably much smaller than I can hold, but it seems worthwhile with no downside. The recoil guide and buffer spring is well-designed with a polymer buffer added to increase life and limit battering. The recoil spring and buffer system added to the pistol's light felt recoil. HK claims significant recoil reduction. The HK45 doesn't recoil more than the Glock 21 .45, which I consider one of the most comfortable of the .45s to fire.

HK offers a number of different actions, including double-action first-shot and LEM (Law Enforcement Modification), and DAO. The pistol as supplied came as a selective double action. Most police agencies use a double-action only type and this is the preferred

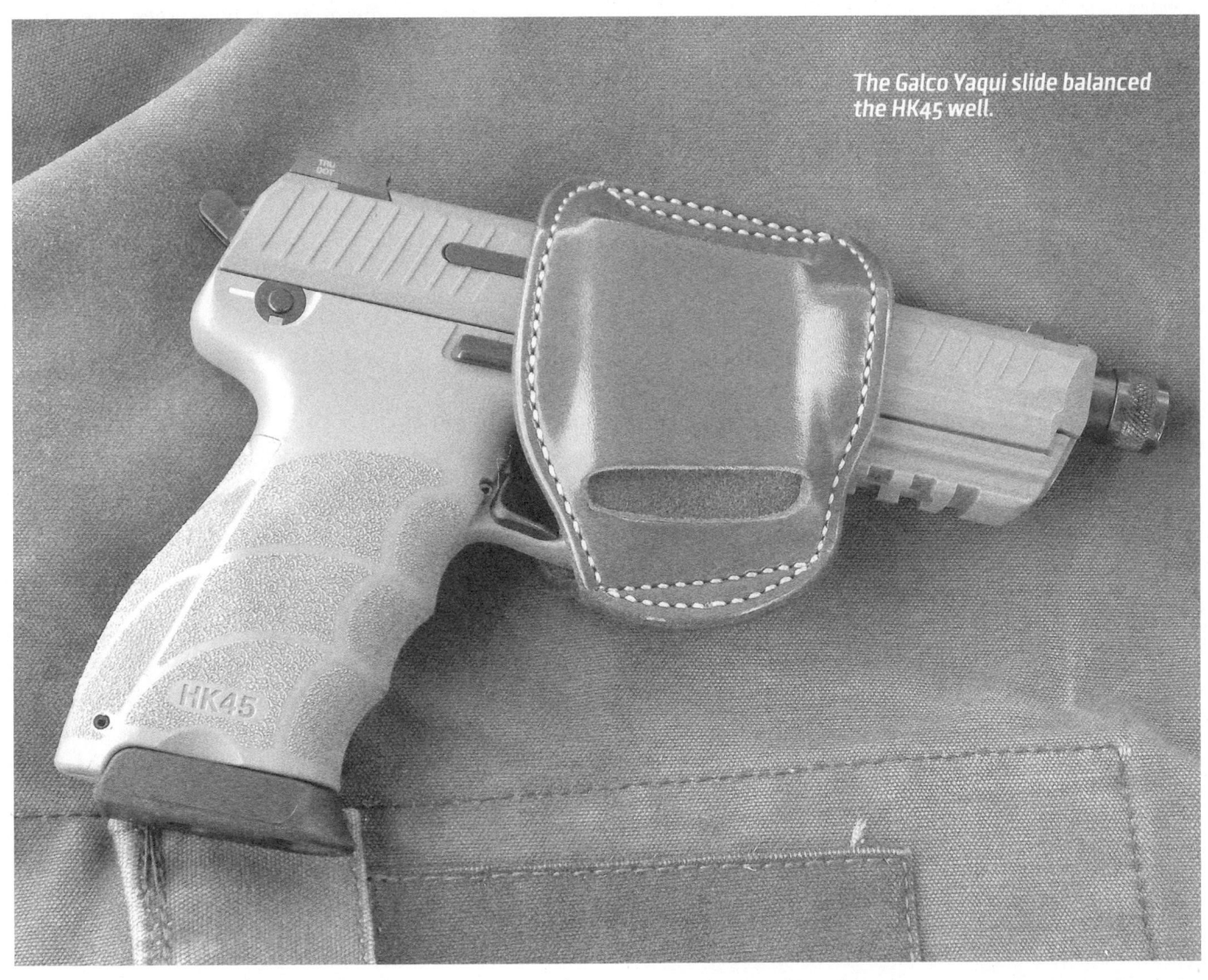

The Galco Yaqui slide balanced the HK45 well.

action for institutional issue. Using the single-action option, a trained individual will be able to connect with a man-sized target at 100 yards. This may be important for the military or for special team use. In terms of functioning, the pistol is loaded and the safety lever is pressed downward to safely lower the hammer. With the hammer at rest, the safety can be pressed into the 'on' position. Despite the size of the pistol, it isn't difficult to thumb the safety lever off as it's drawn from a holster. The long double-action trigger press is heavy at an estimated 14 pounds. It is usable but exhibits stacking at the end of its travel. An alternative is to carry it cocked and locked, hammer to the rear and safety on.

The most likely carry mode for military users is, in my opinion, holstered, safety on, with the hammer down. Unlike pistols with a slide-mounted safety, there is no speed penalty with the frame mounted safety of the HK45. The advantage of the selective double-action system is that once the pistol has fired, you can engage in tactical movement by simply applying the safety — you need not decock the pistol. When properly understood, this system is ideal for all-around tactical use, especially when coupled with the decocker.

A Question of Caliber

Now is a good time to address the reason the .45 ACP is my favorite self-loading pistol cartridge. The advantage of the .45 has been enumerated many times. The only thing that really matters in wound potential is actual damage. Given adequate penetration, the mass and diameter of the bullet means the most. There just are not many men in history with greater experience than Col. Thompson and Dr. La-Garde. They determined over 100 years ago that the military handgun should be a .45-caliber weapon. Nothing has changed. There have been irrelevant, so-called studies that have come to different conclusions in this age of junk science. The validity of secret sources and non-repeatable tests is zero. The .45 makes a larger wound with more total volume, period. The cartridge also operates at relatively low pressure, which ensures long weapon life.

Tests

I have fired the HK45T handgun with a wide variety of ammunition and enjoyed each range session. The pistol is pleasant to fire, accurate, and rated for +P loads. I am not certain we need the +P in the .45 but it may be good to have. Most of my practice has been with handloads and generic 230-grain ball. Fiocchi 230-grain ball is affordable and offers good accuracy. I have also tested the pistol with the sledgehammer Hornady 220-grain +P with good results. As the accompanying table shows, the pistol is clearly accurate enough for personal defense or military use. The HK45T is a great handgun, well-suited to field use or home defense, though it would take a big man and intelligent holster selection to conceal the pistol. There are better choices for concealed carry, but none that are tactically superior to the HK45T. When conducting range drills I carried the pistol in a Galco JAK belt slide holster. This is a custom-quality holster that fits the HK well, offers good retention, and excellent draw speed.

Table 15-2
HK45T Accuracy Testing Solid bench rest, 25 yards

Factory Load	Group
Hornady 185-gr. XTP	2.0 in.
Hornady 200-gr. XTP +P	2.15 in.
Hornady 220-gr. Critical Duty +P	2.4 in.
Fiocchi 230-gr. FMJ	2.65 in.
Fiocchi 230-gr. EXTREMA JHP	2.0 in.
Wolf 230-gr. FMJ	3.6 in.
Handload	
Sierra 230-gr. FMJ/Titegroup/820 fps	2.5 in.
Sierra 230-gr. MATCH JHP/844 fps	1.9 in.

Smith and Wesson M&P

The Smith & Wesson M&P is designed to compete with the Glock, so it is not surprisingly Glock-like. A considerable argument can be made that the Glock is the more proven handgun. Just the same, the M&P has enjoyed much success and has earned its recognition as a reliable handgun. I particularly like the .45-caliber version and find it more shooter-friendly than the oversized Glock 21. The M&P is supplied with three changeable grip straps. This makes good hand fit a real possibility. No complaining about grip size with this handgun.

Its magazine release is well-designed for easy access and some versions are available with a manual safety, which I prefer. The single greatest advantage of the M&P over the Glock is the issue Novak-type sights. These sights allow a good sight picture and enhanced accuracy potential. The Smith and Wesson trigger operates in a similar manner to the Glock; however, the Glock trigger has a lever in the face as a safety feature. The Smith and Wesson features a hinged trigger. That trigger, according to those I know who have tested the M&P, offers better accuracy potential. Like the Glock, it isn't my favorite pistol, but it is too good to ignore. I have fired the M&P in 9mm, .40 S&W and .45 ACP. I particularly like the M&P Shield as a hideout pistol and find it much superior to the mini Glocks for my use. The Shield tends to shoot 'softer' in a given caliber than most polymer-frame handguns.

The M&P .45 is a good shooter, regarded by the author as an all-around service grade handgun.

MAGNUM REVOLVER ACCURACY

The Ruger GP100, above, is one of the strongest magnum revolvers ever made. The Colt Trooper is a vintage revolver with good performance.

When I began this book, I studied the accuracy potential of modern handguns and much of what was written about them. While I have read the works of Sharpe, Keith, Cooper and Skelton, I have also studied contemporary writers. While many of the lightweight polymer frame handguns seem capable of shooting 4-inch groups at 25 yards, to accept such accuracy from a quality revolver is ridiculous.

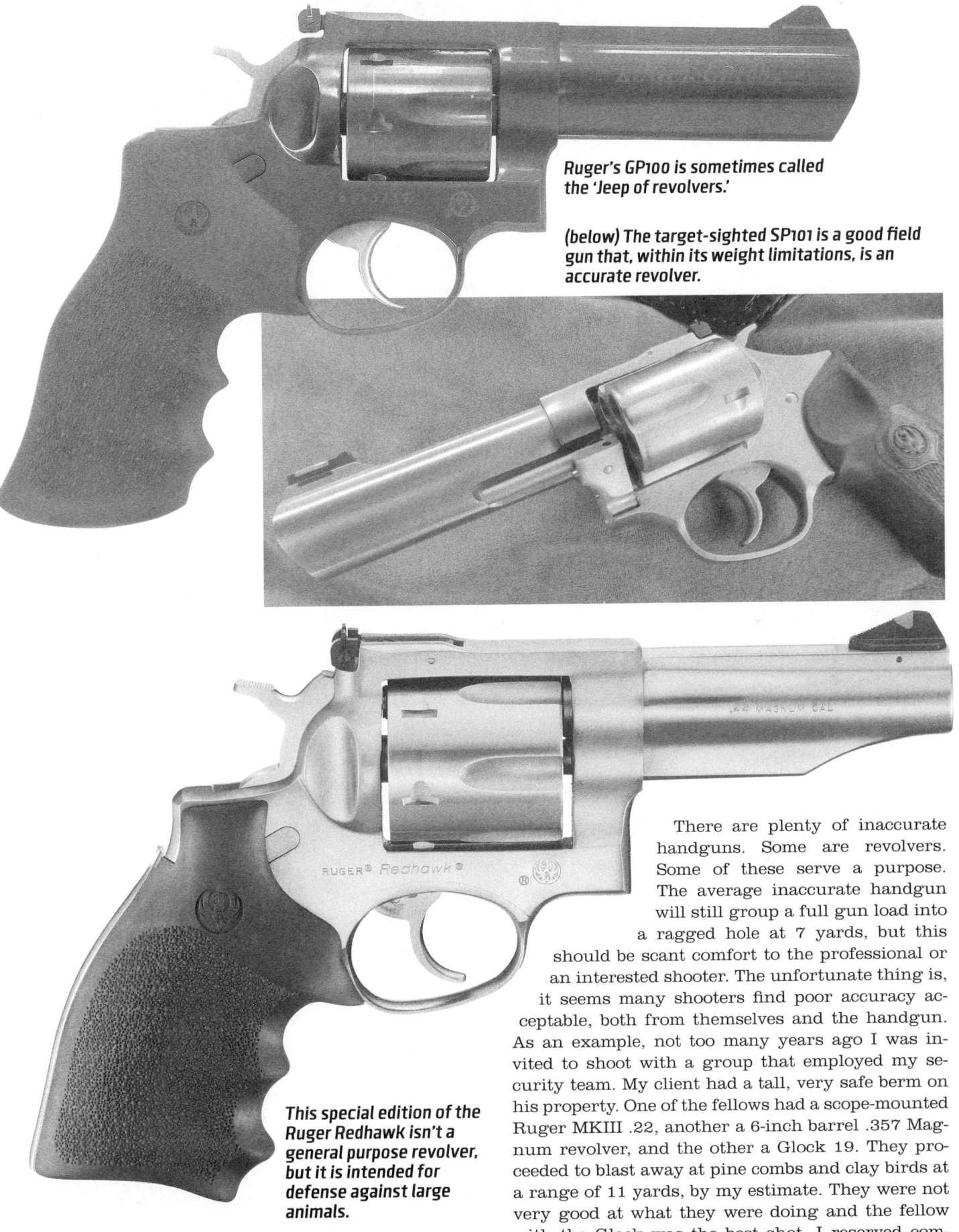

Ruger's GP100 is sometimes called the 'Jeep of revolvers.'

(below) The target-sighted SP101 is a good field gun that, within its weight limitations, is an accurate revolver.

This special edition of the Ruger Redhawk isn't a general purpose revolver, but it is intended for defense against large animals.

There are plenty of inaccurate handguns. Some are revolvers. Some of these serve a purpose. The average inaccurate handgun will still group a full gun load into a ragged hole at 7 yards, but this should be scant comfort to the professional or an interested shooter. The unfortunate thing is, it seems many shooters find poor accuracy acceptable, both from themselves and the handgun. As an example, not too many years ago I was invited to shoot with a group that employed my security team. My client had a tall, very safe berm on his property. One of the fellows had a scope-mounted Ruger MKIII .22, another a 6-inch barrel .357 Magnum revolver, and the other a Glock 19. They proceeded to blast away at pine combs and clay birds at a range of 11 yards, by my estimate. They were not very good at what they were doing and the fellow with the Glock was the best shot. I reserved comment; I was not the instructor, but the guest. At least they were well aware of safety procedure.

Some pistols simply do not shoot well, while others are very accurate. The handgun, shooter and ammunition are the bottom line when it comes to accuracy. Unfortunately, some of the modern revolvers just are not that accurate. I read some reports of modern revolver accuracy by those who tested the lightweight frame .357 wheelguns and certain AirLite .22s. I shook my head. No, they could not be that inaccurate. Once I obtained my own samples, I found that, yes, some were pretty dismal.

Let's face it. You buy a trail gun for beheading reptiles and perhaps to pot game. It is all a very pleasant thing to have. If the revolver will group no better than 4 inches at 15 yards that just isn't relevant to the task at hand. Sometimes, accuracy depends on the caliber. One of my friends obtained a rare bird — a 3-inch Ruger Vaquero chambered for the .40 Smith and Wesson. He thought it was pretty neat, but the best groups I could fire were 6 inches at 25 yards. The long jump through the chamber to the barrel was one culprit, but then again the .40 isn't exactly known as a tack driver. I pointed out that the more powerful .45 Colt was far more accurate on average. He looked at me as if I just didn't get it. Why he wanted such an inaccurate and underpowered revolver is beyond me. If I wanted a .40 S&W, a Glock 23 would do more than his oversized revolver. A .45 Colt revolver, on the other hand, is a good game getter. Another problematic handgun caliber is the .45

The Ruger Blackhawk grips are acceptable in .357 Magnum and .45 Colt, but the author recommends larger grips for the .44 Magnum.

ACP or .45 Auto Rim revolver. I have shot original 1917 revolvers so chambered that were quite accurate and others that were very poor.

Modern production seems hit and miss. It would be better to chamber revolver cartridges in revolvers and self-loading cartridges in self-loaders. A market exists for those demanding revolver accuracy. Custom gunsmiths can cut the forcing cone and smooth the action of certain revolvers. The result is a handgun that will group into 2 inches at 25 yards. The Ruger GP100 and the Ruger Blackhawk come from the factory good to go for handloads and heavy magnum loads of any type. Revolvers can be built to tight tolerances and always work. They do not have to make allowances for dirty powder and lead buildup as is the case with autoloaders. Do not accept less than excellent accuracy from your revolver.

Colt Python

When it comes to a high point in production and absolute quality of manufacture, there is one revolver that stands alone. Some say it is the finest handgun of any type ever made, and I have no argument with that. Others may ask why anyone would pay over two thousand dollars for an out-of-production revolver. The Colt Python was built to exacting standards that would be termed semi-custom today. The Python was eventually turned into a

The Ruger Blackhawk's rugged and adjustable rear and post front sights are ideal for most uses.

520-16833

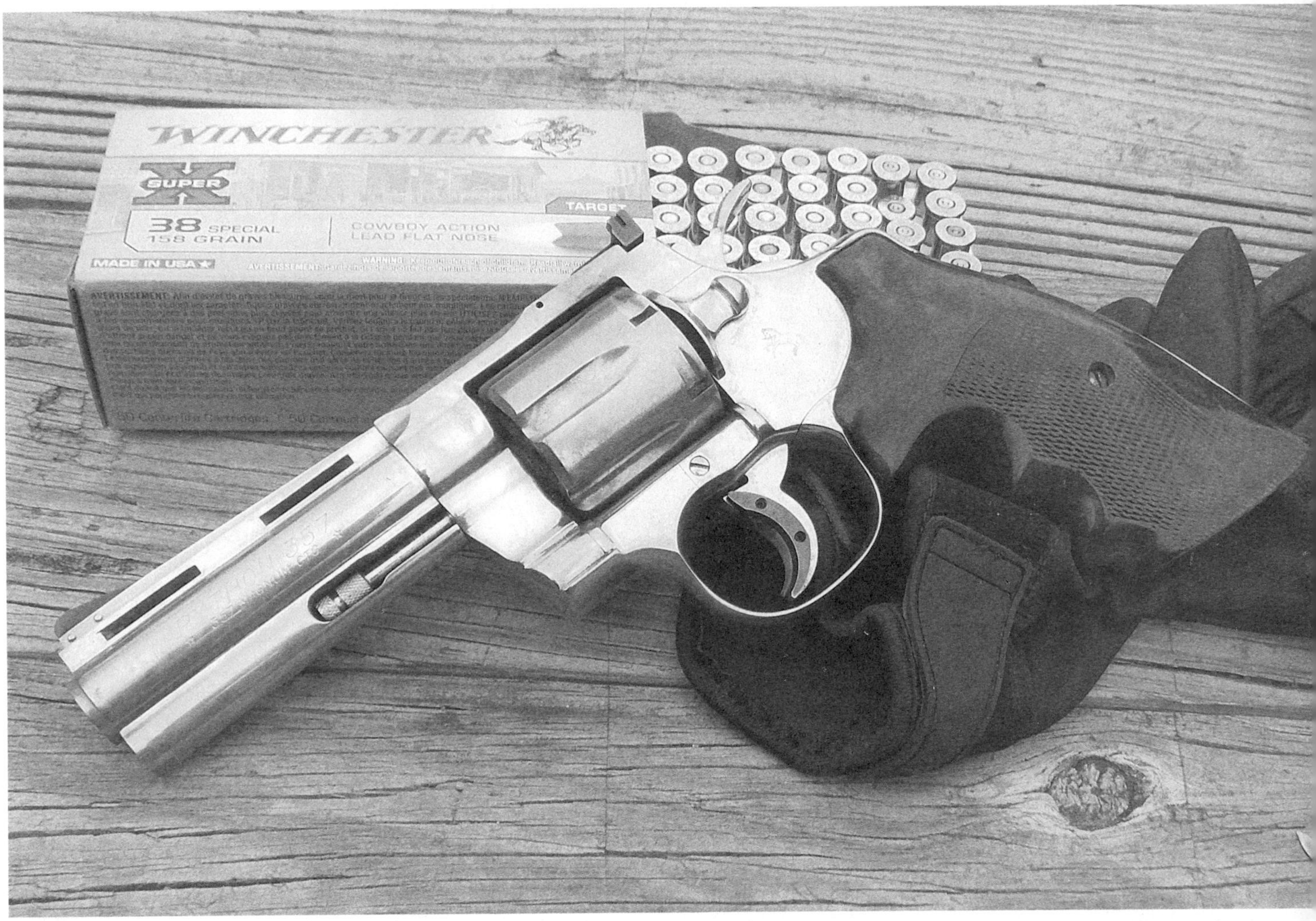

(above) The one and only ... Colt Python. Still a superbly accurate revolver, but used ones fetch a pretty penny on the used market.

(left) In full recoil with the .44 Magnum Blackhawk and Winchester's 1,430 fps, 240-grain JHP. Not for the faint of heart.

Custom Shop item and, truth be told, it was always handled as a custom shop gun on a separate assembly line. A great deal of hand-fitting was part of the Python's construction, and in the end this attention to detail is what made it prohibitively expensive. I think that there is little doubt that the Python was the high point of American revolver production. I don't think you will find any disagreement among revolver shooters — the Python is a wonderful icon of Americana.

The Colt embodied a number of improvements that were spurred on by custom makers during the 1930s. It was intended to win matches, and it did, but it also found its way into the game fields. From the snake's introduction in 1955, it was the front runner for Colt. The bluing was rich — Colt Royal Blue has seldom been equaled — and when offered in nickel was among a few that held its finish for many, many years without chipping and peeling. The upper vent rib and lower heavy lug gave the Python unequaled eye appeal and balance. The fully adjustable target sights are excellent designs for accurate fire. Its cylinder locks up with practically no play. The chamber and forcing cone are precisely mated when the cylinder is locked up. The frame, often referred to as a .41 frame, is the original Official Police that did once chamber the .41 Colt in some variations. The .357 Magnum, which the Python chambers, is a far more useful cartridge. The trigger is superbly smooth. It took a great deal of design effort to make a revolver so smooth, one that always cracks the primer reliably. There is a complete lack of staging or any type of rough motion in the Python trigger action. There is a price to pay for this smoothness, and that is that the Python may go out of time and need adjustment more often than an N frame Smith and Wesson revolver, as an example. But the shooter who fires his Python out of time has to work at it. This means perhaps ten-thousand .38 Special cartridges or considerably fewer .357 Magnum rounds. My personal 1971 nickel 4-inch barrel Python is tight, accurate and functions perfectly. Accuracy is excellent. The following table gives a few examples of the best groups fired with this revolver. I broke it out of the safe, checked the action, and shot it at the range (it's a tough job, but someone has to do it).

With proper handloads the .357 Magnum is as accurate as any handgun cartridge.

Table 16-1

Colt Python Groups at 25 yards (average of three, three-shot groups)

Load	Group
.38 Special Black Hills 125-grain +P	1.2 in.
Federal 148-grain Wadcutter/match	.7 in.
.357 Magnum Black Hills 125-gr. JHP	.95 in.
Fiocchi 158-gr. XTP	1.25 in.
Hornady 158-gr. FTX	1.2 in.
Handloads Hornady 125-gr. XTP /1,200 fps/H110	1.0 in.
Matt's Bullets 175-gr. SWC/WW296/1,000 fps	.9 in.
Hornady 180-gr. XTP/H110/1,055 fps	.85 in.

Ruger Blackhawk

If the Colt Python is the finest revolver ever made, then the Ruger Blackhawk single-action is the most rugged. When the ability to take heavy loads is needed, the Blackhawk is probably the most durable handgun ever manufactured for the purpose. When the Blackhawk was first introduced, a machine and fixture cycled a test gun over 50,000 times; plus, over 10,000 full-powder cartridges were fired in that testing. I am certain the revolver is even stronger today. The revolver is also very accurate. Just the same, the Blackhawk isn't always perfect.

Bullet diameter (which can be controlled with hardcast bullets), a smooth barrel, and a properly

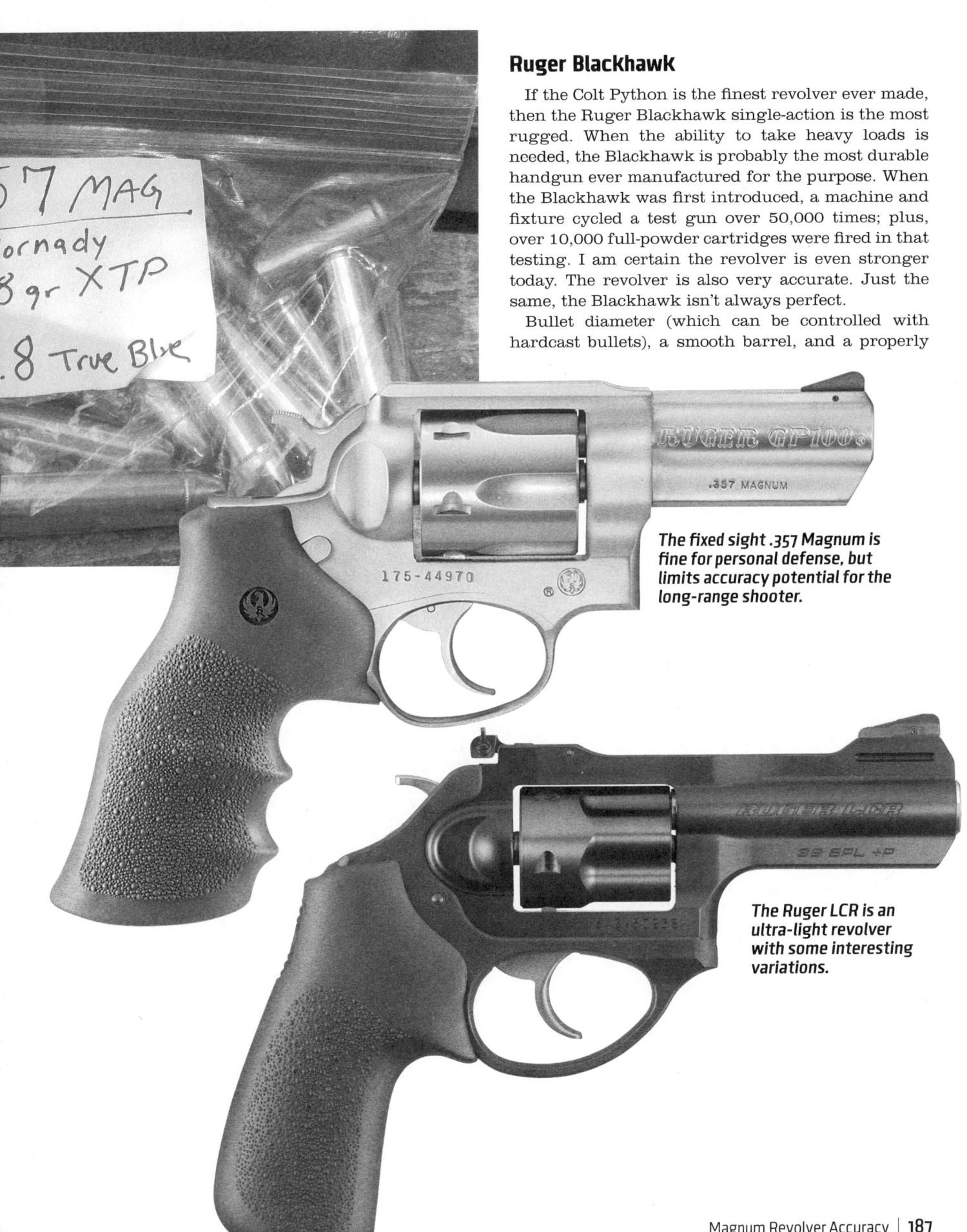

The fixed sight .357 Magnum is fine for personal defense, but limits accuracy potential for the long-range shooter.

The Ruger LCR is an ultra-light revolver with some interesting variations.

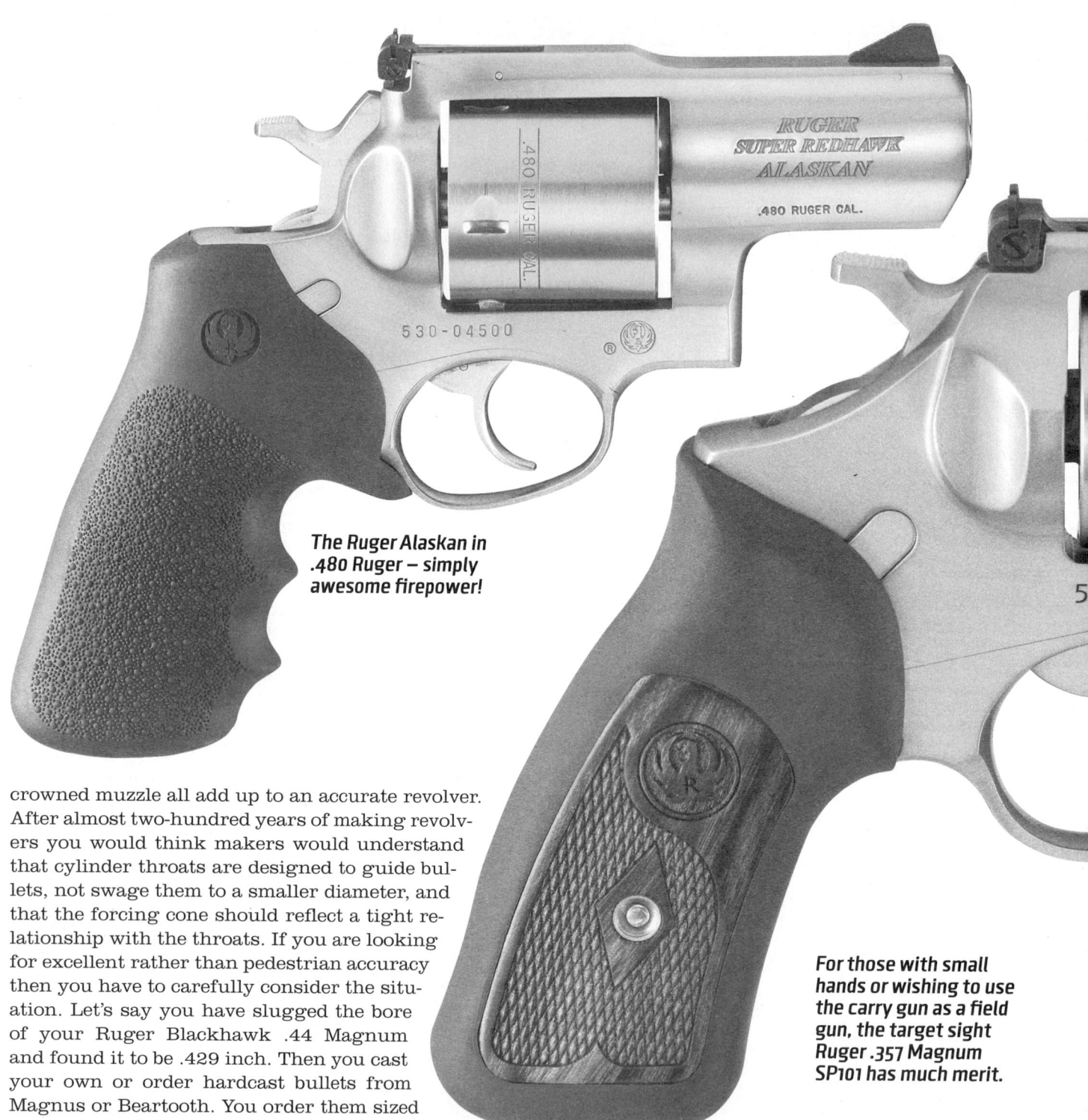

The Ruger Alaskan in .480 Ruger — simply awesome firepower!

For those with small hands or wishing to use the carry gun as a field gun, the target sight Ruger .357 Magnum SP101 has much merit.

crowned muzzle all add up to an accurate revolver. After almost two-hundred years of making revolvers you would think makers would understand that cylinder throats are designed to guide bullets, not swage them to a smaller diameter, and that the forcing cone should reflect a tight relationship with the throats. If you are looking for excellent rather than pedestrian accuracy then you have to carefully consider the situation. Let's say you have slugged the bore of your Ruger Blackhawk .44 Magnum and found it to be .429 inch. Then you cast your own or order hardcast bullets from Magnus or Beartooth. You order them sized .430 and this gives good accuracy. But what if the throats are .428? In that sad state of affairs, the .430-inch bullet will be sized down to .428 and will hit the .429 bore about .001-inch undersize. Gas blow-by makes for less velocity and also less accuracy potential. There are several corrective courses you can take: one is to order parts from Brownells, the other is to choose a reputable gunsmith that will do the work for you. Either course will be profitable in accuracy potential — assuming the revolver indeed has a problem. It seems only certain genera-

tions, or lots of guns have this problem.

I have shot the Ruger Blackhawk revolvers extensively. I have found some more accurate than others, but all accurate enough for most chores. The trigger action should be crisp, with a 3.5-pound let-off not out of the question on a sporting single-action gun. The sights are excellent and the revolver is well-balanced in the hand. The .357 Magnum revolvers are ideal first handguns for those intending to hunt

BUT THE BIG BOY IN HUNTING REVOLVERS IS THE .44 MAGNUM. THERE ARE LARGER HANDGUNS CHAMBERED FOR MODERN MAGNUMS SUCH AS THE .460 AND .500, BUT FOR PRACTICAL USE THE .44 MAG. IS THE BEST ALL-AROUND HEAVY-HITTER THAT ALSO INVITES CONSTANT PRACTICE AND EASY PACKING.

Winchester's modern bullet technology has led to important advancements in magnum cartridge effectiveness.

with a wheelgun. I believe that the 4 5/8-inch barrel .45 Colt is among the most useful Ruger revolvers, at least within 50 yards, for deer-sized game. With quality hardcast bullets or 250-grain XTP jacketed bullets in handloads, these revolvers are often brilliantly accurate.

But the big boy in hunting revolvers is the .44 Magnum. There are larger handguns chambered for modern magnums such as the .460 and .500, but for practical use the .44 Mag. is the best all-around heavy-hitter that also invites constant practice and easy packing. The Ruger Blackhawk in this awesome chambering is affordable and user-friendly for those who practice. In my experience, the Blackhawk revolver in .44 Magnum is more accurate than the .45 Colt. It can be loaded with pleasant-shooting hardcast bullet loads in .44 Special that allow practice with an easy-kicking cartridge. Yet, in the game fields against boar and deer, I have never seen an animal die so quickly as when hit with the .44 Magnum at short to moderate range. Here are a few results with the Ruger .44 Magnum and choice loads.

Table 16-2

Ruger Blackhawk .44 Mag Results 3-shot groups, solid benchrest, 25 yards	
Black Hills 240-gr. JHP	1.9 in.
Black Hills 300-gr. JHP	1.6 in.
Hornady 200-gr. XTP	2.0 in.
Hornady 240-gr. XTP	1.7 in.
Winchester 240-gr. JHP	2.1 in.
Winchester 215-gr. Silvertip	1.85 in.

9MM ACCURACY

The Arex Rex Zero 9mm handgun is among the most accurate new introductions the author has seen in some time.

For many years, shooters regarded the 9mm as a second-rate caliber as compared to the .45 ACP — at least as far as accuracy was concerned. There was little demand for match-grade 9mm ammunition and the handguns were, on average, less accurate than properly set up .45s. In my opinion, much of that has changed. The 9mm is our most popular handgun cartridge and

with good reason. Part of its popularity is economics. It's simply less expensive as a factory cartridge than the .45 ACP. Handloading components are affordable. Modern handgunners shoot more than any previous generation. Concealed carry permit classes, personal defense schools, and IDPA and IPSC competitions account for millions of cartridges fired each year.

Through extensive testing the Rex Zero 9mm has given good results.

The 9mm is more comfortable to shoot than larger calibers. When engaging in long practice sessions, the difference in recoil between the 9mm and .45 is pronounced. With the 9mm you need not go home and rub your wrists after firing a few hundred rounds of ammunition. Accuracy potential of the 9mm is considerably improved with modern bullets and powder combinations. There are those who state that with modern projectiles and +P velocity, the 9mm is as effective in personal defense as the

.45 ACP. Some use murky logic, poor science and unverifiable and unrepeatable 'studies' to support these claims. Of course, the 9mm doesn't have the wound potential of the .45 ACP. Physics do not allow such a leap. But the 9mm is a respectable cartridge with good performance. Its balance of control, accuracy and reliable expansion make it a viable choice for many shooters. You do not have to dismantle one cartridge to build up another and the 9mm can stand on its own merits. Those who practice little will appre-

(above) An important component of modern handguns is the ability to mount a light on a receiver rail. The Rex Zero is one such gun.

Springfield's long-slide XD is an accurate shooter. It's little wonder why so many XD fans prefer this system.

(right) The Glock 19, like many medium-sized 9mm handguns, is easily concealed yet offers good power and a decent reserve of ammunition.

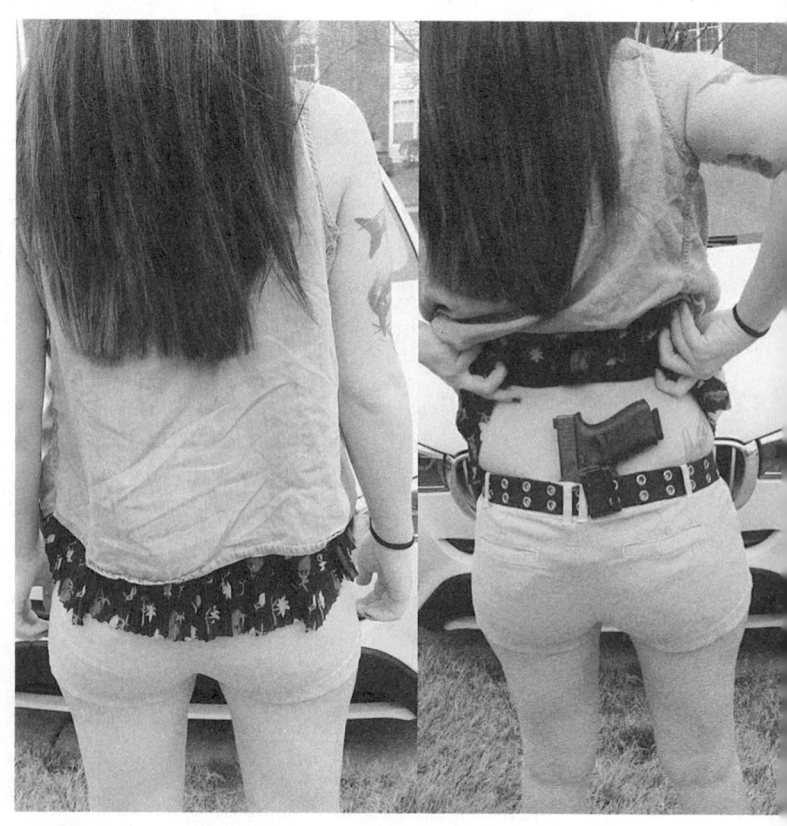

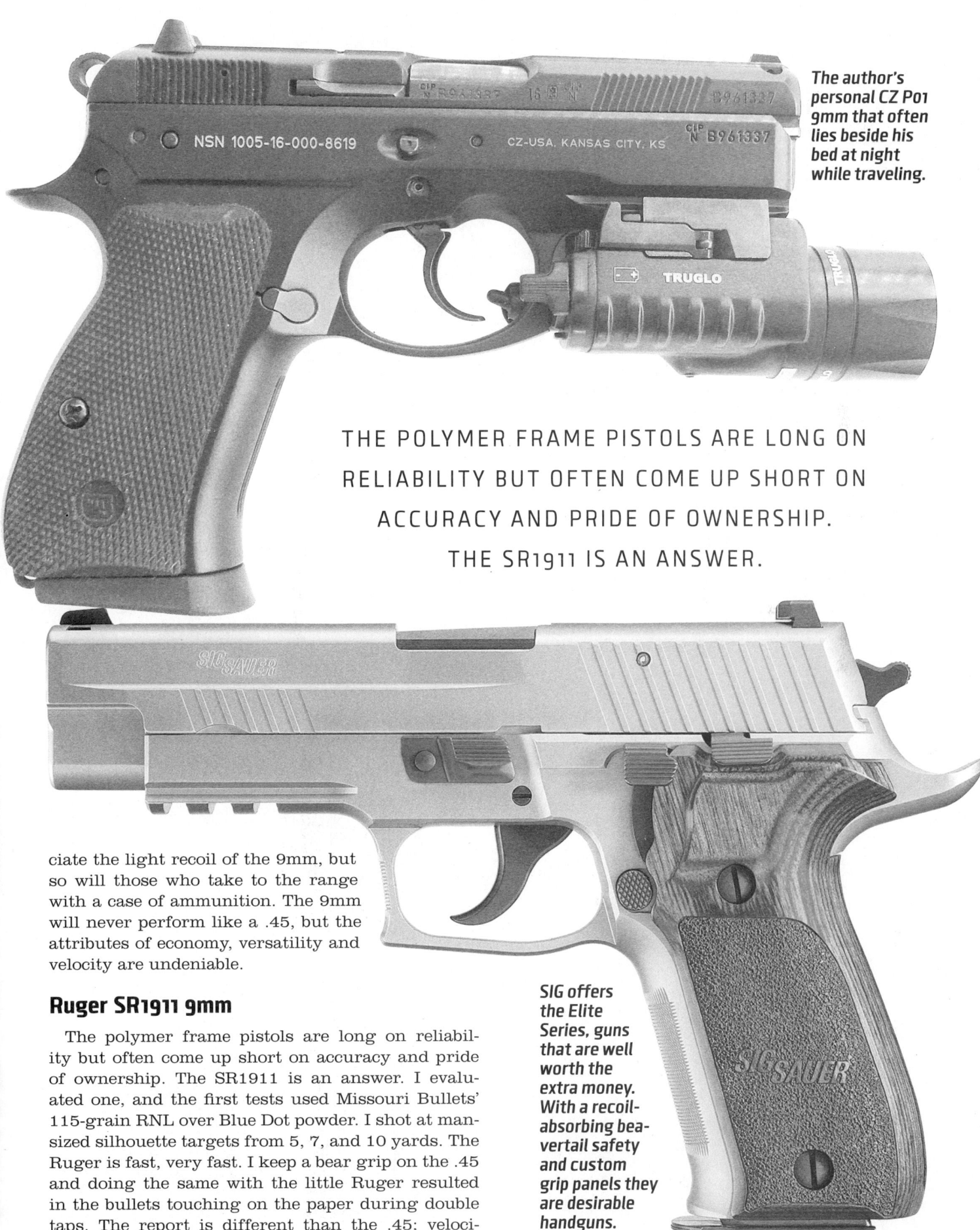

The author's personal CZ P01 9mm that often lies beside his bed at night while traveling.

THE POLYMER FRAME PISTOLS ARE LONG ON RELIABILITY BUT OFTEN COME UP SHORT ON ACCURACY AND PRIDE OF OWNERSHIP. THE SR1911 IS AN ANSWER.

ciate the light recoil of the 9mm, but so will those who take to the range with a case of ammunition. The 9mm will never perform like a .45, but the attributes of economy, versatility and velocity are undeniable.

Ruger SR1911 9mm

The polymer frame pistols are long on reliability but often come up short on accuracy and pride of ownership. The SR1911 is an answer. I evaluated one, and the first tests used Missouri Bullets' 115-grain RNL over Blue Dot powder. I shot at man-sized silhouette targets from 5, 7, and 10 yards. The Ruger is fast, very fast. I keep a bear grip on the .45 and doing the same with the little Ruger resulted in the bullets touching on the paper during double taps. The report is different than the .45; veloci-

SIG offers the Elite Series, guns that are well worth the extra money. With a recoil-absorbing bea-vertail safety and custom grip panels they are desirable handguns.

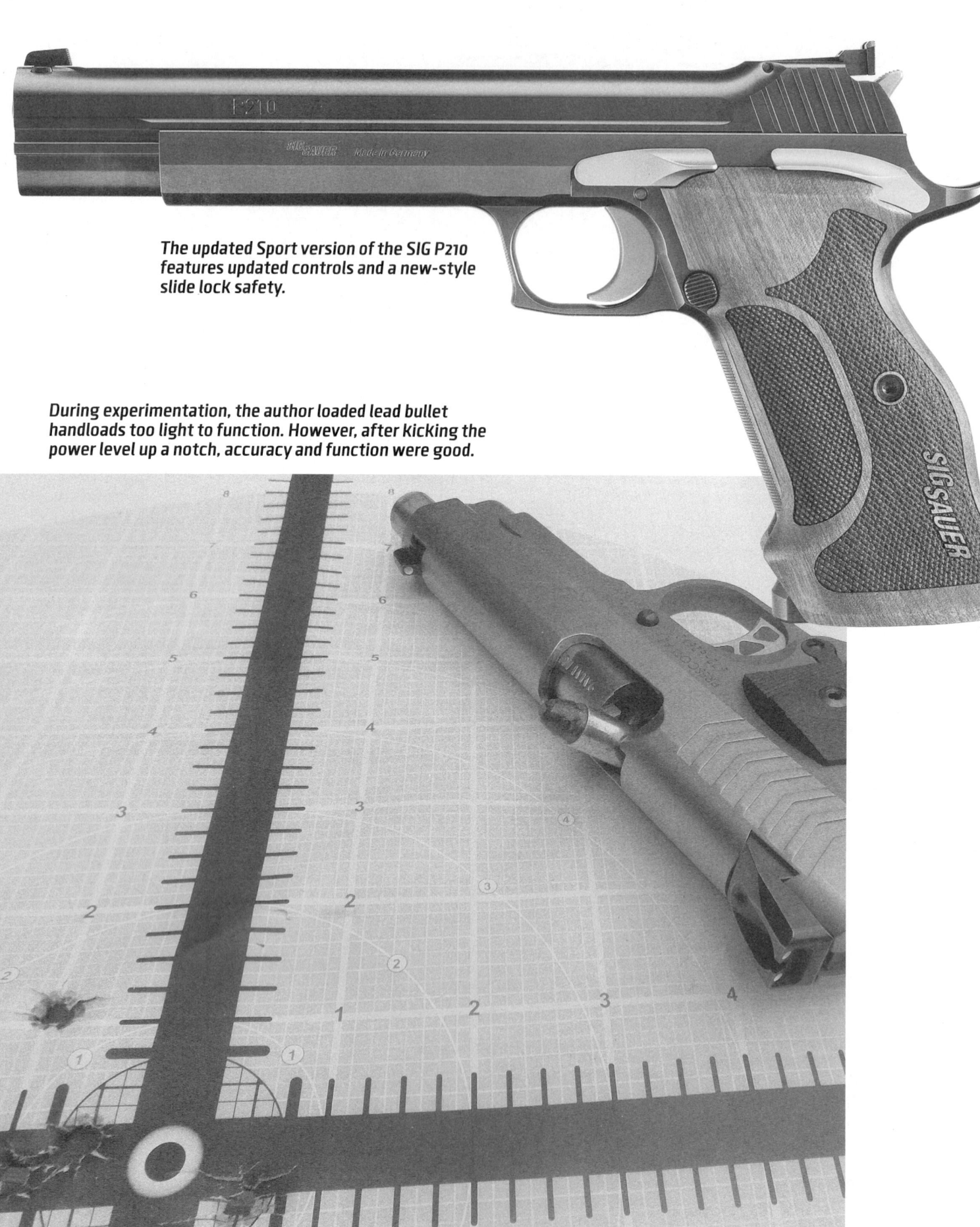

The updated Sport version of the SIG P210 features updated controls and a new-style slide lock safety.

During experimentation, the author loaded lead bullet handloads too light to function. However, after kicking the power level up a notch, accuracy and function were good.

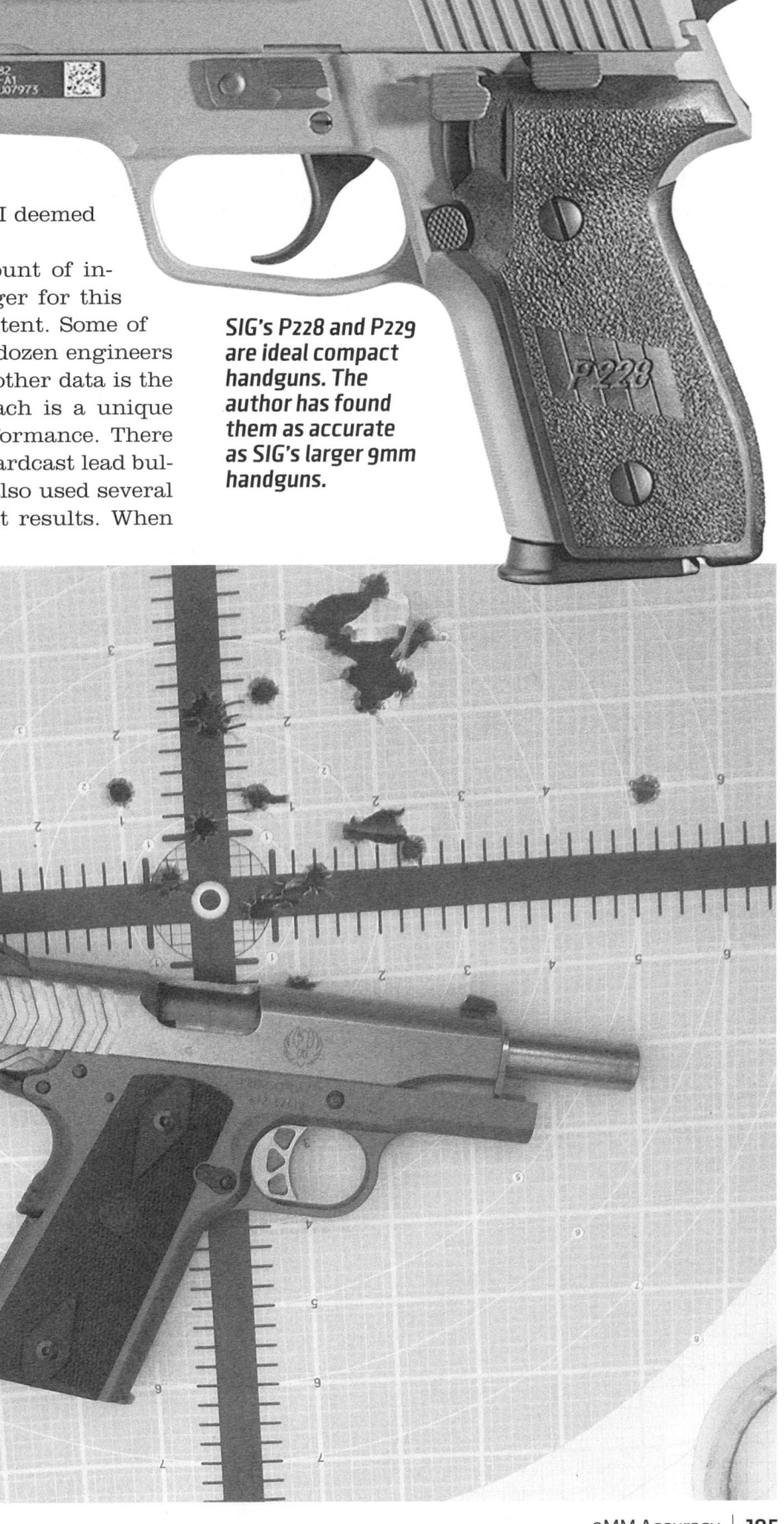

ties of tested ammo ranged from 890 to 1,400 fps. After shooting for accuracy with factory loads I deemed the pistol worth a loading project.

I carefully studied the huge amount of information on loading the 9mm Luger for this project. There is a mountain of content. Some of the information is the product of a dozen engineers with a huge budget at work, while other data is the result of one man's experiment. Each is a unique personality with a passion for performance. There are several routes for 9mm loads. Hardcast lead bullets offer economy and accuracy. I also used several powder-coated bullets with excellent results. When working with light loads the Ruger worked well and functioned reliably in the 950 fps range. These are useful practice loads. Past experience tells me that reduced pressure handloads of this type add to the pistol's longevity. Next, I tested standard loads that propelled a 115- to 124-grain jacketed bullet at 1,050 to 1,150 fps. Then shot were the high performance, or +P loads. These are among the most accurate and the most interesting. I used the Hornady XTP bullet primarily for these but also enjoyed good results with the Speer Gold Dot. Both bullets produced excellent performance in every load. The difference in expansion at 1,200 fps is stark when compared to 1,100 fps. And at 1,300 fps you

SIG's P228 and P229 are ideal compact handguns. The author has found them as accurate as SIG's larger 9mm handguns.

In both slow and rapid fire the SR1911 9mm was a joy to shoot.

are really getting somewhere! The difference is substantial enough to give you reasonable confidence in the 9mm for personal defense. Some of these loads printed surprising accuracy.

While this isn't a long-term test program, it is reasonable to suggest the SR1911 is capable of handling a steady diet of such loads. The 9mm is versatile. The light loads listed below gave good accuracy and would be well-suited to introducing a beginner to centerfire pistol shooting, while the heavy loads will handle small game, predators and two-legged attackers. The Ruger's superb trigger and sights are an aid in this pursuit. In combat shooting, the Ruger is an excellent pistol. Hang onto it like you would a .45 and you will see good results on paper. As the tables below show, accuracy is good to excellent. There are no dogs in the show, all loads I worked up gave acceptable results but a few produced outstanding groups. I was particularly impressed by the heavy loads. The SR1911 9mm just may see more use than I originally intended. I like this pistol — it is tight, accurate, light enough for daily carry and pleasing to own. Ruger has succeeded on both the technical and commerce side.

Table 17-1
Ruger SR1911 9mm Load Data

Bullet (grains)	Powder (grains)	Velocity (fps)	25 Yard Group (in.)
Lead Bullets Missouri Bullet Company			
115-gr. RNL	4.8 True Blue	990 fps	2.8
	6.0 Unique	1,135 fps	2.5
125-gr. Hi-Tek	4.4 WW231	1,166 fps	2.0
	6.0 Unique	1,154 fps	1.9
	4.8 True Blue	1,020 fps	2.5
Bayou Bullets (Coated) 115-gr. RN	5.8 Unique	1,125 fps	2.5
	4.2 Red Dot	1,040 fps	2.9
124-gr. TCG	6.0 Unique	1,170 fps	1.9
	4.5 W-W WSF	990 fps	2.25
	4.4 W-W 231	1,011 fps	2.3
135-gr. RN	4.0 Unique	950 fps	2.6
	4.1 Unique	974 fps	2.65
	4.8 Titegroup	1,070 fps	2.4
147-gr. FP	3.0 Titegroup	890 fps	2.0
Jacketed Bullets Speer 115-gr. Gold Dot	7.0 HS6	1,201 fps	2.25
	8.2 HS6	1,290 fps*	2.5
	4.8 Titegroup	1,150 fps	2.0
	7.0 Power Pistol	1,270 fps*	2.25
Hornady 115-gr. XTP	6.8 VV 3n37	1,313 fps*	1.9
	5.6 WW WSF	1,190 fps	1.8
	5.4 Power Pistol	1,259 fps*	2.4
Hornady 147-gr. XTP	4.4 Unique	930 fps	2.0

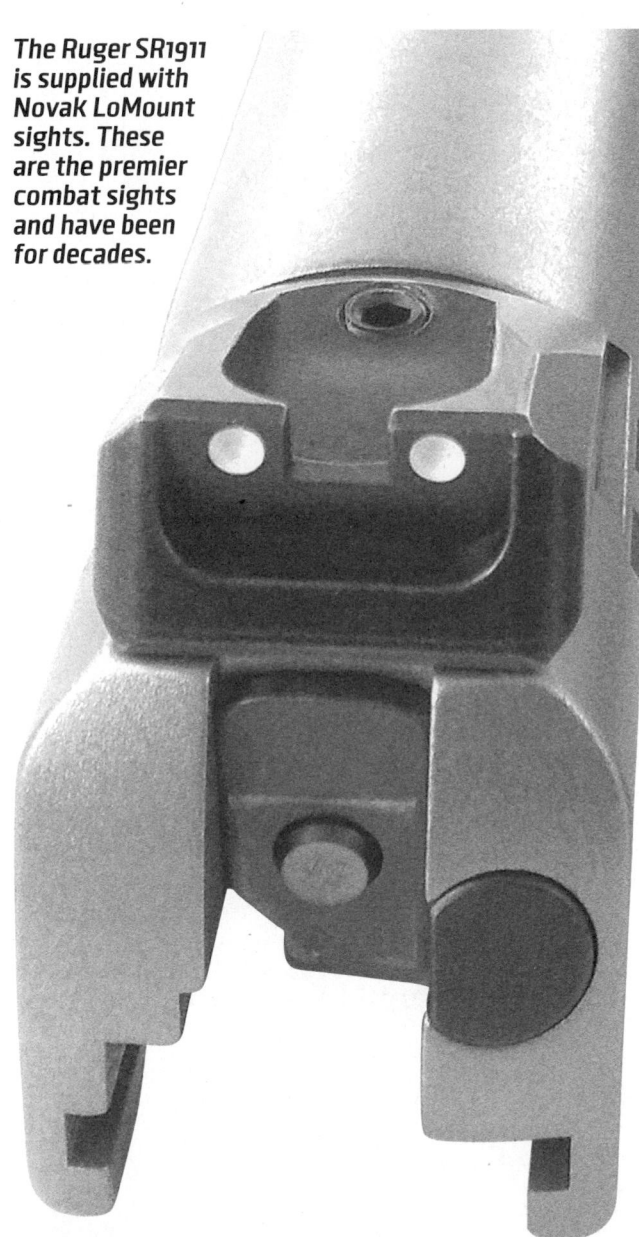

The Ruger SR1911 is supplied with Novak LoMount sights. These are the premier combat sights and have been for decades.

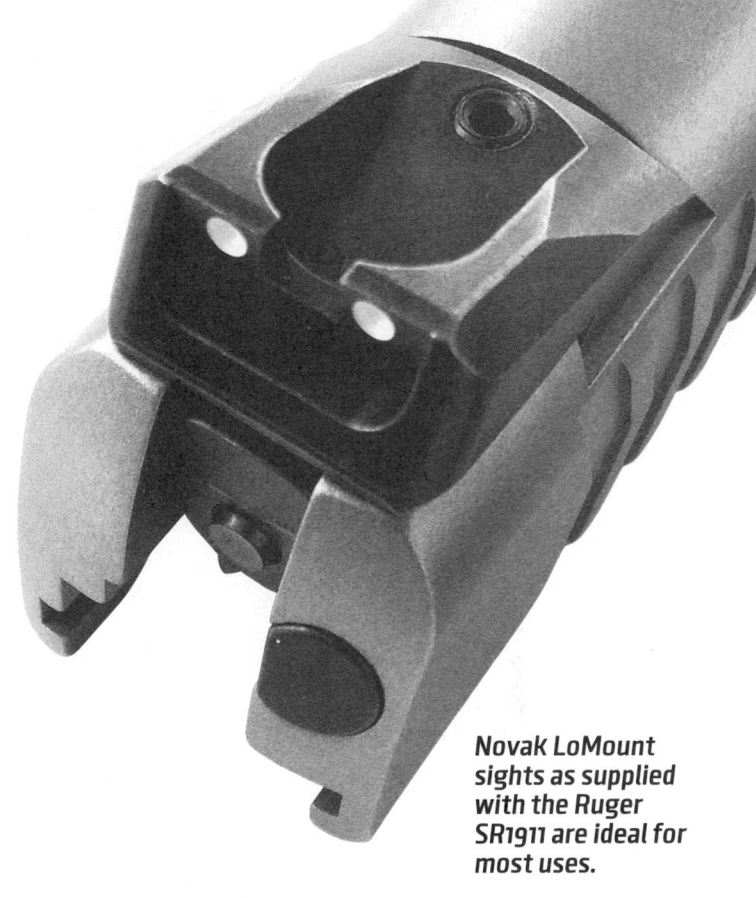

Novak LoMount sights as supplied with the Ruger SR1911 are ideal for most uses.

Table 17-2

Factory Load Testing		
Black Hills 124-gr. JHP	1,080 fps	1.9
Black Hills 115-gr. EXP	1,256 fps	2.3
SIG Elite 115-gr. FMJ	1,170 fps	2.9
SIG Elite 124-gr. V Crown JHP	1,167 fps	2.25

Table 17-3

Comparison Velocity, Browning Hi Power, 5-inch barrel			
Missouri Bullet 115-gr. RNL	4.8 True Blue	1,035 fps	N/A
Hornady 124-gr. XTP	6.2 Unique	1,172 fps	N/A

Shot in Rex Zero FDE 9mm			
Hornady 115-grain XTP	6.8 VV 3n37	1,330 fps*	2.3
	5.6 WW WSF	1,179 fps	1.8
Hornady 124-grain XTP	6.0 Unique	1,160 fps	2.5
	4.4 Titegroup	1,137 fps	2.4
	5.4 Power Pistol	1,272 fps*	1.8

(right) Control with a 9mm 1911 is excellent; such pistols are a joy to shoot.

(below) Even compact handguns such as the Honor Guard 9mm are easy enough to control in 9mm.

SIG's V-Crown 9mm hollowpoint is not only accurate and clean-burning, its wound ballistics cannot be faulted.

FACTORY AMMUNITION AND ACCURACY

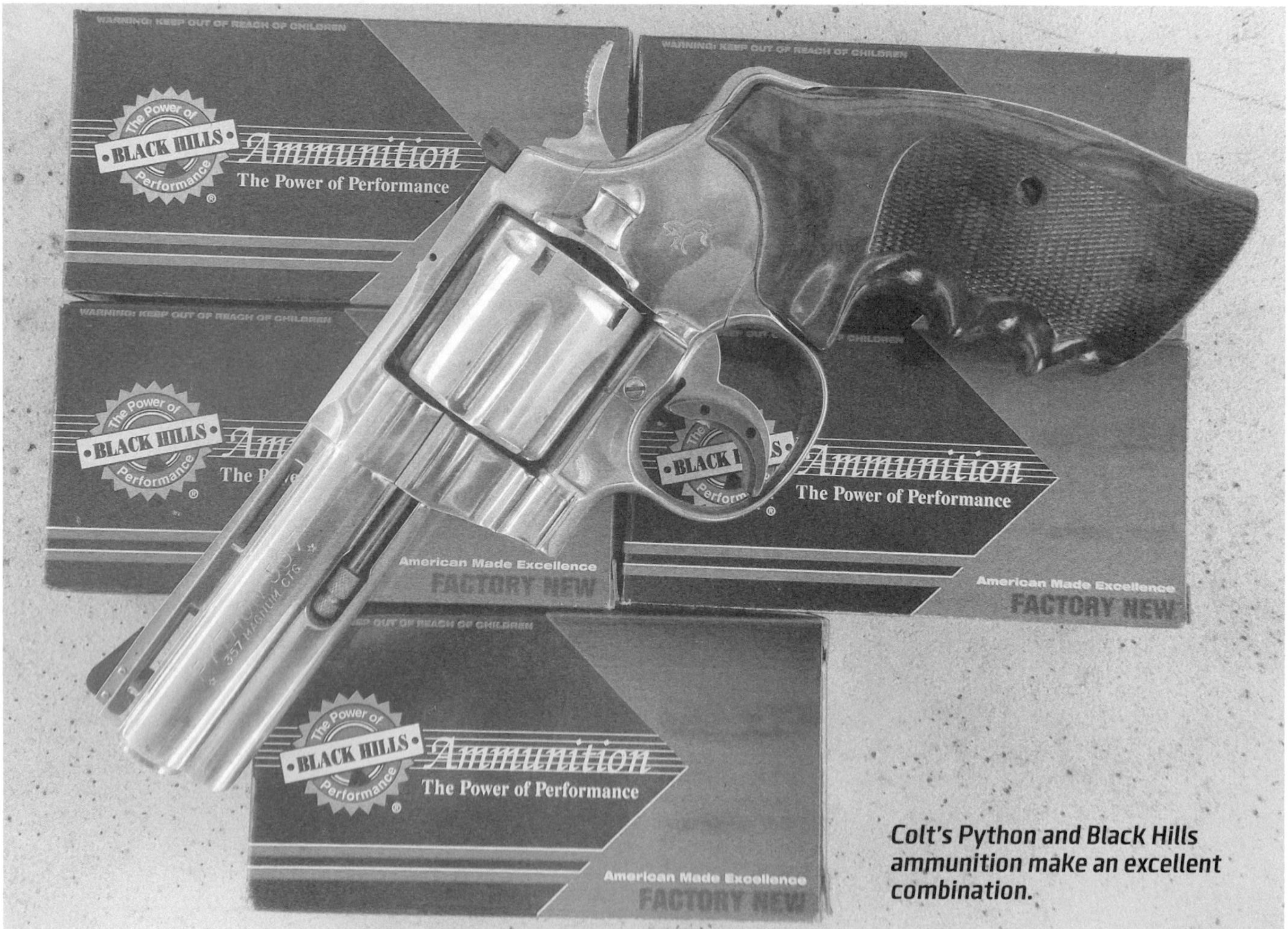

Colt's Python and Black Hills ammunition make an excellent combination.

There are many phrases repeated concerning factory ammunition and accuracy. Some of them are true, many are misconceptions. Others are terribly off base. Over the years, I have shot most of the factory loads available from the major makers. I have seen manufacturers come and go. Some of the now-defunct ones were skilled, but the loads filled a narrow niche or the economic downturn took its toll. Others found making hardcast pistol bullets more profitable. Some were simply swept aside by the vagaries of a niche market and changing demands.

The big three — Federal, Remington and Winchester — have survived based on quality and brand loyalty. They have been around a long, long time and have supplied billions of cartridges in times of war

Black Hills ammo in .45 ACP has given excellent results in a wide range of handguns.

Modern ammunition is highly developed for accuracy, reliability and terminal effect.

and peace. Following the big three we have Black Hills Ammunition and Hornady Manufacturing. These are no small concerns, manufacturing billions of cartridges for the police and military as well as civilian users. These companies manufacture ammunition for practice, hunting, and personal defense.

There is Fiocchi, originally an Italian company, now employing many skilled workers in a plant in Ozark, Missouri. CorBon and Buffalo Bore manufacture high-performance ammunition. Double Tap began supplying true 10mm loads and now offers many good choices in the popular calibers. They offer good-quality loads in 9mm and .38 Super that are effective and accurate. Buffalo Bore makes hard-hitting loads with heavy, hardcast bullets that offer real performance in the field. Several traditional calibers, such as the .45 Colt, are maximized by them.

Single-action revolvers are more accurate than most shooters realize, given the right ammunition.

CorBon produces fast-stepping personal defense loads with real power. Gorilla Ammunition is a new company with much promise, concentrating on personal defense loads with all copper JHP loads. SIG Sauer has introduced a line of cartridges that use FMJ bullets for practice and a well-thought-out V-Crown JHP option for personal defense. Quality is high. Barnes Bullets has a notable line of personal protection ammo with their all-copper bullets. Nosler's personal defense line includes a number of excellent choices in 9mm, .40 and .45.

These ammunition companies use a combination of automation and human hands so there is sometimes a variance from perfect accuracy. Yet, arguably, the makers offer the finest ammunition ever produced in Amer-

Buffalo Bore maximizes the .44 Special and provides excellent performance.

Double Tap loads are recommended by the maker for the Honor Guard pistol.

ica and the world. As just one example, in 1916, Winchester was awarded an ammunition contract with the stipulation that primer failure be kept to one in 100,000 cartridges. The standard was met and exceeded; yet, the standard is much higher today.

Is there one maker or one load with a proven superior product that is apt to prove more accurate in your handgun than another? In a real sense, you get what you pay for. There are bargain basement loads and foreign loads with inferior powder technology and quality control. Even the big makers offer generic ball that doesn't have the reputation of factory match loads. It is no secret that quality handguns will prefer one load over the other. Just the same, a load that proves accurate in one handgun will seldom prove to be a dog in another. The major makers offer lines of ammunition with RNL, or non-expanding FMJ bullets for practice. Federal's American Eagle and Winchester's USA lines are among these. Black Hills Ammunition offers a Blue Box remanufactured line that uses recycled brass. While affordable, it is reliable and accurate enough for training.

Companies such as Buffalo Bore produce only premium loads. CorBon puts out JHP loads exclusively, save for some hardcast hunting cartridges. In general, the less expensive lines from various makers offer good utility for shooting and action competition. A primary cost-cutting measure is the elimination

38 Super +P
115gr. Barnes TAC-XP
1425fps / 5" bbl.
20 cartridges

38 Super +P
125gr Bonded Defense® JHP
1350fps / 5" bbl.

38 Super +P
115gr Controlled
Expansion™ JHP
1495fps / 5" bbl.

Double Tap ammunition makes some fast-stepping, very accurate loads in .38 Super.

Super
nded Def
50fps / 5"

Ammunition can be both powerful and accurate. Don't assume that light target loadings are required for match-grade accuracy. Sometimes you can have it both ways.

of both primer seal and case mouth seal. These seals aren't necessary in bulk practice ammo. Now, such generic loads are plenty reliable and affordable. In fact, I have seen thousands of them fired in my training classes without a hiccup. But they should not be chosen for critical use — for everyday carry, for example. They lack the proper primer seal for use in defensive applications and their non-expanding bullet limits terminal effectiveness. Still, they are among the most useful factory loads for function testing or IDPA and IPSC competition for those who do not handload. For 50-yard bullseye competition, perhaps a more accurate loading is needed, such as standouts like the Black Hills remanufactured line, which offers better accuracy than you would expect. Sometimes quality manufacture trumps mismatched cartridge cases, as any careful handloader will tell you. Fiocchi doesn't offer a burner line but

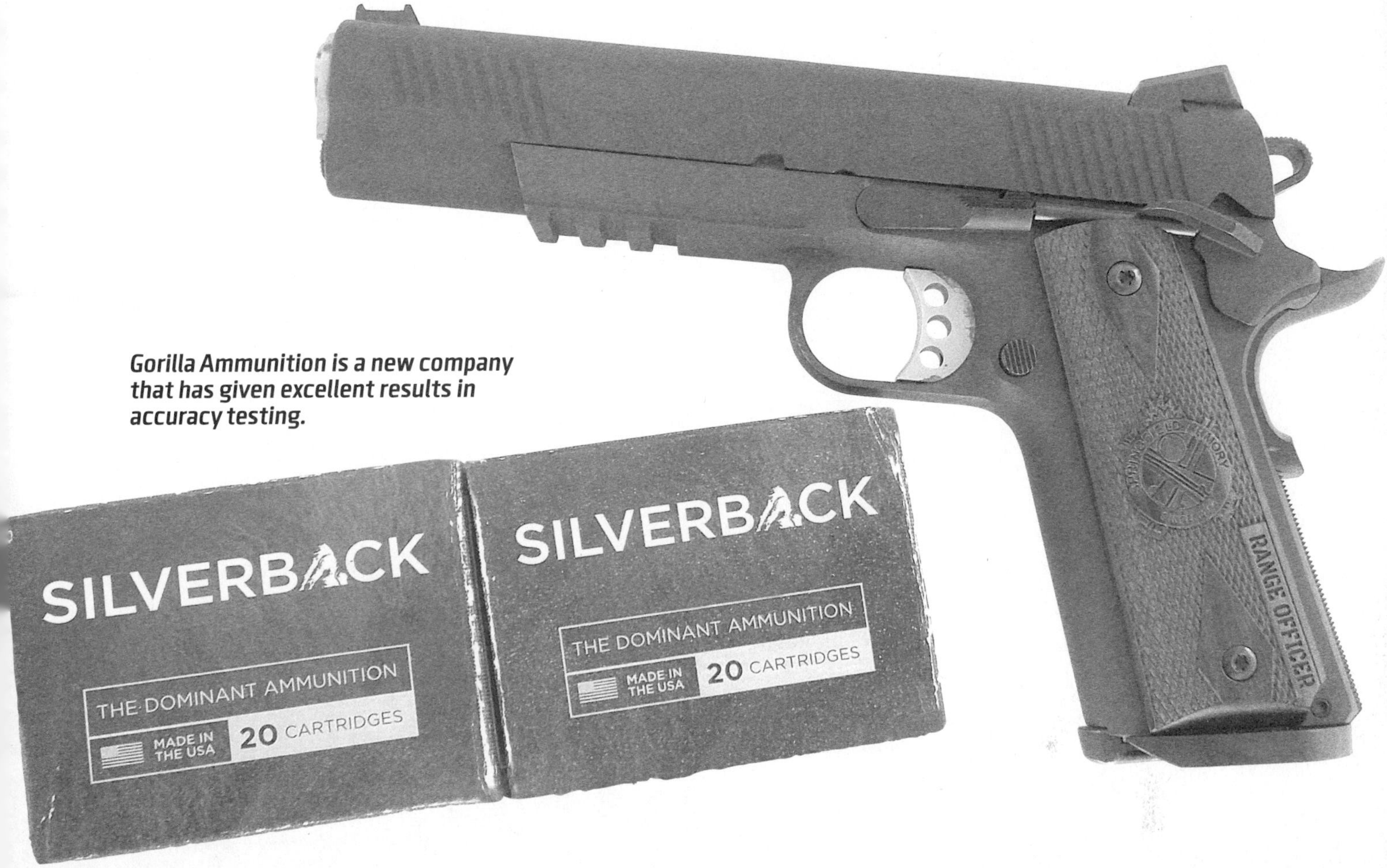

Gorilla Ammunition is a new company that has given excellent results in accuracy testing.

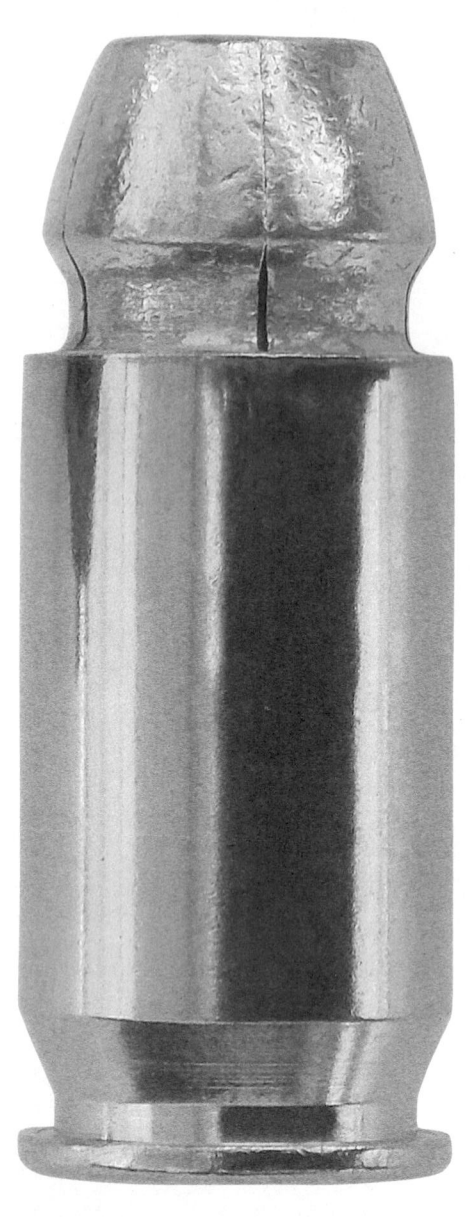

The FBI-level penetration of .45 ACP from a Gorilla Ammunition load. You can do things with all-copper bullets that cannot be done with cup and core projectiles.

POWDER TECHNOLOGY ISN'T AS HIGHLY DEVELOPED IN SOME COUNTRIES AS IT IS HERE IN THE U.S., AND OVERSEAS LOADS ARE SOMETIMES DIRTY AND INCONSISTENT.

The author has found CZ and Hornady to be a good combination.

concentrates on affordable FMJ loads. Their ammunition consistently gives good accuracy results. There are a number of pretty lousy offerings from regional makers and steel-cased foreign loads that are not up to snuff for many uses.

Not long ago, I tested an ammo sample that refused to properly feed and eject in my CZ 75 pistol. As described earlier, the military-grade CZ is famous for digesting anything reasonable, so I immediately suspected this load was off spec. It turned out that the cartridge case rim was too small for proper function. This was an aggravation and accuracy, as may be expected,

NSN 1005-16-000-8619

Hornady 9MM LUGER
115 gr XTP®
#90244
Muzzle 50 yds 100 yds
1155 fps 1038 958

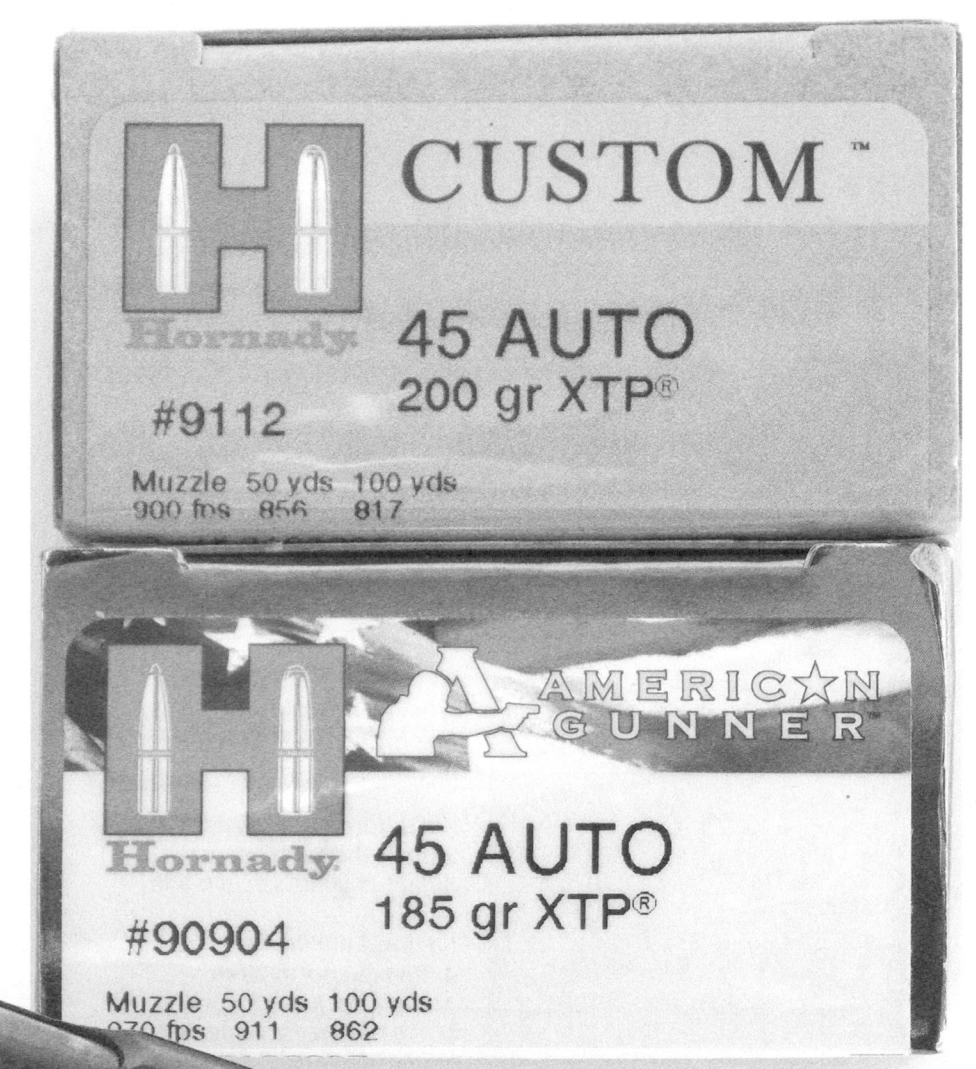

CUSTOM™

Hornady

45 AUTO
#9112   **200 gr XTP®**

Muzzle 50 yds 100 yds
900 fps 856   817

AMERICAN GUNNER™

Hornady

45 AUTO
#90904   **185 gr XTP®**

Muzzle 50 yds 100 yds
970 fps 911   862

Hornady offers a new branding called American Gunner that features affordable but accurate loadings.

And, often, factory generic ball isn't any more expensive when purchased from the major retailers. With proper care in loading and market pressure demanding quality ammunition, generic loads should offer a similar value and accuracy on par with the big three, and they often do. For the most part, the accuracy produced by these loads is enough for the task at hand. For most of us, brand loyalty is important. I grew up shooting Winchester ammunition. The difference in quality was significant compared to experiences with other makers at the time. Then Federal offered a special run of .38 Special at a very good price and I recognized the quality of these loads in my first experience with them. The morale: Try all types and brands with an open mind.

Some factory ammunition is loaded to match-grade standards. Among my favorites are Federal 230-grain Match .45 ACP and the Black Hills 148-grain wadcutter in .38 Special. Winchester's 158-grain .38 Special SWC is another gem. These loads are useful in testing the accuracy of any handgun and realistically expecting the best performance. They are manufactured to exacting standards and suitable for the most demanding matches. The only loads superior to these will be carefully crafted han-

was inconsistent. Powder technology isn't as highly developed in some countries as it is here in the U.S., and overseas loads are sometimes dirty and inconsistent. Achieving a full powder burn with minimal ash is a product of the proper powder charge, good bullet pull, and intelligent powder choice. While I understand the concept of the least expensive loads for practice, meaningful accuracy testing isn't possible with these loads.

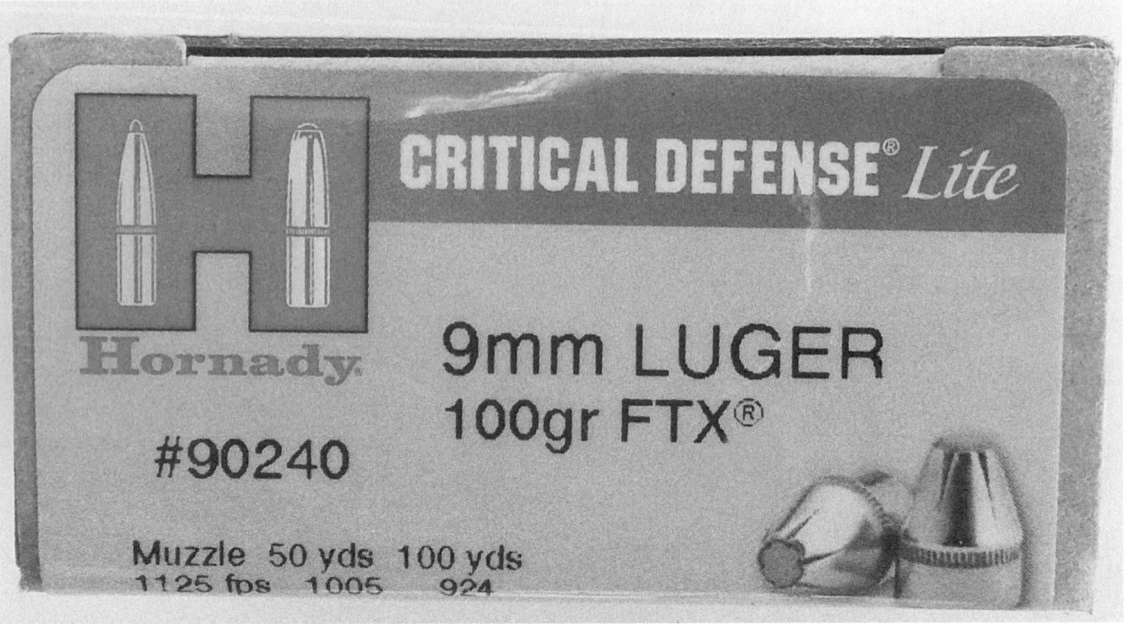

(above) Hornady offers a low-recoil line that, incidentally, is also quite accurate.

(left) Hornady's XTP is among the most accurate handgun bullets ever made.

(below) Looking for good ammo quality at a fair price? Check out Fiocchi's stand out loads, some of which are consistently accurate.

dloads loaded to exacting standards. Quality handloads with much research and development behind them can exceed the accuracy potential of many match factory loads in some handguns. So, match-grade loads are more accurate than generic or standard loads and they should be.

But there is another class of cartridge that often exhibits sterling accuracy. These are the highly developed personal defense loads. Exacting quality control and tight tolerances are the reason. For obvious reasons, service and personal defense loads must be reliable. Cartridge

integrity must be high. Such high-pressure ammunition demands strict quality control. Defensive loads must be consistent. The Black Hills 124-grain +P and the Federal 124-grain HST 9mm are rock solid reliable. You cannot afford otherwise in a personal defense or service grade loading. By the same token, the expense of these loads, while justified, precludes firing them at every range outing. That is why you need to handload! The best of these loads — Black Hills Defense, Federal HST and Hydra-Shok, Speer Gold Dot, Hornady XTP and Critical Defense and Winchester PDX — are often very accurate in quality handguns. There are certain loads that have developed an excellent reputation among professional handgunners. One is the Hornady .45 ACP 200-grain XTP, a wonderfully accurate bullet, which is available as a handloading component. The question is, does the load suit your tactical, hunting or competition needs? Accuracy is

GM45A

FEDERAL PREMIUM

45 AUTO
230 GRAIN FULL METAL JACKET
GOLD MEDAL® MATCH

(above) Federal Gold Match is legendary ammo that really does win pistol matches.

(below) SIG offers three good choices in .45 ACP. The author finds all of them accurate and reliable, but prefers the 230-grain loading.

This is an expanded Federal HST. Not only is the load a dynamic defense load, but accuracy is excellent.

relative, but when you can have sterling accuracy you should take it along with bullet performance. That is a large point of this book: The final determiner of accuracy is quality control and consistent manufacture.

The powder charge must be consistent and the bullet weight the proper grains for good bullet pull against the powder gas expansion to achieve full powder burn and limited muzzle flash. Muzzle flash is unburned powder, something to be avoided. The crimp must be consistent. The bullet should have plenty of bearing surface to meet the bore. A jack-

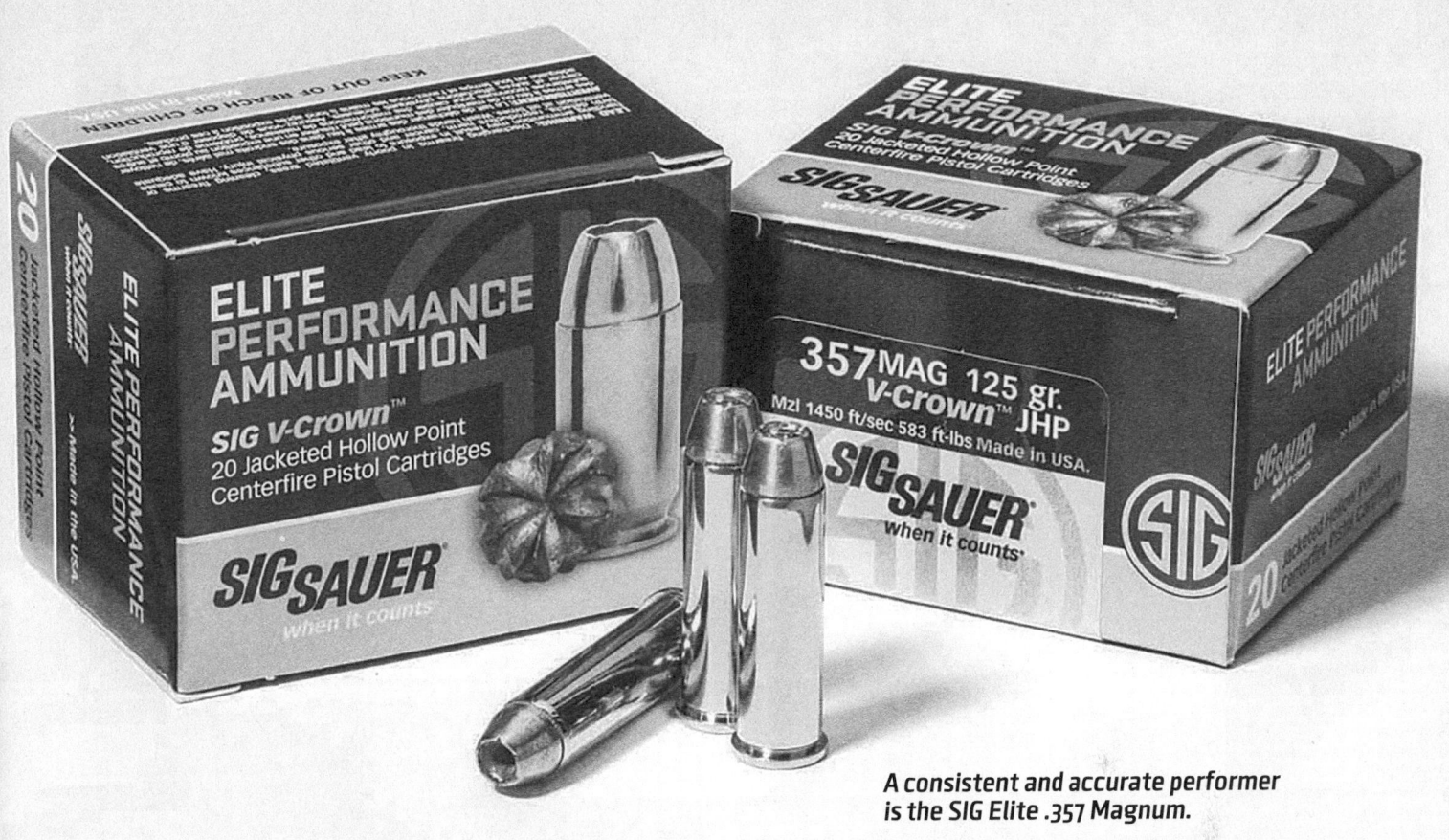

A consistent and accurate performer is the SIG Elite .357 Magnum.

eted hollowpoint bullet is better balanced than a full metal jacket bullet. Therefore, hollowpoints will generally be more accurate. A semi-wadcutter bullet is also more accurate than a round nose one. While I am primarily concerned with accuracy in a quality load in an accurate handgun, the JHP often is most accurate and best suited for personal defense. For target shooting, whatever is less expensive is good and a JHP isn't necessary. I keep coming back to the Hornady XTP in super accurate handloads. The XTP gives good feed reliability, is very consistent in bullet weight and diameter, and has the perfect balance for accuracy. The design takes the bore well with plenty of bearing surface. The XTP is a good bullet to start with and many will remain with it.

A popular and highly developed type of projectile found in factory ammunition is the solid copper hollowpoint. Pioneered by Barnes, these bullets offer good performance. However, they are expensive. On average, I believe other types are more accurate, but it takes a lot of shooting to prove this out. For what they are designed to do, the slight differences in ac-

curacy at personal defense ranges do not matter. The cup and core type JHP bullets offered by Hornady, Speer and Sierra are accurate, and some are among the most accurate choices. The all-copper bullets take the bore in a different manner and, while accurate, may not be match-grade accurate — no surprises there. In some ways, the discussion is irrelevant as the solid copper bullets are prohibitively expensive for constant use.

The question of factory load accuracy is best answered by consistent and proper testing over a long period of time. There are tiers of performance among factory loads with many offering basically the same performance. There are some safe assumptions: generic ball loads are generally less accurate. They are useful for offhand fire, for action competition, and for training. They have the advantages of relatively modest expense compared to other loads and that they are full powder and suited for use in IPSC competition. Few shooters are able to shoot up to the potential of these loads in offhand fire. For bullseye and other competitions that demand absolute accu-

When testing ammunition, be certain to use a quality chronograph and take careful notes. Both accuracy and the standard deviation of velocity between shots is important.

I KNOW MANY ACCOMPLISHED SHOOTERS WHO DO NOT HAVE TIME TO HANDLOAD OR TEST FIRE EVERY LOADING. TIME AND MONEY ARE IN SHORT SUPPLY. MANY PURCHASE THE LEAST EXPENSIVE AMMUNITION AND HOPE FOR THE BEST. THE MORE EXPENSIVE HUNTING AND PERSONAL DEFENSE LOADS ARE NOT PRACTICAL FOR CONSTANT USE. THERE ARE ALSO ACCOMPLISHED SHOOTERS WHO USE ONLY HANDLOADED AMMUNITION. SOME SHOOT INEXPENSIVE GENERIC BALL LOADS FOR TRAINING AND SHORT RANGE COURSES OF COMPETITION, RETAINING THE MATCH LOADS FOR LONG-RANGE USE

racy, match-grade loads are best. When coupled with a capable handgun, match loads are amazingly accurate. Next are premium service loads, which may be match grade in some offerings. They are highly developed. Service grade loads can be pleasantly accurate due to demands placed on makers by various agencies.

When the FBI was looking for a new SWAT pistol, the agency demanded that it place five shots of the service load, a readily available factory 230-grain JHP, in 1.25 inches at 25 yards. The Springfield Operator 1911 fed with Remington's 230-grain Golden Saber load met this criteria. That is an incredible showing even after 20,000 rounds of ammunition were fired. I was skeptical at the time, but as I followed the testing I became convinced.

I know many accomplished shooters who do not have time to handload or test fire every loading. Time and money are in short supply. Many purchase the least expensive ammunition and hope for the best.

The more expensive hunting and personal defense loads are not practical for constant use. There are also accomplished shooters who use only handloaded ammunition. Some shoot inexpensive generic ball loads for training and short range courses of competition, retaining the match loads for long-range use. This is a good program. Even an advanced handloader will need a factory load as an exemplary load to test and confirm accuracy. Factory ammunition is far higher quality today than when I first became a handgunner. At one time, the accuracy of factory ammunition was a poor second to handloads. Today, the spread has narrowed and the handloader is challenged to meet and exceed the standard set by factory ammunition. For the shooter who understands his needs, factory ammunition offers acceptable performance. The tests performed in the accompanying tables show my results with a number of the finest loads available. These loads will give you every advantage for accuracy.

Winchester's reputation for reliable ammuntion is second to none.

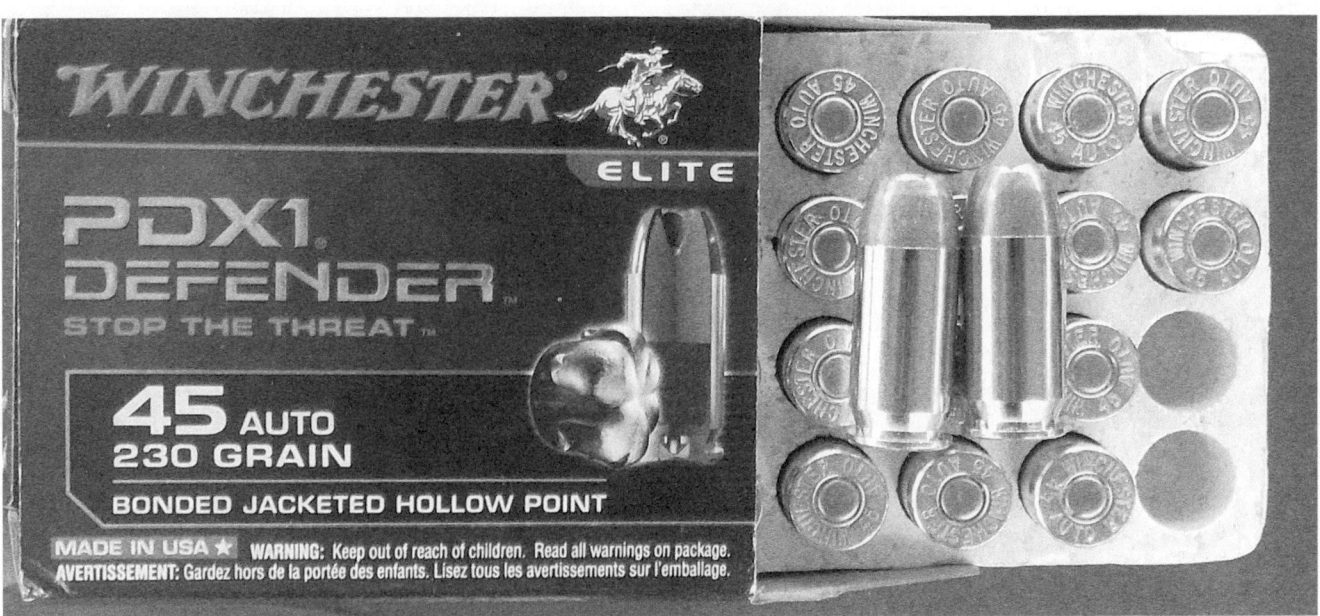

Accuracy Testing Factory Ammunition

Table 18-1
Handgun CZ75B 9mm

Load		
Black Hills 124-gr. JHP	1,090 fps	2.0 in.
Hornady 124-gr. +P	1,187 fps	2.1 in.
Fiocchi 115-gr. Extrema	1,101 fps	1.9 in.
SIG Sauer 124-gr. JHP	1,167 fps	2.3 in.
Federal 124-gr. HST	1,180 fps	2.25 in.
Winchester 124-gr. PDX +P	1,198 fps	2.5 in.
Gorilla Ammo 135-gr. JHP	960 fps	2.45 in.

Table 18-2
SIG P226 9mm

Load	Velocity	25-Yard Group
Black Hills 124-gr. +P	1,190 fps	2.25 in.
Winchester 115-gr. JHP	1,155 fps	2.5 in.
Hornady 147-gr. XTP	960 fps	2.0 in.
Speer 147-gr. Gold Dot	980 fps	2.25 in.

Table 18-3
CZ P01 9mm

Load	Velocity	25-Yard Group
Black Hills 115-gr. TAC +P	1,149 fps	2.5 in.
Hornady 115-gr. Critical Defense	1,160 fps	2.0 in.
Winchester 124-gr. PDX +P	1,180 fps	1.8 in.
Fiocchi 124-gr. JHP Extrema	1,099 fps	2.25 in

Table 18-4
Glock 22 .40 S&W

Load	Velocity	25-Yard Group
Hornady 155-gr. XTP	1,109 fps	3.0 in.
Winchester 155-gr. Silvertip	1,160 fps	3.2 in.
Fiocchi 170-gr. FMJ	1,020 fps	2.5 in.
Nosler 200-gr. JHP	890 fps	2.75 in.

Table 18-5
CZ 75B .40 S&W

Load	Velocity	25-Yard Group
Black Hills 180-gr. JHP	970 fps	2.5 in.
Winchester 180-gr. JHP	980 fps	2.4 in.
Hornady 155-gr. JHP	960 fps	2.65 in.
Federal 165-gr. Hydra-Shok	990 fps	2.3 in.

Table 18-6
Smith and Wesson M&P .38 Special

Load	Velocity	25-Yard Group
Black Hills 148-gr. WC	760 fps	2.0 in.
Winchester 158-gr. SWC	830 fps	2.5 in.
Buffalo Bore 158-gr. SWCHP +P	1,010 fps	2.6 in.
Federal 129-gr. Hydra-Shok	970 fps	1.9 in.

Table 18-7a
Ruger GP100 .38 Special

Load	Velocity	25-Yard Group
Black Hills 148-gr. WC	730 fps	1.2 in.
Black Hills 125-gr. JHP +P	1,020 fps	1.1 in.
Winchester 158-gr. SWC	819 fps	1.25 in.
Hornady 125-gr. XTP	870 fps	1.0 in.
Speer 135-gr. Gold Dot	910 fps	1.65 in.

Table 18-7b
Ruger GP100 .357 Magnum

Load	Velocity	25-Yard Group
Black Hills 125-gr. JHP	1,410 fps	1.25 in.
Hornady 125-gr. Critical Defense	1,380 fps	1.4 in.
Winchester 145-gr. Silvertip	1,307 fps	1.3 in.
Winchester 158-gr. JHP	1,258 fps	1.5 in.
Fiocchi 158-gr. XTP	1,140 fps	1.2 in.
Buffalo Bore 180-gr. HC	1,355 fps	1.25 in.

Table 18-8
.38 ACP Super RIA

Load		
SIG Sauer 125-gr. FMJ	1,220 fps	3.0 in.
SIG Sauer 124-gr. JHP	1,201 fps	2.9 in.
Winchester 125-gr. Silvertip	1,220 fps	3.5 in.
Winchester 130-gr. FMJ	1,220 fps	3.5 in.
Federal American Eagle 115-gr. JHP	1,209 fps	3.25 in.

Table 18-9
SR1911 9mm (converted to .38 ACP Super/Bar-Sto barrel)

Load		
SIG Sauer 124-gr. JHP	1,180 fps	2.0 in.
Winchester 125-gr. Silvertip	1,200 fps	1.75 in.
Federal American Eagle 115-gr. JHP	1,170 fps	2.25 in.
Double Tap 115-gr. JHP	1,380 fps	1.9 in.
Double Tap 124-gr. JHP	1,340 fps	2.1 in.

Table 18-10
Smith and Wesson Model 21 .44 Special

Load	Velocity	25-Yard Group
Buffalo Bore 190-gr. SWCHP	1,040 fps	2.5 in.
Hornady 180-gr. XTP	870 fps	2.0 in.
Black Hills 210-gr. FP	770 fps	2.5 in.
Fiocchi 200-gr. JHP	810 fps	2.1 in.

Table 18-11
Remington 1911 Commander .45 ACP

Load		
Black Hills 230-gr. FMJ	820 fps	2.8 in.
Fiocchi 230-gr. Extrema	780 fps	2.5 in.
Gorilla Ammunition 230-gr. FBI	790 fps	2.25 in.
Hornady 200-gr. XTP	944 fps	2.6 in.
SIG Sauer 200-gr. JHP	910 fps	2.9 in.

Table 18-12
SIG 1911 (with target sights)

Load	Velocity	25-Yard Group
Black Hills 230-gr. FMJ	839 fps	2.0 in.
Black Hills 230-gr. JHP	865 fps	1.5 in.
Hornady 200-gr. XTP	960 fps	1.25 in.
SIG Sauer 200-gr. JHP	935 fps	1.5 in.
Winchester W1911 230-gr. JHP	870 fps	1.8 in.
Speer 200-gr. Gold Dot +P	1,050 fps	2.0 in.

Table 18-13
Springfield Range Officer Operator .45 ACP

Load	Velocity	25-Yard Group
Gorilla 230-gr. Personal Defense	815 fps	2.75 in.
Black Hills 230-gr. JHP	859 fps	2.0 in.
Black Hills 185-gr. TAC +P	1,060 fps	2.6 in.
Hornady 230-gr. XTP +P	915 fps	2.5 in.
Winchester 230-gr. PDX	862 fps	2.25 in.
Fiocchi 230-gr. FMJ	822 fps	2.6 in.
Speer 200-gr. Gold Dot +P	1,038 fps	2.25 in.

Among the author's top picks is the Winchester .38 ACP Super Silvertip.

HANDLOADING ACCURACY TIPS

Like many enthusiastic handgunners, I own firearms that are shot often and a few that seldom get used. Among the latter is a .44 Magnum revolver. While I appreciate the capability of the .44 Magnum — and sometimes the piece is carried when hiking — I do not fire it often. However, I recently put a 20-round box of handloads through it to keep my hand in with the hard-kicking beast. They had been assembled back in 1998. All rounds fired off without any type of problem and with good accuracy. I realize that there have been advances in bullets and powder, but for my informal shooting these loads remain ideal. No improvement will appreciably alter the utility of my handload.

My go-to 9mm and .45 handloads are a different story. I suppose few are more than six months old. They get turned around quickly. In considering my needs and the ammunition situation, I have planned for the inevitable shortages as supply and demand take their effect on the market. While panic buying and hoarding are important factors, the reality is we shooters are using more ammunition than ever before — IDPA, IPSC, PPC, steel silhouette competition and handgun training courses require a lot of ammo. The best means of ensuring a good supply is to handload. Ammunition loaded by a competent individual is safe, reliable, accurate, economical and useful. As for your needs, like a good doctor, prescribe a realistic amount for your use. Practice loads are loaded in greater quantity and service loads in a smaller amount.

Spent brass is resized and reloaded with powder and a projectile. This is the real economy of handloading.

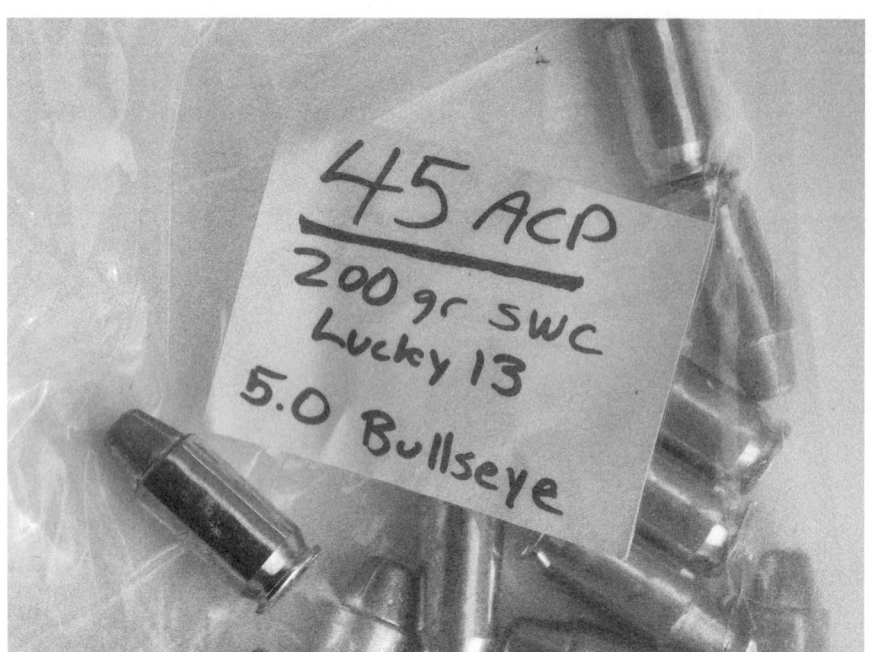

Mark your loads and carefully store them.

Handloads can be tailored to the game or the mission. These loads are for knocking down bowling pins.

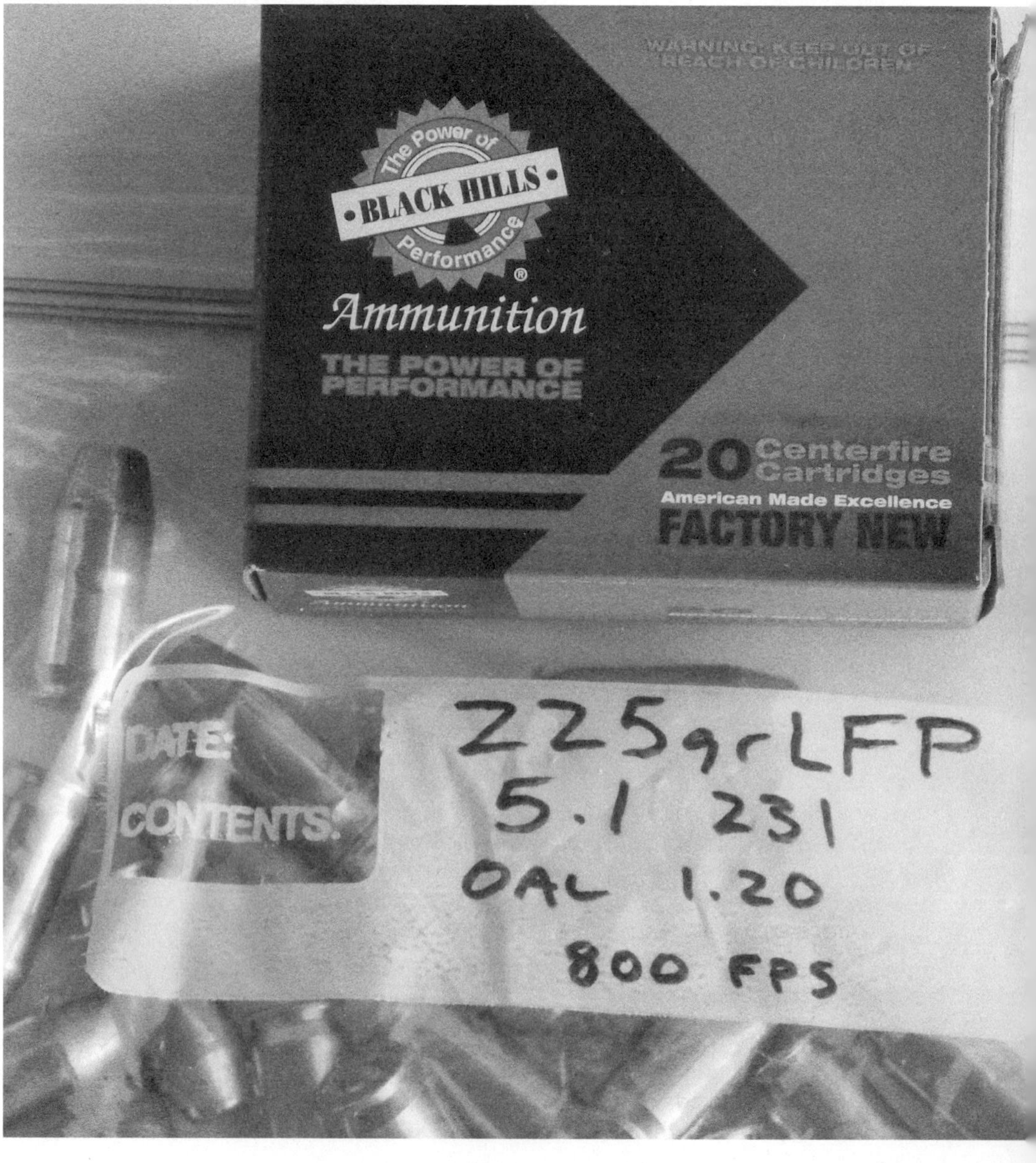

Reloading Tips

The mechanics of reloading are covered by loading manuals. Get two or three manuals and study. Take an NRA handloading course. Check out the how-to reloading books and videos available at GunDigestStore.com. Brass cartridge cases are the heart of reloading and a renewable resource. Save yours or purchase a quantity of once-fired brass from a commercial source. Or get off to a good start with Starline Brass. I do not sort brass for high volume practice loads in 9mm, .38 Special, or .45 ACP. I seldom sort brass in .45 Colt and .44 Special because I use Starline and the stuff is so consistent it isn't necessary. Revolver brass can be simply stuck back in the box after firing. With the self-loaders, you get plenty of practice bending the knees and flexing the back. Sorting brass isn't that difficult, but offers little real advantage in personal defense practice. I do not sort 9mm burner loads, though I do go through .357 brass for the

The Innovative steel target is a great training aid that has absorbed many thousands of handloads.

Python. Handloads should be at least as reliable as factory ammunition and, if you are a careful loader, will be more accurate than most factory loads.

Tips for Long-Term Use

Use standard velocity 9mm and .45 loads. Standard velocity is ideal with hardcast lead bullets. Factory FMJ bullet standard velocity is good for practice loads. If you can produce practice ammunition that functions well at slightly below factory pressure level, all the better for comfortable practice and economical shooting. Wear and tear on the handgun is decreased with standard pressure loads, while +P ammo produces more flash and muzzle blast as well as recoil. When loading service loads with expanding bullets, good velocity is fine but not at the expense of reliability and function. A good standard for service loads is 1,200 fps with the Hornady 124-grain XTP, 930 fps with the 200-grain XTP in .45 ACP and 830 fps with the 230-grain XTP. The target will never know the difference if you put the bullet in the right place. If you do not place the shot precisely, high velocity will not help.

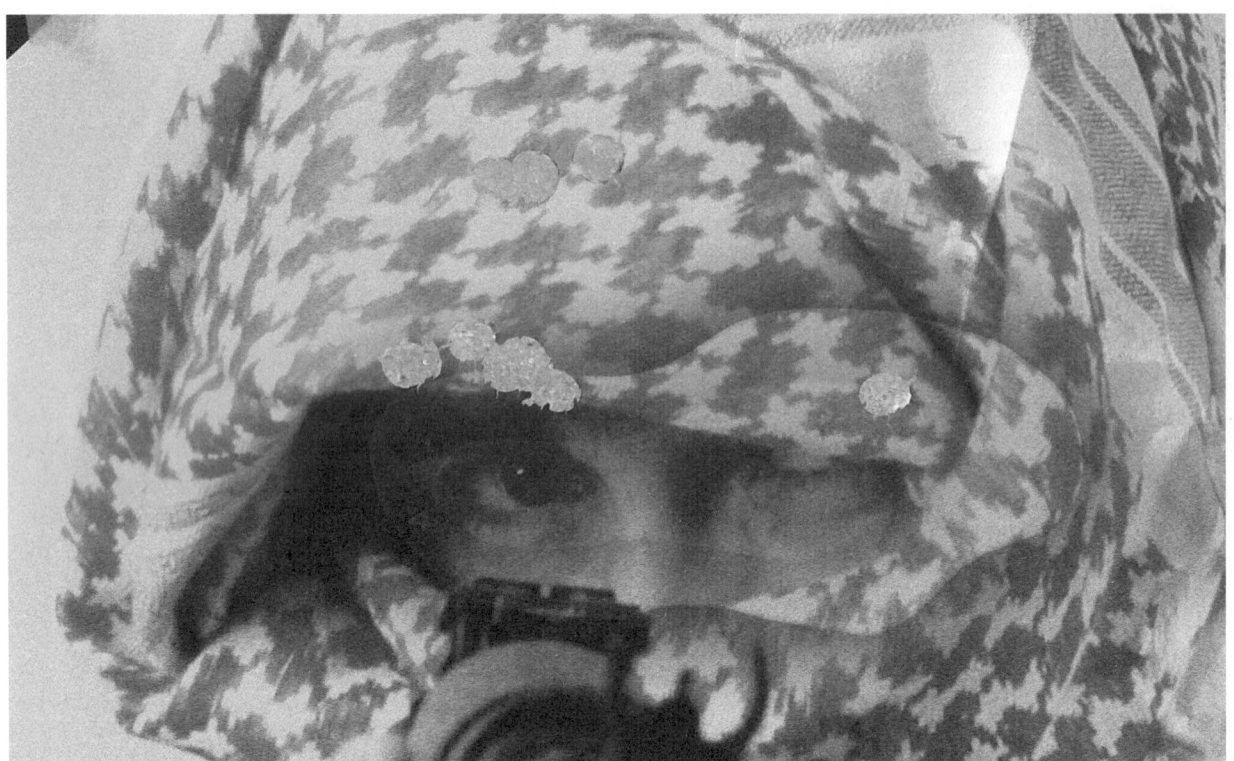

For intense training, very accurate loads are needed.
The author's handloads have performed well in all drills.

(below) These bullets from Precision Bullets have given
good results in many handloads.

A coated bullet such as the ones from Precision Bullets have performed exceptionally for the author.

Powder selection is based on economy and a clean burn. AutoComp, Titegroup, Clays and Universal give excellent results. I moved to Titegroup as soon as it was introduced. I still use WW231 as well, but if I had to live with a single handgun powder, Titegroup would be the one. Old standards such as Unique and Bullseye will still do what they have done for over one-hundred years. Pay attention to your reloading process and particularly the crimp. A self-loader demands a taper crimp for good function while a revolver must have a solid roll crimp. Use a headspace gauge or a barrel removed from the handgun to check proper chambering.

Choosing Bullets

Bullet selection is easy. Hardcast bullets have given good results for decades. As mentioned in earlier chapters, hardcast isn't the same as lead. Lead

Gateway Bullets makes some dandy coated bullets that are worth checking out if you reload.

is soft, hardcast is an alloy. Leading is limited and accuracy excellent when shooting hardcast projectiles. Standard weight bullets are best for loading for the bunker, storage and to be certain of function in every handgun. It is fine to experiment with lightweight bullets such as the 90-grain 9mm. The 152-grain .45 is very interesting. But if you have

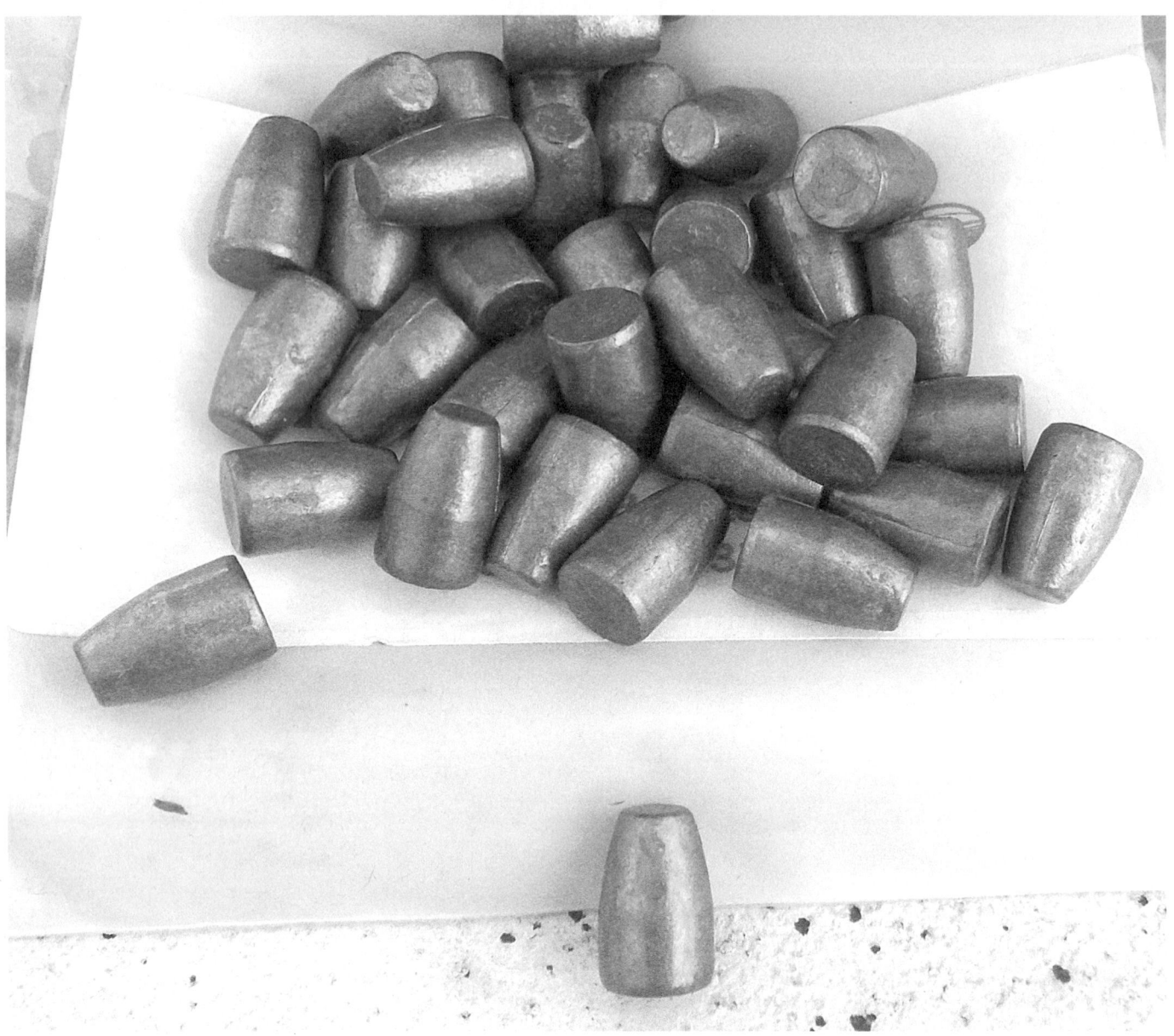

Heavy 9mm bullets from Bayou Bullets are quite accurate and economical as well.

a safe full of 9mm handguns and wish the load to be reliable and accurate in every handgun, then 124-grains at 1,100 fps for a practice load is ideal. By the same token, the .45 ACP should be 230 grains at 800-820 fps.

With revolvers, you have more leeway. For use in a number of calibers straight across the board, nothing beats the Hornady XTP. I use the 124-grain in both 9mm and .38 Super loads. The 230-grain XTP is ideal for .45 ACP loads. In the .38 Special, the 125-grain XTP is useful and offers stunning performance in the .357 Magnum. These service grade loads will serve you well in a worst case scenario. When loading for critical use I perform extra procedures. These include applying case mouth seal to the inside mouth of the cartridge case before seating and crimping the bullet. I also add a dot of finger-nail polish across the primer of handloads that are intended for long-term storage and possible critical use. Achieving a seal when the primer is seated is sufficient for most use, but this is simply an extra step that ensures reliability. Be certain to properly mark each loading. Factory ammo boxes are fine, but MTM plastic boxes are better. I have many that have been in use for decades. Ammo shortages — caused by hoarding and panic buying — are real. When an ammunition drought is on the horizon careful reloading and storage will lessen the hardship.

There are many new and interesting products for the reloader. I have used the new generation of coated bullets with good results. I have also enjoyed fine results with the Barnes Tac bullet. I saw really good results with the CorBon 95-grain 9mm and Black Hills 115-grain 9mm loads. I obtained a supply and

This press from RCBS will provide years of trouble free service.

THERE ARE MANY NEW AND INTERESTING PRODUCTS FOR THE RELOADER. I HAVE USED THE NEW GENERATION OF COATED BULLETS WITH GOOD RESULTS. I HAVE ALSO ENJOYED FINE RESULTS WITH THE BARNES TAC BULLET. I SAW REALLY GOOD RESULTS WITH THE CORBON 95-GRAIN 9MM AND BLACK HILLS 115-GRAIN 9MM LOADS.

loaded several interesting loads in the .38 ACP Super. I have also painstakingly weighed each powder charge and came up with a combination that would group five shots into less than an inch at 25 yards — using a 1913 6-inch barrel Smith and Wesson .38 Special revolver. The load used a hardcast 165-grain SWC at a solid 900 fps. What an improvement it was over factory loads! Today, I load volume batches for combat practice, but still take my time and make certain the magnum revolver ammo is loaded with the same care as those early .38 Special loads. It pays off in accuracy and economy.

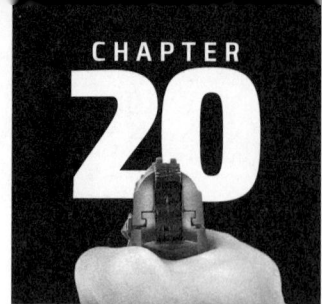
CUSTOMIZING THE 1911

This handgun is a parts gun, yet it offers excellent performance. Note Bomar sights and Ahrends grips

There are speed bumps with every project and most of them revolve around cost. Others may entail a lack of experience or mechanical ability. When it comes to the 1911 handgun, many desire to build their own pistol or at least modify an existing type to their specifications. A quality 1911 isn't inexpensive. But there are good buys among quality handguns. Among the best values is the Springfield Range Officer line. These handguns have a pedestrian matte finish, but the rest of the handgun is first-class, including a match-grade fitted barrel. The Range Officer, in my opinion, isn't an upgraded Loaded Model, but more similar to a National Match-type handgun with a less expensive finish.

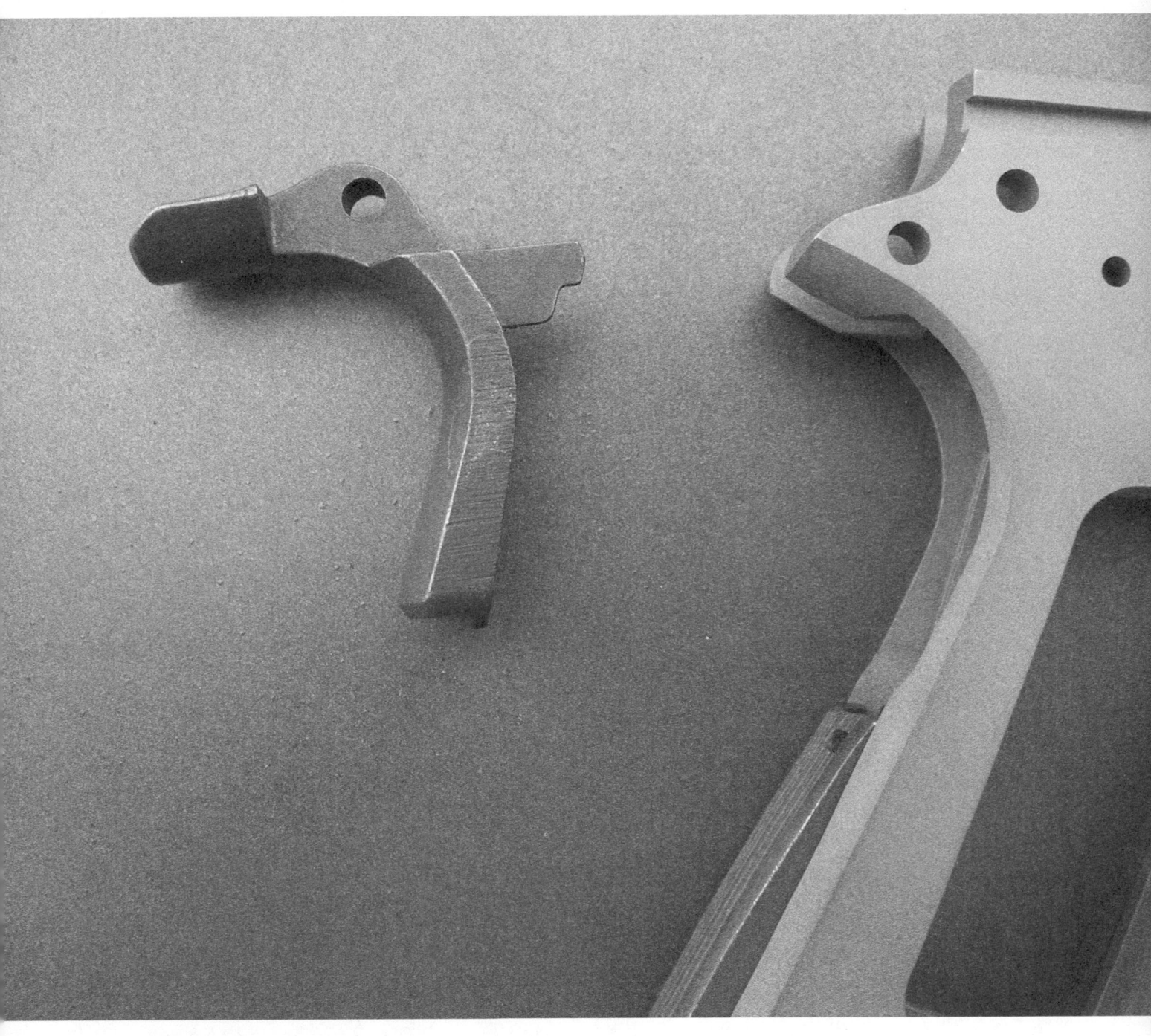

No matter how good the particular 1911 may be, the bug to build your own or upgrade an existing handgun is a strong one. There are many avenues available to scratch your itch, including purchasing a Caspian slide and frame. I have experience with a number of aftermarket slides and frames. Some have required more work and fitting than others. A reasonable beginning is the Rock Island Armory 1911. Using a cast frame and slide rather than the forged slide of the Colt and other high-end pistols, the Rock Island is worth its modest cost. I have worked with several upgrades. Recently, I worked with a particular Rock Island Armory 1911 and fitted a number of upgrades that turned out well. The result was a

A little mechanical ability goes a long way in building a 1911 handgun.

much more capable handgun.

After some forty years of working with the 1911, I realize that parts interchangeability is always a concern. No matter how reliable or well-made a pistol, either it will eventually break or you will desire to modify it. Inexpensive handguns end up in the shop most often. One of the most popular inexpensive handguns — and by all reports the present best-selling 1911 in the world — is the aforementioned Rock

Island Armory 1911. Rock Island 1911s are patterned after World War II GI guns, but with several changes. The Rock (as it is known) features a long trigger and flat mainspring housing. This makes it easier to fit a beavertail safety compared to the original GI gun's arched housing and short trigger. The pistols are finished in a dull Parkerized finish and are Series 70 without a firing pin block. After working on sixteen or more of these pistols during the past few years I am able to make several observations. While we call them Series 70, what we really mean is Mil-Spec or GI. They will accept most 1911 parts with a minimum of fitting. The 1911 handguns that are less likely to accept aftermarket slides, barrels and other parts without fitting are high-end handguns with a tighter fit. Off-spec economy handguns sometimes suffer the same complaint. My purpose in writing this chapter is to outline my experience with the Rock Island and High Standard pistols. (The same pistol under a different name.) My own projects with this handy little gun involved determining how well the pistol accepts popular aftermarket parts and what type of improvement could be had.

Rock Island Armory 1911

Many of us were skeptical of the new Philippine-made Rock Island 1911. After all, we had seen the terrible Llama 1911, which was 1911-like, not a true clone. The other Philippine 1911s do not enjoy the good reputation of the Rock Island. I have observed quite a few 1911 handguns in my training classes, and many of them were Rock Island Armory pistols. Like most quality 1911s, when they arrive for class lubricated and with good magazines and ammunition they have proven reliable. One of the .38 Super Rock Island handguns needed the extractor tuned out of the box and the ejector properly staked. Another needed a new extractor at less than one thousand rounds, but those were unusual. One student subjected his pistol to a heavy practice schedule without a complaint. Another suffered the indignity of having a handload blow in the chamber of his High Standard 1911, a Rock by another name. The slide lock was blown out of the frame, the magazine was wrecked and the floor plate never found. The shooter had to pick brass out of his cheek. Thank God he wore shooting glasses. The culprit, he believed, was a bullet that was jammed into the cartridge case on feeding due to a poor cartridge crimp. The pistol was reassembled and test fired and functioned normally. Since the magazine was blown out — along with the slide lock — this was no proof load, it was well above that standard! The pistol did not suffer permanent damage.

The Rock seems free of the problem of the firing pin stop coming loose as it did with the GI gun. The

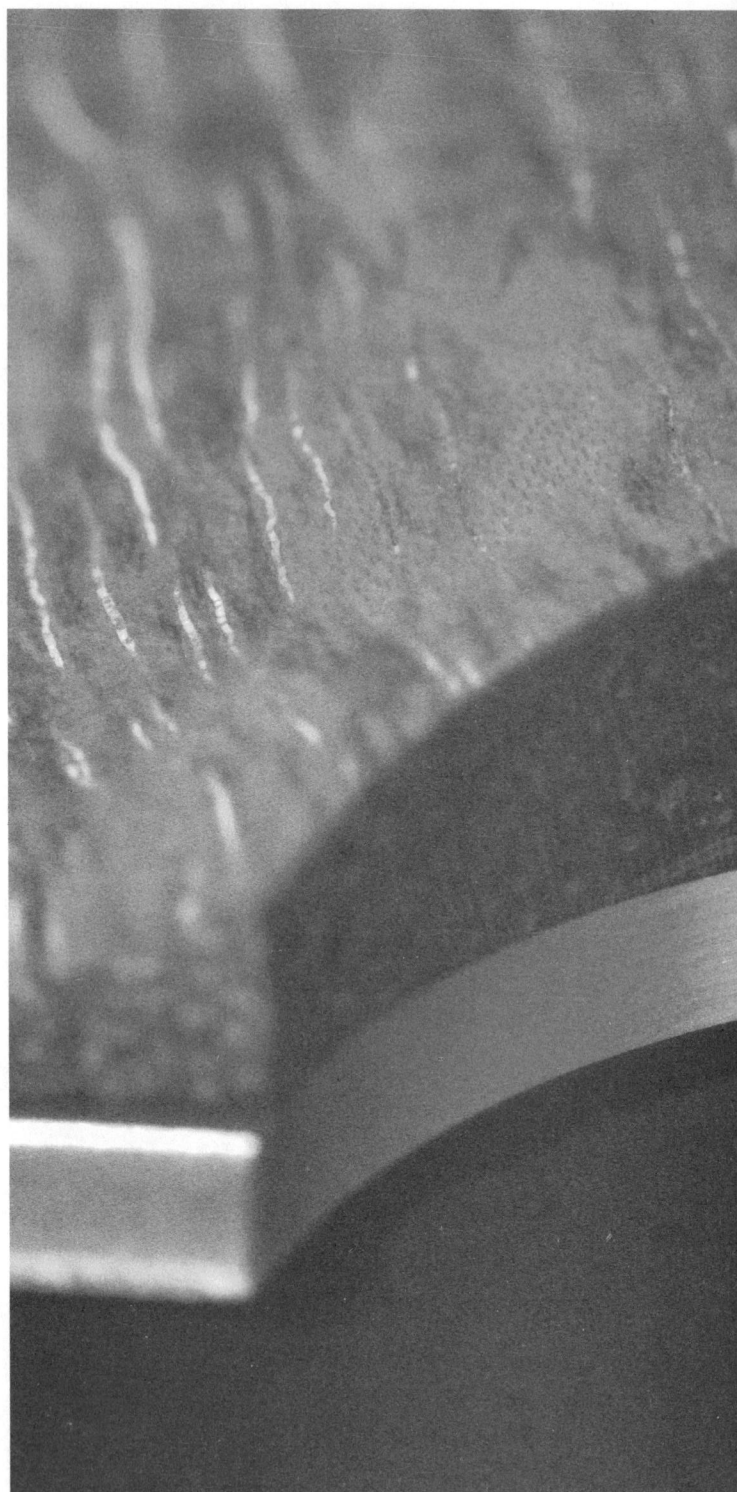

Challis grip screw is a great start for a personal handgun and avoids a lot of trouble down the road.

front sight seldom comes loose, but it did with my test gun, the only Rock I have ever seen suffer this indignity. The plunger tube also seems properly attached. As for feed with JHP bullets and handloaded lead semi-wadcutter bullets, I have yet to see a problem with the Rock Island pistol. The typical one is

Grip Screw
Grip screw O-ring
Challis Hex Drive Bushing
Bushing O-ring
Frame

reliable, while the atypical Rock is easily repaired with an extractor or changing magazines. There are versions with adjustable sights and an ambidextrous safety, but the prospect of upgrading the Rock with quality aftermarket parts was my concern.

There are many who prefer the 1911 as close to GI as possible. There is little to go wrong, less weight and less protrusions with the GI gun. If the Rock is your recreational or competition shooter then the modifications listed are not needed. However, if you carry the Rock for personal defense — and many do — and wish to bet your life on the pistol, then these upgrades are needed. I would be confident upgrading a customer's gun on his request and, while there are pistols I would not recommend to anyone regardless of the time spent in modifying the piece, the Rock is a gun worth the effort. What follows is my experience with parts interchangeability.

Test Gun

The test gun was a stock High Standard GI 1911 purchased at a retail outlet. It was test fired for function and accuracy and proved both service grade accurate and reliable with JHP and SWC ammunition. With a total of five-hundred rounds fired through it, the pistol proved reliable and, within the parameters of a GI .45, accurate enough. With the Black Hills 230-grain FMJ loading the handgun would put five rounds into the target in a cluster of 3 1/2 inches. The Black Hills 230-grain JHP would group slightly better.

Next, I decided to take the High Standard and see if it would accept a number of quality aftermarket parts that I thought would produce a pistol that was more than the sum of its parts. Most were purchased from Brownells. I added the new Challis hex head grip screws, which is SOP with a hard use handgun. In the first step to test parts compatibility, I dropped in a Wilson Combat, then a Colt, and finally an Ed Brown Series 70-type firing pin. Each fit as designed. I left the original firing pin in place for the time being. A problem observed in some RIA pistols is the clocking extractor. This is simply an extractor that moves in the extractor tunnel. A new extrac-

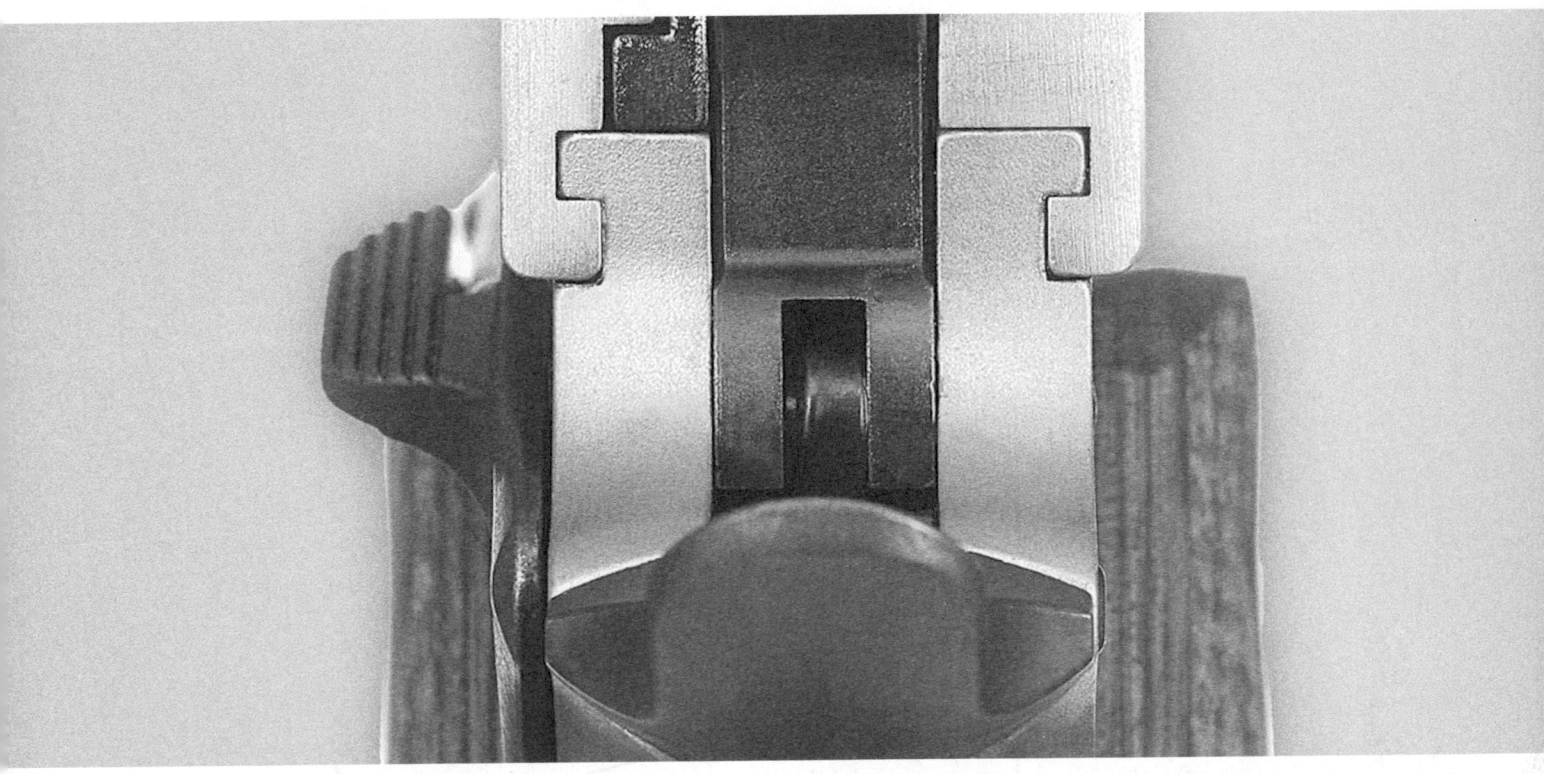

Fit and finish of the Ruger factory firearm can be equaled with careful procedure, but few will exceed this standard.

The slide is Colt, but the frame is Essex. This is a combination that works very well.

tor might be a cure, but in one case the extractor looked fine, yet the firing pin stop was loose. The pistol functioned, but brass was thrown back into the shooter's face. The original firing pin stop could have been peened for improved fit, but a Wilson Combat oversize firing pin stop was installed. Filing was minimal and in the end a good, tight fit was achieved — more expense but cheap life insurance in a carry gun. To fit the oversized firing pin stop, small strokes with a jewelers file was used and the stop lubricated and bumped into place for final fit. Field stripping will require more effort due to the tight fit, but this is secondary with a defensive handgun. You are never in need of a speed field strip!

I had a rather simple problem come to my attention with another Rock Island 1911. The magazine did not drop free when the magazine catch was actuated. The mag had to be extracted by hand. The problem was that the trigger bow was contacting the magazine. In this case, the bow was lightly filed and this solved the problem. A standard of custom pistolsmiths is to tune each magazine to the trigger. Although we do so to prevent trigger binding on the magazine for a smooth trigger action, achieving the proper drop with the mag is also a good reason. Another problem that can be addressed with training is that those using the thumbs-forward firing grip sometimes raise the palm off of the 1911 grip safety, resulting in a failure to fire. It is simple enough to tune the Rock Island 1911 to release a bit easier. You

Be certain to obtain a credible fit in the barrel bushing and barrel for good accuracy.

never want to make the safety inoperable, but simply to make it easier to activate.

First, understand how the leaf spring works. If you look from the back of the 1911 you will note that the leaf on the right pushes to the rear and exerts pressure on the grip safety. You can bend the leaf forward to reduce the pressure needed to depress the grip safety. Replacing the grip safety is another option, but for the gun to remain GI in appearance — and for less expenditure — bending the spring is an option. Care must be taken in this modification as you may increase the likelihood that the inertia of the grip safety would overcome the spring in the case of a dropped pistol. Perhaps this modification should be limited to a competition pistol such as a Wild Bunch CASS-class handgun. The grip safety doesn't really need much pressure to be activated, but it does need movement. Remember, the contact area is where the bump on the grip safety contacts the trigger stirrup.

Safety Check

Let's go over the safety check that must be done when any work is performed on the 1911.

It is a shame, but sometimes the safety operation of 1911 handguns leaves something to be desired. The home gun butcher is responsible for a lot of this type of action, but occasionally so is the haphazard factory worker. To check the safety, you should rely upon

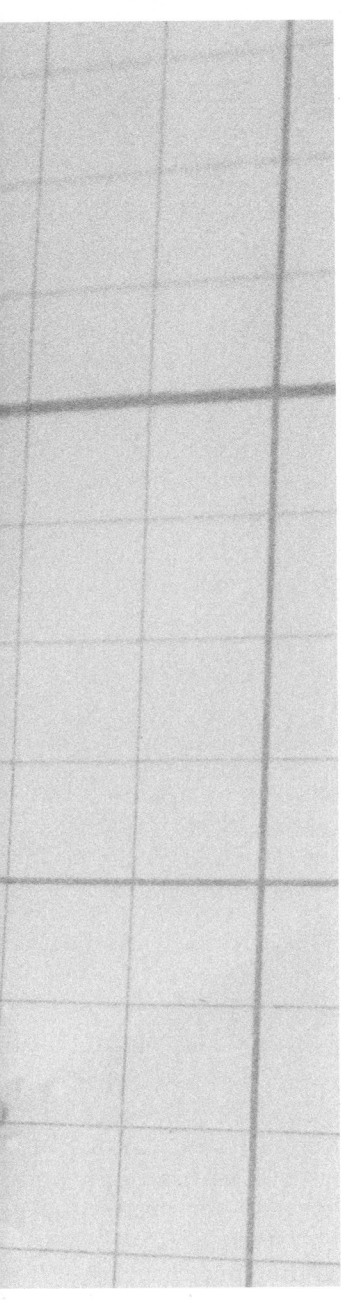

a method first used around 1912. Check to see that the gun is not loaded. The hammer should be cocked and the thumb safety on for the first check. While pressing the grip safety, pull the trigger. The hammer should not fall. Next, try to move the cocked hammer to the rear. It should show no movement. If a faint click is heard, it means the sear moved slightly when the trigger was pressed with the safety on. One particular brand of 1911 has this problem a lot, even though the trigger action is sometimes good. The safety is quite soft and spongy on these pistols. Replace with quality aftermarket parts. Next take the safety off. The hammer should not fall.

Further Upgrades

The Rock Island pistol was fitted with Cherokee Hills custom grips. The design is a bold and personal one and the adhesion during firing was excellent. Note that Rock Island Armory pistols often have cheap slabs that are not the best fit. High Standard handguns have checkered grips that fit better. It is a good idea to obtain a quality set of aftermarket ones. Next, I fitted a Wilson Combat slide lock safety. This safety seemed to demand more fitting than is usual with the 1911, but it was very doable and maintained a good, sharp action.

Trouble came when I fitted the U-Notch rear sight from Harrison Design and Consulting. Sometimes called the 'old man's sight,' this open rear notch allows real speed in finding the front sight and is recommended for speed shooting at close range. Advertised to fit the GI rear sight notch, the sight did not fit the High Standard. Considerable file work was needed to mount the sight, too much for practical use in my opinion. The dovetail is simply too wide for a GI rear dovetail. Sometimes, and it depends on the individual 1911, you will need to remove .008

to .010 inch of material from the bottom of the retro sight. It takes time and care to keep the surface even. Make the cut and then bevel the front and rear corner of the sights, then lubricate the sights and try to get it started in the dovetail. You will probably make the cut and then have to file with a large bastard file some more. Be aware of this work before you take the job in. It is really a lot of fussing. File a little bevel into the dovetail in the slide to relieve pressure required to push the sight in. Again, this is a difficult operation, but the sights do work well. The sight provided a quick sight focus that gave the shooter a real advantage in speed shooting at moderate ranges.

As a long-time 1911 shooter, I never throw anything away that may be useful. After working the High Standard up, I had a Colt 1911 come in with a damaged rear sight. This was a GI gun and, while a good shooter, not collectible or worth a lot of money. The pistol had been dropped on the rear sight and there was practically no rear sight notch. The rear sight was bumped out with a brass hammer and the rear sight that was formerly on the High Standard was bumped into the Colt notch. The High Standard rear sight is GI-type, after all!

Trigger Thoughts

The smoothness that you experience as an improved function of trigger compression is most evident after takeoff and before the hammer falls. Stoning the sear is fine, but you must maintain .020-inch engagement in the hammer hooks. It is easy to see if the hammer hooks are taller than .020 using a feeler gauge. At the same time, the hammer hooks must be checked to be certain they are perfectly square. When performing this type of work, I set the stone in the vise rather than the part to be stoned. I keep the stone in the vise and work the part over the stone. I have had better results with this technique. Of course, if you purchase aftermarket parts, stoning and polishing must not be undertaken. As an example, when purchasing a set from Ed Brown, simply installed the parts. This set includes the hammer, trigger, sear and disconnect. I want to stress that these parts are the highest quality and give excellent function. This is the recommended course rather than attempting to modify the existing trigger action. Some will wear rapidly once the hardened finish is broken. Other parts, such as those found in Colt pistols, are very hard and will last a lifetime or two. The Ed Brown parts are properly cut for engagement and do not require additional smoothing. Such work is unnecessary for smoothness and proper function with these quality parts — leave custom-grade, first-quality factory parts as they are delivered.

Understand the relationship between parts such as the magazine and the magazine catch, and their function before you begin.

For standard guns, study the hammer hook and sear and how they fit together. When polishing, it is fine to produce a smoother surface, but you must always maintain the original angles. And it is not all in the hammer and sear. The sear spring is another part that bears close study. It places resistance on the trigger bar and on the bottom, or foot of the sear. I have checked many factory sear springs and you must be familiar with what a proper sear spring feels like. The spring is sometimes adjusted by bending to reduce pressure on the trigger. This expedient works.

After putting the High Standard pistol together, the owner enjoyed excellent results. The sights were what he wanted and the pistol exhibited a personal look that he found pleasing. However, fewer than 200 rounds after the modifications were completed, the staked in front sight came loose. Since replacing a single tenon front sight is problematic for longevity, the decision was made to cut a front sight beavertail and permanently modify the slide. This was a good answer; however, it was an expense not originally expected. Now, I have not seen the front sight come loose on other Rock Island guns, but it is a GI gun and should have been expected.

In the end, is the Rock Island/Armscor pistol compliant with GI/Mil-Spec parts? Yes it is. Is it a worthwhile modification? I say yes, as the project gun turned out well. Could a good-quality pistol with equal features — a Springfield Loaded Model for example — have been purchased for the same outlay? Probably. But it would not have been as unique.

Other Options

If you wish to start from the ground up, you can always purchase a Caspian slide and frame. These are high-quality parts with excellent histories. The slides and frames are bare and will need every part fitted. If you are confident and willing to learn, this is a great project. If you tend to rush and leave things half done, never attempt such a project. You need to make a commitment to the type of 1911 you want to build. A straight-up GI gun is fine, but they are inexpensive from the factory. A good, solid shooter with adjustable sights and smooth trigger is never a bad choice. Many folks have a good eye for detail and can obtain a schematic and piece together practically any machine. If you work in maintenance in a plant or you are a car mechanic, I do not think the 1911 will be a challenge. When you are done you will have a pistol that is unique or at least personalized. Get the idea in mind of the type of pistol you need and then consider the parts and expense.

Before you order, make sure parts will be compatible with the type of pistol you want to build. It isn't unusual to find various quality builds at a pawn shop, and they can be a decent source for frames and slides if purchased cheaply enough. Essex frame handguns seldom bring good money no matter what the slide and modifications. If you are planning on

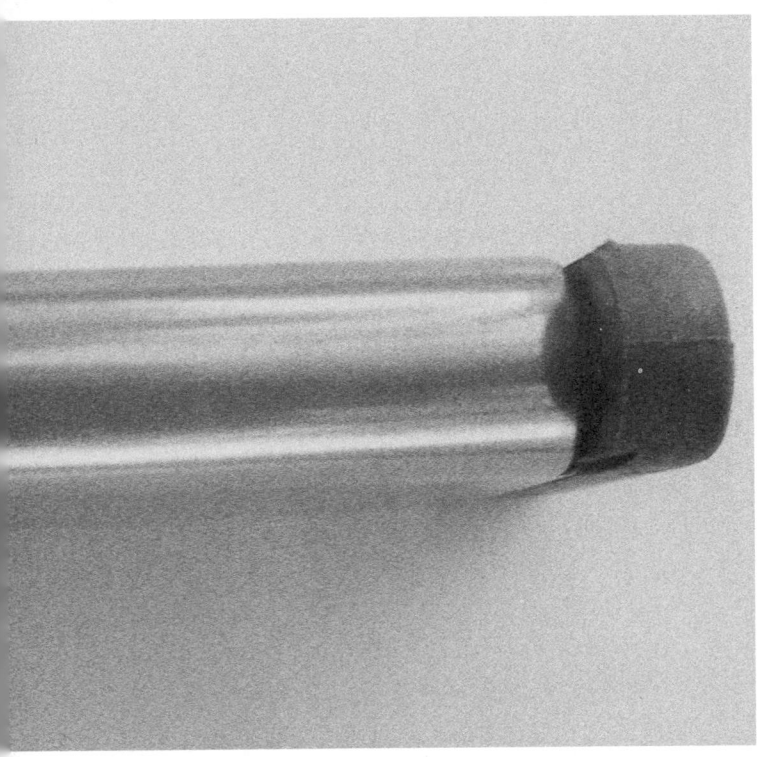

keeping such a pistol that is fine, but remember a parts gun no matter how well done will not recoup your expenses (unless the frame and slide say Wilson Combat or Ed Brown, but that is another story). Before you begin, research the parts needed. Just as importantly, consider the knowledge needed. If you are able to put together everything save the trigger job and wish that done by a professional, that is one course, but if you need someone to put the gun together you really should simply purchase a target-grade 1911 from the showcase, it will be less expensive. The procedure includes fitting the frame and slide, fitting the barrel and bushing and also fitting the small parts such as the magazine catch. Fitting the trigger action together takes some finesse. When you are working with the 1911, the primary concern is safety and then reliability.

Like most machines, the 1911 is only as good as the parts and the assembler. There are a number of quality firearms costing well over a thousand dollars and others such as the Springfield Mil-Spec and the Remington R1 that run well at a modest cost. Decide if you are more concerned with reliability or accuracy. If the piece is a carry gun, then reliability comes first. But remember: a well-fitted handgun is often more reliable in the long run as eccentric wear is kept to a minimum. A tightly fitted gun is good, but it must be done correctly.

Also consider the 1911's method of operation. It is a controlled feed handgun. Along with the controlled feed Mauser bolt-action rifle, the 1911 is a model of reliability in a wild variety of inhospitable environments. The pistol is loaded and when it is cycled — by hand or via discharge — several things occur. The cocking block catches the rim of the cartridge and moves it forward from the magazine. The cartridge rim moves into the extractor groove. The extractor grasps the cartridge rim as the bullet nose contacts the feed ramp, snugging the cartridge into the breech face as the round is chambered. The 1/32nd-inch gap between the two halves of the feed ramp ensures good function. The cartridge chambers, the pistol fires, and the slide moves to the rear as the extractor pulls the spent cartridge case from the chamber. The ejector kicks the case clear of the slide.

The author found that, overall, the fit of GI guns (Mil-Spec or Series 70) is good. Aftermarket parts seldom present a problem.

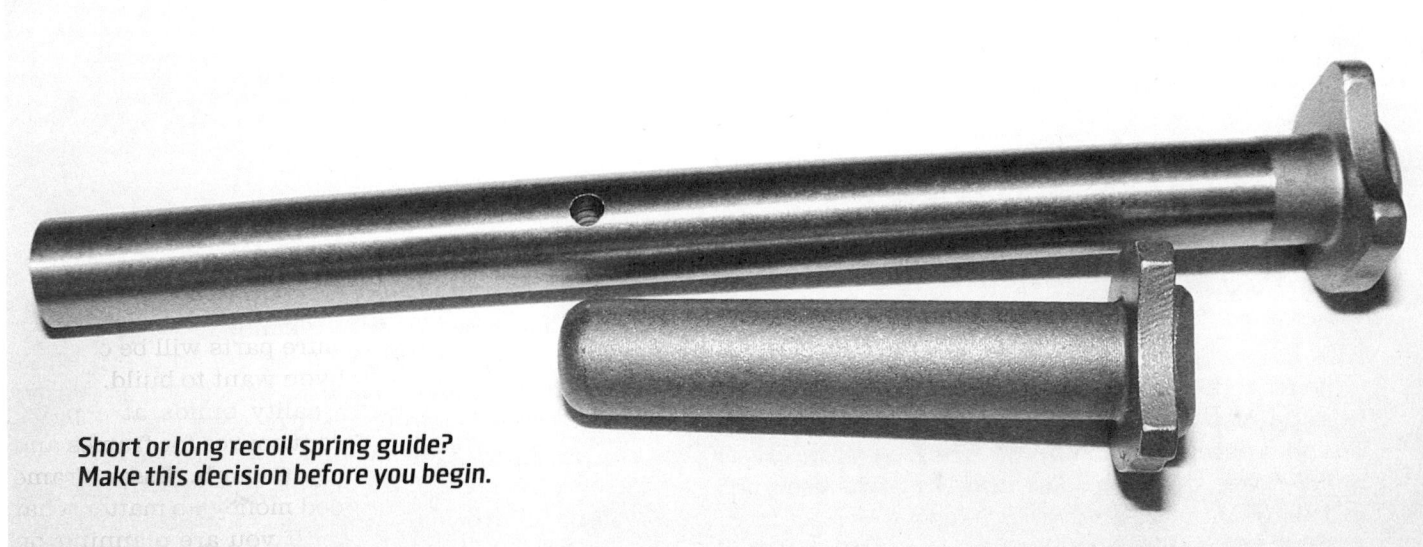

Short or long recoil spring guide?
Make this decision before you begin.

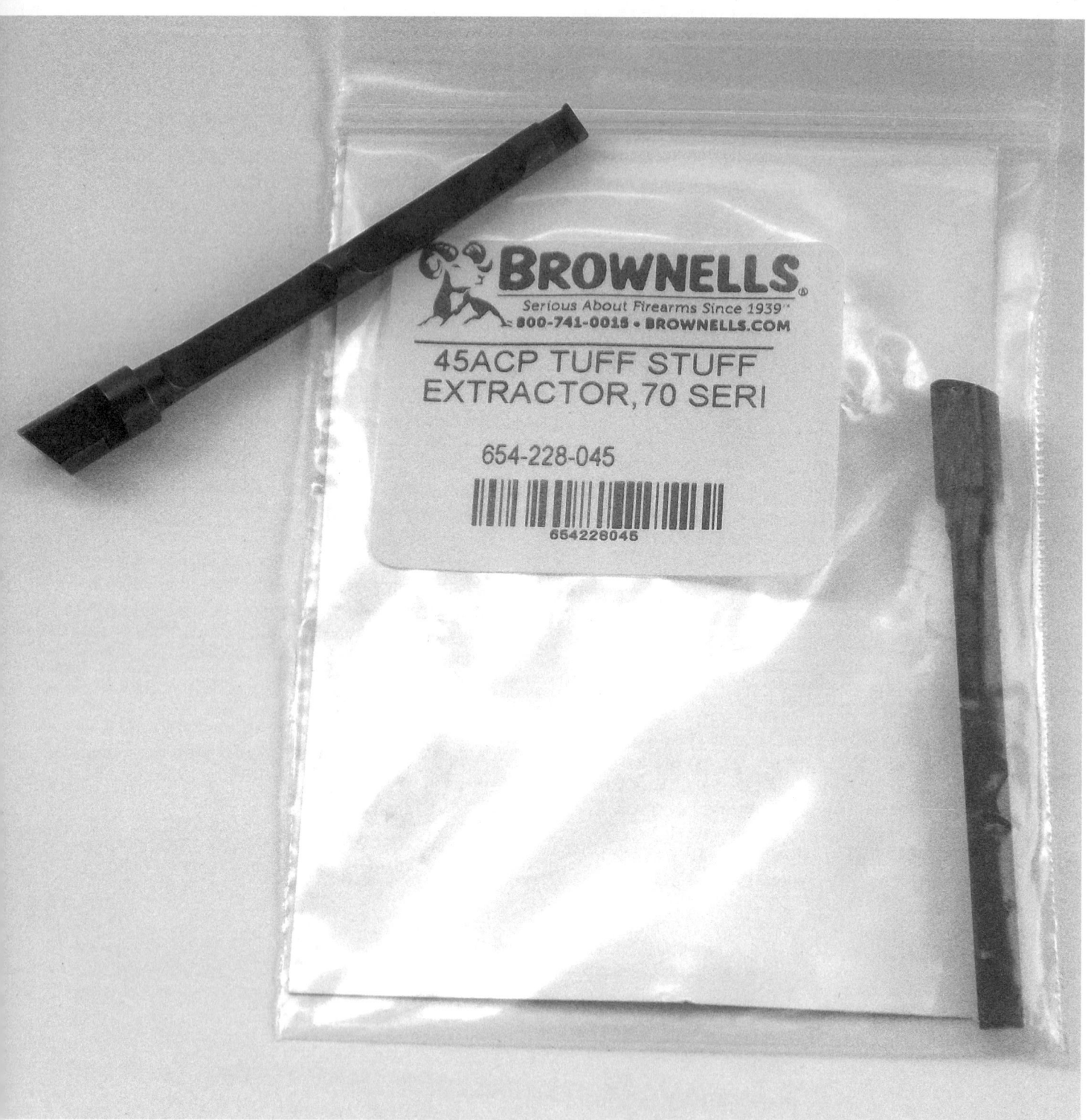

Brownells is the number one source for 1911 parts, in the author's opinion.

Modern 1911 handguns tend to feed reliably. The fit and finish is much better than a few decades ago. The feed ramp is smooth and will feed a variety of bullet noses. Just the same, the 1911 was designed to feed loads with an overall length of 1.250 inches and, when this is adhered to, the 1911 will feed properly. A properly designed magazine is essential. The Ed Brown, Brownells and Wilson Combat mags work well and ensure feed reliability.

Modern 1911s feature a larger ejection port. While I like the retro look of a Colt Series 70, the larger slide window should be used in your build gun for many reasons. The lowered port makes for more positive clearance of the spent case, and in the case of a dud round easier clearance of a loaded cartridge. For best reliability, a service pistol should feature a

The author found that, overall, the fit of GI guns (Mil-Spec or Series 70) is good. Aftermarket parts seldom present a problem.

lowered ejection port. The breech face is sometimes rough and should be polished. I began polishing the breech face when converting calibers many years ago. Whether converting a 1911 Colt 9mm to .38 Super, or simply plugging in a .400 CorBon barrel, I found that a breech face polish makes for smoother

feeding. Be certain you never change the angle of the breech face, though — only make it smoother. Be particularly careful that you do not damage the firing pin channel and that this channel remains smooth.

As mentioned, the 1911 is a controlled-feed firearm and the extractor is very important. Never drop the slide on a chambered cartridge. Always feed the cartridge into the chamber from the magazine! If you wish to top the load off, first load the cham-

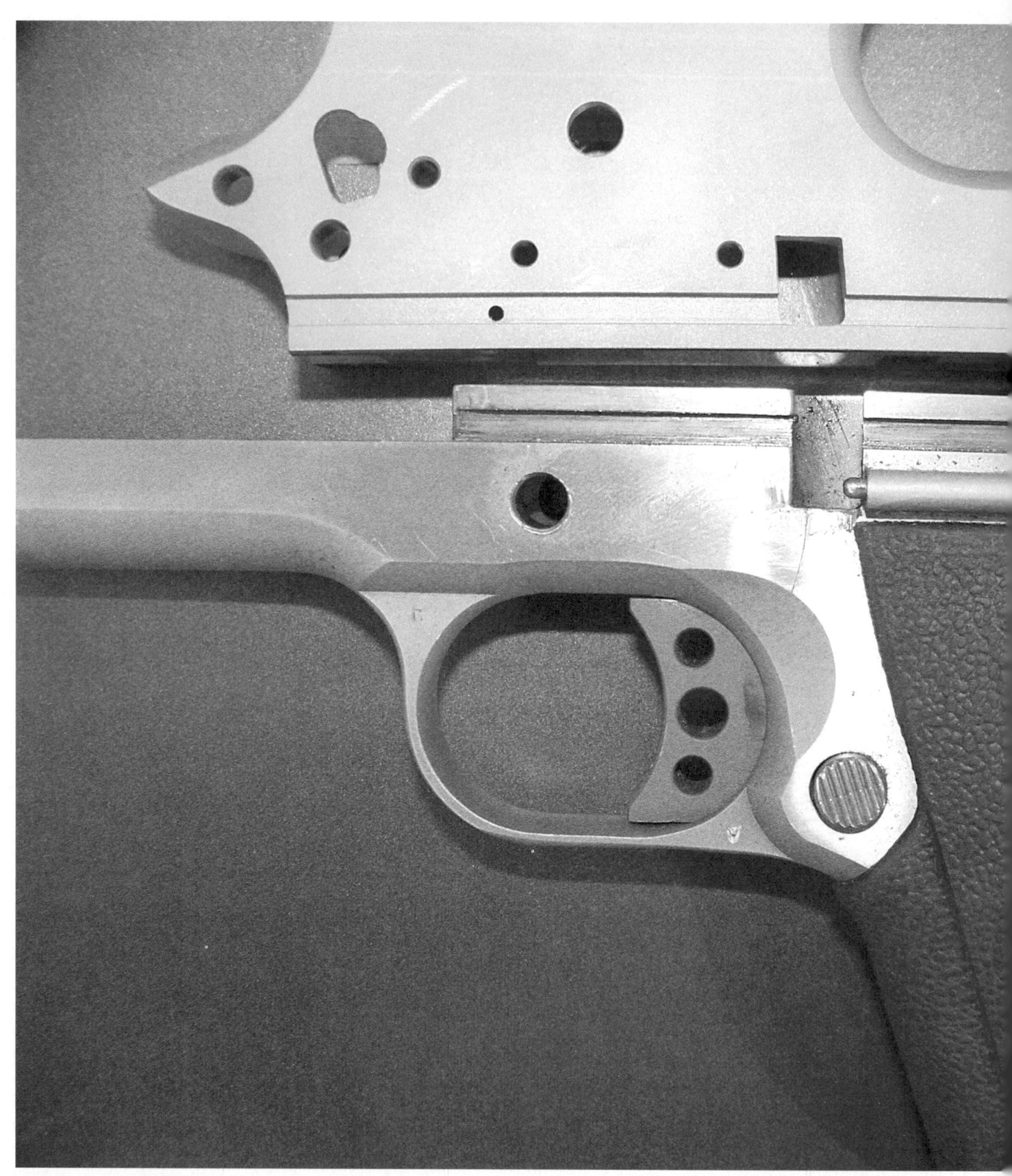

ber, then remove the magazine, and top the magazine off. When you drop the slide on a loaded cartridge, the extractor is forced over the cartridge case rim and over-stressed. The extractor is designed to capture the cartridge case rim as it is fed from the magazine. It doesn't take many of these abusive slide drops to ruin the extractor, either by robbing the extractor of tension or breaking the extractor hook. The means of testing extractor tension is to strip the barrel, bushing and spring from the slide and insert a loaded cartridge into the extractor hook. The slide should be rotated in every direction, and in the case of a properly tuned extractor, the cartridge will be retained and not fall out.

An old axiom is that the recoil spring should be replaced every 3,000 rounds. I have personally fired 1911 handguns with the original recoil spring that were at least thirty years old. Yet, I have examined recoil springs with far less use that needed replacement. Once the spring has lost an inch of free length it is overdue for replacement. Replacement springs are inexpensive, widely available, and should be kept on hand. The proper spring weight depends upon the load used, but the original 16-pound weight is ideal in the Government Model .45. For heavy pin loads or the +P defense loads 18.5 pounds works well. The Commander takes a 20-pound spring. Be certain that you use the correct poundage. A recoil spring that is too heavy can be hard on the extractor. A good test of a recoil spring weight is to shoot the pistol with one hand. You do not have as firm a grip in one handed fire, and the recoil spring will cause a malfunction more readily than with the rock-solid two-handed grip.

The 1911 is my favorite handgun and the one a serious shooter in search of accuracy should have. To build your own is the dream of many handgunners. I am no Bill Wilson or Ed Brown, but I have assembled quite a few 1911s. Build may be too strong a word for what I have done, but the individual handguns have turned out well. I have taken my time and ended up with a credible handgun that served well. You can do the same by taking your time, setting a goal, and doing plenty of research. The end result — the accurate handgun — is well worth the time and expense.

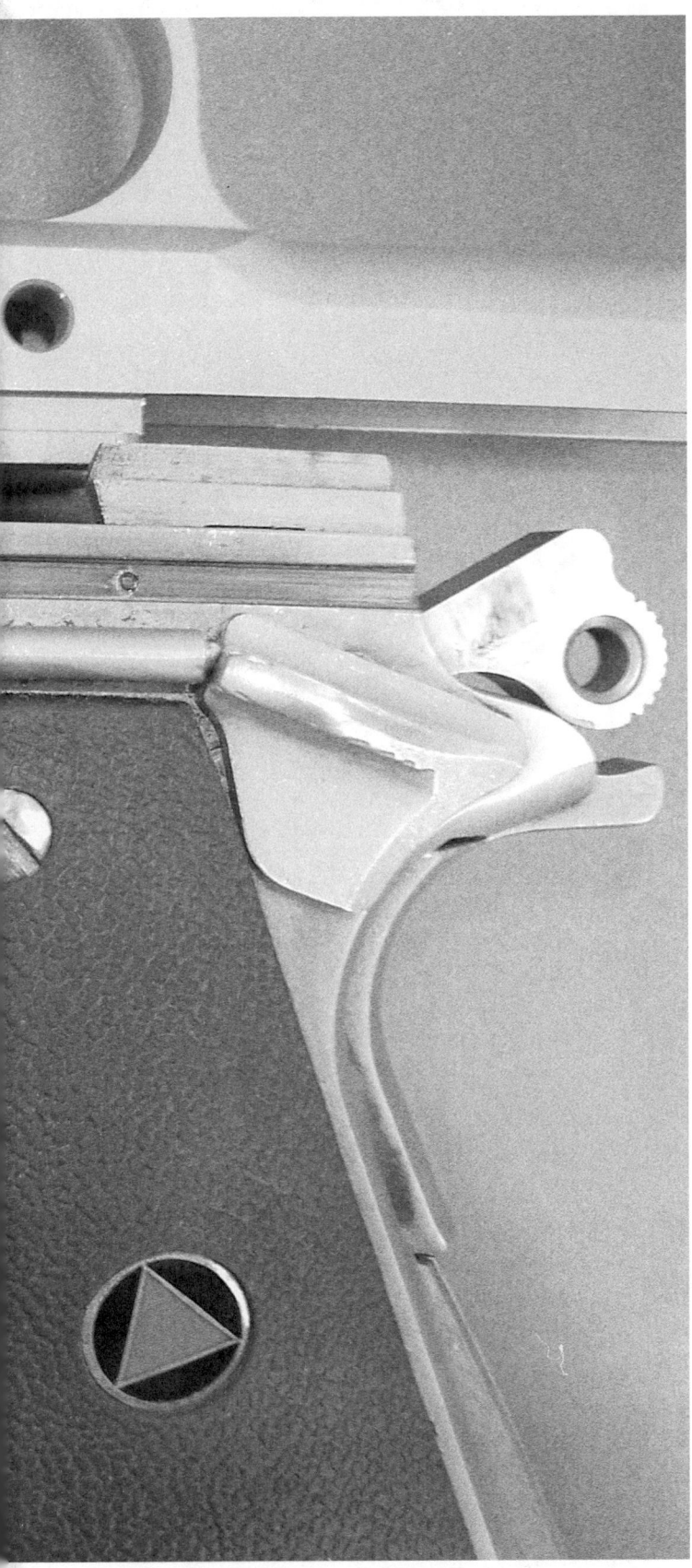

Some things are harder to do than others in a build. The Caspian frame, top, is first-class. The Colt 10mm frame, however, has a cutout to relieve stress when firing the powerful 10mm cartridge.